EVENINGS WITH HOROWITZ

EVENINGS WITH HOROWITZ

A PERSONAL PORTRAIT

by David Dubal

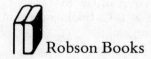

Robson Books

First published in Great Britain in 1992 by
Robson Books Ltd, Bolsover House, 5–6
Clipstone Street, London W1P 7EB

British Library Cataloguing-in-Publication Data
A catalogue record for this book is available
from the British Library

Printed and bound in Great Britain by
W.B.C. Print Ltd and W.B.C. Bookbinders Ltd,
Bridgend, Mid-Glamorgan.

For Eri Ikezi
With all my heart

If by some dispensation a man born deaf were to be given hearing for a single hour, he might well spend the whole time with Horowitz. Indeed, when I listened to Horowitz for the first time, it was almost like that—as if I had never heard the piano before—as if the instrument itself had never known what it could do until Horowitz came along.

—James Hilton

TABLE OF CONTENTS

ACKNOWLEDGMENTS

During a lunch, my agent, Richard Curtis, questioned me about my relationship with Horowitz. Like many music lovers, he was fascinated with the pianist. He emphatically remarked, "There must be a book lurking in you about the many evenings you spent with him."

I was certain no such book existed in me. But that night, I had dream after dream about Horowitz. The next day, I found myself looking through old appointment books where I had jotted down copious notes on what had occurred during my evenings with the Maestro. Still, I had no conscious intention of writing a book.

About a week later, while practicing the Brahms A Major Intermezzo, I was flooded with memories and discussions I had had with the great virtuoso. I left the piano, found my pen, and began the book.

I am grateful to Richard Curtis as the catalyst for *Evenings With Horowitz* and for his encouragement throughout its composition. Thanks are also due to Leslie Curtis, who provided excellent advice.

I extend special thanks to my editor, Hillel Black, the president of Birch Lane Press, for his enthusiasm, guidance, and his well-known skills.

My thanks to Peter Goodrich, Director of Concerts and Artists at Steinway & Sons, for photographs of Horowitz and for many kindnesses shown to me.

At RCA, now BMG Classics, my appreciation goes to John Pfeiffer, Daniel Gorgoglione, Bonnie Levine, Joseph Stelmach, Marilyn Egol, and Elizabeth Costello.

Thanks are in order to Carol Shookhoff for a splendid job of copy editing.

Others who must be thanked are Susan Schiffer, Richard Probst, Peter Rosen, Lola Cantor, and Donald J. Davidson.

Thanks are due to Glenn Plaskin, whose biography of Horowitz is the pioneering work on the pianist's life.

My gratitude to Mordecai Shehori for providing me with photographs of Horowitz as well of myself. To Shawn Randall, who took the only photograph of me with Horowitz, as well as for sending me others for use in this volume

My deepest appreciation is to Eri Ikezi. Her unlimited help and sensitivity to me cannot be estimated.

AUTHOR TO READER

It is deeply human to want to know and understand our great personages. Even trifles count. John Keats wrote, "It would be a great delight as to know in what position Shakespeare sat when he began 'to be or not to be.'" This book is simply a record of my own view of Vladimir Horowitz, a complex man and musician whom I came to know during the last years of his life.

My relationship with the Maestro spanned three and a half years. I first entered Horowitz's world in November 1979 when I interviewed him for New York's radio station WNCN, where I was music director. These interviews are described in the book. Although I thought then that we got on splendidly, I never pursued a further relationship.

In 1983 I began teaching the piano literature classes at the Juilliard School. In the autumn of 1985 my close friend Thomas Frost, Horowitz's record producer, told me that Horowitz had asked about me. The great pianist had hinted to Tom that he might like to do an interview with me for the Juilliard students.

Soon after, I began visiting the Maestro and Mrs. Horowitz at their lovely town house off Fifth Avenue on East Ninety-Fourth Street. These visits, too, are described in the book. There are also chapters recounting my impressions of hearing two of Horowitz's famous recitals, his return to the concert stage in 1965 at Carnegie Hall after an absence of twelve years, and his Metropolitan Opera House recital after another retirement which lasted from 1969 to 1974.

The book begins with a biographical profile of the pianist until his retirement in 1953.

Naturally, *Evenings With Horowitz* pertains greatly to music, the great composers, and the art of piano playing. However, I have kept in mind that my readers will certainly not all be pianists or musicians. At the same time, many things Horowitz and I discussed will be of little interest to the general reader and music lover. Therefore, I have attempted to solve this dilemma by retaining all that is musically pertinent without getting bogged down in technical language.

I was trained as a pianist, and my career, besides broadcasting and programming music, always included piano teaching, recording, and giving concerts, mostly lecture-recitals. It was my knowledge of the piano literature which attracted Horowitz to me.

For my part, I will never forget the wonderful feeling of being close to a pianist who played a principal role in the history of the instrument I love. For pianists, Horowitz was what Heifetz was to violinists, but more, much more.

To my generation, he had become a living legend, but he was an enigma, too. After his sudden retirement in 1953, there seemed no chance of ever hearing him play in public. Still, as a young student, I was constantly aware of him, and this was true of all my peers at Juilliard.

Although he disdained "live" appearances at this time, Horowitz fortunately continued making recordings at rare intervals. Whenever a new record appeared, we would literally devour the performance, listening to it repeatedly. Whatever the repertoire he recorded, those same pieces were soon heard pounded to death in every practice room of the school.

In the early sixties, nobody played much of the keyboard music of the Italian eighteenth-century master Domenico Scarlatti. But listening to Horowitz's new Scarlatti album was a dazzling revelation. Soon many students began their school recitals with a group of Scarlatti sonatas.

Piano talk abounded in the school's cafeteria. Cups of coffee were consumed as we passionately discussed the repertoire we were studying. If one worked on the Liszt Sonata, the Horowitz recording was the standard of measurement. How did the man achieve those glistening runs? How did he get that particular sound? If you were studying Liszt's *Funérailles,* you knew you were a failure if you could not play the mighty left-hand octave section as fast as he, not to mention the sheer kinetic power that made the piano sound frightening.

One of Horowitz's specialties was the Rachmaninoff Third Concerto. In fact, he owned it. It is the ne plus ultra of the Romantic concerto literature, a work reserved for only the heroes of the keyboard. The copy of his recording in the Juilliard library was well worn and had to be frequently replaced. I remember half the pianists at school walking around with the score conspicuously in view, but in reality, only a select few had the technical equipment to play it properly.

Oh, certainly we talked of other pianists, of Dinu Lipatti and William Kapell. Both had died young. We were stunned by eccentric Glenn Gould's Bach; we were proud of Juilliard's own golden-toned Van Cliburn. We went to hear Serkin's and Arrau's Beethoven; we would never miss a heavenly Rubinstein concert; we admired wholeheartedly the two Russians, Gilels and Richter. But still, all these and many others were eclipsed in our minds by Horowitz. He dominated our pianistic thinking; we talked of him endlessly. He was an obsession.

When Horowitz invited me to his home, I felt more honored than if Elizabeth II had invited me to Buckingham Palace. Indeed, it resembled a royal command. Horowitz was used to being treated like royalty. People were simply awestruck being near him.

Many of the most telling moments of an evening with Horowitz were nonverbal. One had to be aware of and understand his varied expressions: looks of disdain, humor, or approval. His moods flickered like a lit candle, and his enthusiasms could change abruptly.

Our evenings were often long, sometimes lasting five or six hours. Horowitz was an old man, but never once did I see him succumb to a snooze in my presence. When I said good night, he looked as fresh as when I entered. Of course, he slept quite late and might have breakfast at two or three in the afternoon.

Mr. and Mrs. Horowitz always dressed immaculately in very expensive clothing. Only once in my many visits did I see him unshaved.

Naturally for me, the great moments of our evenings came when the Maestro played the piano, which he usually did. Suddenly, as if he had waved a magic wand, life changed. To hear him play for me in his own living room was enthralling beyond any of my thousands of musical experiences.

When he played, critical judgment was suspended. Even when I disliked some of his conceptions or thought them facile or vulgar, it didn't matter. His individuality was devastating and blinding. I knew there would never again be a pianist of his emotional power and force of temperament.

Horowitz's art was inexplicable. Goethe called this indefinable element in an artist "the daemonic something which intelligence and reason cannot account for." He says, "The daemonic manifests itself in absolutely positive energy. It likes to attach itself to outstanding personalities."

Clearly, every great performer has this energy in varying degrees. Paganini, Chopin, Liszt, Paderewski, Caruso, Toscanini, Rachmaninoff, Rubinstein, Callas, and Glenn Gould possessed it on a high level.

Whatever the quality, something seemed to ooze from Horowitz. The air in the room crackled with an electrical charge when he played. In concert, this energy penetrated to the last row of the concert hall. Horowitz on stage had nothing flamboyant in his manner, yet his presence glowed with a special aura.

This aura translated to the man himself. As a person, he was immensely charismatic. A great performer does not suddenly wilt the moment he or she leaves the stage. Liszt's and Paderewski's personalities were colossal, as were Nijinsky's, Isadora Duncan's, Sarah Bernhardt's and Laurence Olivier's. Every performer of genius appears larger than life. When Horowitz walked into his living room, his presence dominated.

Mrs. Horowitz, possessed of the Toscanini genes, also had something of a daemonic nature. It was fascinating to watch their complex interactions. She had been strong enough to survive her father's overpowering personality, and she knew how to maintain her own individuality as the wife of an impossibly demanding man.

My own feelings about Horowitz remain complicated. As the text will show, he disappointed me several times. I tried not to put myself in any situation which implied any kind of expectation from him.

Although we talked together as fellow pianists, he showed no interest in my career and never asked me to play for him. If he had, I would have felt unprepared and intimidated, and would have refused vehemently.

When I left him, I sometimes found myself deeply inspired to practice, while other times I felt it was silly for me to continue playing the piano. I was always conscious of the distance that separated my ability from his. Out of respect, I never called him Volodya, as he once asked me to do. "No, Mr. Horowitz," I said, "I shall only call you Mr. Horowitz or Maestro."

My instinct told me, as I think his did, that my playing for him would have upset the delicate balance of our friendship. I was there as an interviewer, a Juilliard professor, and lover of the piano literature and its lore. Horowitz needed me as a younger musical confidant. Above all, he loved talking of music and the piano.

After one of my early visits, Mrs. Horowitz said to me, "Come often, he needs you." I felt that was true, and in those last years, Horowitz had very few good friends left. My function was to talk to him of Chopin and Liszt. In my way, I was there to help keep him going.

From the beginning, our chemistry "clicked." Our natural intensity included Mrs. Horowitz. Without her tacit approval that I was "good" for her husband, my many visits would never have happened. I owe her much.

During our evenings, he was mostly relaxed and expansive. I was able to see him with napkin tucked under his shirt collar, eating his soup with eyes tightly shut, savoring the liquid with the same high concentration he had when entering the harmonic labyrinth of a Scriabin sonata.

I could enter the room and smell the emotional climate. After I kissed Mrs. Horowitz's hand, she would vent her many dramas. I was able to convince Mr. Horowitz that the composition he was practicing was, without doubt, the most important thing happening on the planet.

In turn, they let me rant and rage on anything from the decline of art to the evils of overpopulation. They would hear me spout off on Voltaire or the work ethic, or I would give them a long lecture on the birth of the piano. They were wonderful listeners. Mr. Horowitz loved saying, "Mr. Dubal, I am normal [nor-*mall*] compared to you."

I would arrive, sit down, and ask, "Maestro, did you ever study a Kalkbrenner etude?" Friedrich Kalkbrenner was an important figure in the world of early nineteenth-century piano playing. At once we would be launched on Kalkbrenner.

"You know," Horowitz said, "everyone laughed at him because he was so pompous."

I concurred. "But I loved Kalkbrenner telling his pupils 'What did God give us wrists for if not to play octaves?'"

Horowitz laughed. "I think he was right. Can you imagine, Kalkbrenner told Chopin that he had to study with him for *three* years, and only then he would be a finished pianist? To Chopin, he say this. *He would have ruined him!*" Horowitz cried.

"And, Mr. Horowitz, Kalkbrenner said this to the young Chopin of twenty-one who had already completed his études, which revolutionized piano technique."

Horowitz went on. "But you know, Chopin refused. He wasn't dumb. Kalkbrenner was a powerful man then, and Chopin healed his wound by dedicating his E minor Concerto to him."

"Yes," I continued. "Chopin was always a good careerist. But not one note of Kalkbrenner's music survives in the permanent repertoire."

At that, Horowitz lifted himself off the couch with some difficulty and a great grimace, saying, "Let's see if some Kalkbrenner survives in me." To my amazement, the master played a Kalkbrenner etude perfectly. Afterward, looking at me, he exclaimed, "I learned it when a boy. Maybe ten or eleven. I don't play it for a hundred years."

"But, Maestro, how can you play it so perfectly after all these years?"

Horowitz smiled modestly, saying simply, "I learned it well." Horowitz never ceased to astonish me with such feats of musical-muscular displays.

Fame came to Horowitz early, and his celebrity grew each year. The less he played, the more the world wanted to hear him. He was terribly spoiled. Certainly, in his long career, Horowitz got away with more ludicrous behavior than most people ever dream of. His demands on tour concerning accommodations and food as well as his many eccentricities were unthinkable for others.

Horowitz was almost totally narcissistic. However, I feel in his case, for his talent to thrive, his narcissistic self-absorption was necessary. Those people sensitive to him, especially his wife, understood this. To keep him functioning and to keep him "playing" was a burden and, for some, a responsibility.

Aldous Huxley wrote, "The neurotic who succeeds as an artist has had to overcome a tremendous handicap. He creates in spite of his neurosis, not because of it."

Horowitz spent most of his existence battling to overcome his deeply troubled nature. It was a war he waged for years at a time, winning battles sporadically and, finally, in his last few years, making some real psychological progress. The giving part of his nature—his love for his art and the force of his musical gift—needed an ever-increasing worldly expression.

Horowitz at eighty-five said to me, "I'm afraid life is a little bit too short." It was said with deep sadness because in some ways he was just beginning to live.

At his best, he was humorous and displayed a childlike playfulness that all artists must retain if they are to continue developing. Nietzsche declared, "In every real man, a child is hidden that wants to play." In Horowitz, this child was constantly peeping out.

For the public at large, Horowitz was the last representative of Romantic piano playing. His death was more than the end of an era; he was the culmination of a great tradition stemming from Liszt and Anton Rubinstein. It is a concept of piano playing based on the Romantic repertoire, which emerged from the poetic and turbulent geniuses of Chopin and Schumann as well as the pictorial virtuosity of Liszt.

Such pianists as de Pachmann, Paderewski, Sauer, Rosenthal, Carreño, Godowsky, Rachmaninoff, Scriabin, Lhévinne, Hofmann, Friedman, Moiseiwitsch, Barère, Arthur Rubinstein, and others reveled in color, gorgeous tone, and delicately poetic effects. Their hallmark was supertechnical prowess, which they used to thrill and astound. They were a mighty breed of virtuosi, highly individualistic, wayward, sometimes musically eccentric. They were temperamental, explosive, and instinctive. In short, they were *Romantic*.

During the last years of his life, Horowitz was undeniably the most famous pianist in the world, yet he was—musically speaking—lonely and alone. Ironically, his way of playing music was out of fashion during much of our century.

Modern performance practice, as a reaction to the self-indulgence of the late nineteenth century, has held the composer's score sacred. A more academic point of view has prevailed in our conformist world. Trusting the letter of the score has too often passed for respect for the composer. This and the deadly perfection of recording have helped to homogenize musical interpretation, producing a blandness which threatens musical life and alienates many young performers from the spirit of music.

Horowitz suffered deeply over the prevailing musical pedanticism of our time. He never played any composition the same way twice. And because of the emotion his playing produced in any audience, the adulation he received was immense. I even felt that in an increasingly historyless and traditionless world, where many young pianists had never even heard of Paderewski, mature music lovers doubly cherished Horowitz for being unique. In fact, he *was* "the Last

Romantic," and the world held on to him tightly. He was a final link to and a symbol of another age, where passion and beauty seemed essential to life.

Horowitz's involvement with the piano was so absolute that he actually wondered what people who were not pianists did with their time. With Flaubert, he could ask, "Why is he in the world? And what is he doing here, poor wretch? I cannot imagine how people unconcerned with art can spend their time; how they live is a mystery to me."

Although Horowitz lived in New York for half a century, his English remained faulty, often extremely so. He was not always easy to understand. He could repeat the same word over and over, or, in looking for the next word, would say, "da, da, da, da." His sentences could produce awful traffic jams. Sometimes everything was tangled or he would use the wrong word. He was verbally lazy.

He had a strong, rather deep voice with a thick Russian accent. He did not speak fast, but his speech could become very heated in short spurts, when his voice became hysterical-sounding and high-pitched.

When in good form, he laughed in great outbursts. Or he would emit a rather frightening cackle, with a smile showing the entire range of his teeth, an effect that could look seedy and vulgar. He had a wide range of facial expressions, and when excited, his face would be vividly heightened by color. He could also look amazingly glum. Photographs by no means show the great variety and expressiveness of his face.

Horowitz often sang when we were discussing certain compositions. Many musicians punctuate their speech by singing fragments. Horowitz did this mostly to compare his tempi to those of others. Of course, this marvelous aspect of our conversation cannot be reproduced. Nor can the many varieties of laughter that peppered his speech. Here are a few examples of his constant difficulty with finding the right word:

"I don't like television—I like, the—eh, eh, da, da, how do you call it—radio!" Or, "The piano has those eighty-eight—things—what we call 'em—keys."

In the midst of a conversation, he could have a mini-anxiety attack. "By the way, I hope they have my juice there. How do you call that juice—orange juice? If they don't have it, I will walk out of there—from the restaurant. But they, they have everything."

Or in the middle of a topic, he would ask, "I hope maid did my shirt for tomorrow. That is the most important!"

I would ask "What kind of man do you think Mozart was?"

"Was *terrible person*, absolutely terrible, awful man. He died because he was drinking too much. He was—eh—um—drunk all the time, you know. A terrible man [followed by five high-pitched laughs]. Be-*tho*-ven, Be-*tho*-ven's brother was a uh, uh, was a— criminal, I think [laughter]. He was not clean with money. Be-*tho*-ven, too, not at all. *No*, eh sure! And even in nineteenth century, take Wagner. What he did with money—with people—*whew*—*he used everybody* [loud]. Liszt [Leest] was a nice person [reverential tone]."

In recreating our discussions, I have erased Horowitz's stammering and modified many tangles which would prevent intelligibility, while, hopefully, retaining his color and manner of speech.

Evenings With Horowitz is not, of course, a literal transcription of our conversations, but rather a distillation of our talks over three and a half years based on notes and tapes. He once said to me, "I believe in your integrity." I hope that this account of some of our evenings would not have displeased him. In writing about them, I relived the electricity I felt the moment we shook hands on our evenings together.

Even at eighty-six, Horowitz's piano technique remained wondrous. It was a blessing that he passed away so easily in the midst of a conversation. For Horowitz, the greatest virtuoso of them all, to have suffered the ignominy of a crumbling piano technique would have been pain beyond his endurance. Playing the piano was all he had, all he ever wanted.

A Brief Chronology
of the Life of Vladimir Horowitz

1903	October 1: Born near Kiev, the Ukraine
1909	First piano lessons from his mother Sophie
1912	Begins studies at the Kiev Conservatory
1914	Meets and plays for Alexander Scriabin
1919	Learns the Rachmanioff Third Piano Concerto
	Leaves Sergei Tarnowsky after five years of piano study with him for Felix Blumenfeld
	Performs the Rachmanioff Third Concerto at his graduation from the conservatory
1920	Solo debut recital in Kiev
1921	Solo debut in Kharkov
1922–25	Concerts throughout Russia
1925	Leaves Russia in the fall
1926	Solo debut in Berlin
	Performs Tchaikovsky Concerto No. 1 with the Hamburg Philharmonic
	Solo debut in Paris and Rome
1927	Concerts in Holland, Austria, England, Belgium, Hungary, and Italy
1928	New York debut in the Tchaikovsky Concerto with the New York Philharmonic, followed by a solo recital and an extensive American tour
	Plays Rachmanioff's Third Concerto for the composer
1928–32	Nonstop concertizing in Europe and America

1930   Records the Rachmaninoff Third Concerto with Albert Coates conducting the London Symphony

1932   Records the B minor Sonata of Liszt in London

1933   December 21: Marriage to Wanda Toscanini

1934   October 2: The birth of the Horowitzes' only child, Sonia

1936–38 Retirement from public performance

1939   Resumes career: On August 29, Horowitz and Toscanini perform the Brahms Second Concerto.

The Toscaninis and the Horowitzes leave for America because of the war

1940   Records the Brahms Second Concerto with Toscanini

1941   Records the Tchaikovsky Concerto with Toscanini

1942   Gives the American premiere of Prokofiev's Sixth Sonata

1943   Tchaikovsky War Bond Concert at Carnegie Hall; his playing of the Tchaikovsky Concerto with Toscanini raises over $10 million

1944   Gives the American premiere of Prokofiev's Seventh Sonata

1945   Gives the American premiere of Prokofiev's Eighth Sonata

Becomes an American citizen

Gives the world premiere of Samuel Barber's *Excursions*

Composes his transcription of Sousa's *Stars and Stripes Forever*; performs it in Central Park on "I Am an American Day"

Records Prokofiev's Seventh Sonata

1947   Gives the American premiere of Dimitri Kabalevsky's Second Sonata

1948   Gives the American premiere of Kabalevsky's Third Sonata

1949   Gives the world premiere of Barber's Piano Sonata in Havana, Cuba

1951   Second recording of the Rachmaninoff Third Concerto, conducted by Fritz Reiner

First performances in Europe after the war

1953   Gala concert at Carnegie Hall to celebrate the twenty-fifth anniversary of his American debut

1953–65   Retires from concert activity although periodically releases recordings

1957   January 1957: Toscanini dies

1965   Returns to the concert stage in a recital at Carnegie Hall which is recorded

1968   Plays a one-hour "Television Concert at Carnegie Hall" on CBS

1969–74   Once again withdraws from concert activity

1974   Plays the first piano recital at the Metropolitan Opera House at Lincoln Center

1975   January 10: Sonia Horowitz dies in Geneva at age forty

            Steinway & Sons honors Horowitz on the occasion of the fiftieth year that he has played the Steinway piano exclusively

1978   The Golden Jubilee of his American debut is commemorated with Horowitz's first concerto performance in a quarter century, the Rachmaninoff Third Concerto, with Eugene Ormandy conducting the New York Philharmonic

            Performs at the White House for President and Mrs. Carter

1979   Performs the Rachmaninoff Third Concerto on NBC television, with Zubin Mehta conducting the New York Philharmonic, also his first appearance at Lincoln Center's Avery Fisher Hall

1981   Solo recital at the Metropolitan Opera House

            Wins eighteenth Grammy Award for Best Classical Performance by an instrumental soloist without orchestra for *The Horowitz Concerts: 1979/80*

1982   First recital in London in thirty-one years, "at the invitation of Prince Charles"; recital filmed and televised in Europe and the United States

1983   Concerts in Japan

1985   Documentary film, *Horowitz: The Last Romantic*

1986   Returns to Russia for concerts in Moscow and Leningrad,
         followed by recitals in Hamburg, Berlin, London, Frank-
         furt, Amsterdam, New York, Milan, and Tokyo.
         Awarded the Legion of Honor (France), Distinguished
         Service Cross (West Germany), and the Medal of Freedom
         (U.S.A.)

         Concert film, *Horowitz in Moscow*

1987   Records Mozart Concerto in A Major, K. 488, in Milan,
         with Carlo Maria Giulini conducting; a one-hour film is
         made from the rehearsals

         Recitals in Amsterdam, Berlin, Hamburg, and his first
         concert in Vienna in fifty-three years; the film made of the
         Vienna recital is released in 1991

1988   No public performances during 1988–89

1989   Records "The Last Recording"; it wins the Grammy for
         the best solo classical album in 1991

         November 5: Dies at home of a heart attack. Horowitz is
         buried at the Cimitero Monumentale, Milan, in the
         Toscanini family tomb

EVENINGS WITH HOROWITZ

1

THE FIRST TWENTY-
TWO YEARS

Vladimir Horowitz was born October 1, 1903, not 1904 as many sources indicate. He was probably born in the town of Berdichev, not Kiev, as Horowitz claimed.

Berdichev was a bleak industrial settlement, some fifty miles from Kiev. Russian settlement laws had prevented most Jews, unless prosperous, from living in the large Russian cities, but these were relaxed somewhat by the time of Horowitz's birth. His father, Simeon, a well-educated electrical engineer, did not wish to remain in a province, and quite early he moved his family to Kiev, a city of wealth and beauty, and also the cultural capital of the Ukraine.

Jews, nonetheless, lived in mortal danger. In 1905, Kiev underwent a hideous pogrom intended to destroy the emerging power of the city's Jewish merchant class. The Horowitz apartment was fired upon, and the child just missed being killed by bullets flying through the windows. Like all Jews in the Ukraine, Horowitz had the fear of the Cossack etched in his bones.

However, compared to most Russian Jews, the Horowitz family was extremely privileged. Simeon became increasingly prosperous.

Volodya (the diminutive of Vladimir), as he was called, was the youngest of four children. Both parents were musical, and his uncle on his father's side, Alexander, had studied piano and composition with Alexander Scriabin, one of Russia's great composers. Sophie, his mother, known as a woman of beauty and talent, gave the children their first training. Regina, his older sister by three years, was highly musical. Horowitz told me he was proud of his sister, who played very well. His two brothers, Jacob and George, also had talent, but both were strange, unhappy boys.

The youngster's home life during his first decade was comfortable and financially secure. Volodya was lavished with love, and as the favored child, he was profusely spoiled. He was not forced to practice, nor was he exploited as a child prodigy. In fact, at home, his every whim was a command. Horowitz said to me, "I got away with everything. The whole family tiptoed around me." As a child, Horowitz was willful, selfish, and often lazy.

Volodya was not a wonder-child, but by age ten, his unusual talent began to bloom, and Sophie knew that her son had to enter the Kiev Conservatory, considered an excellent training ground. There he studied with Vladimir Puchalsky, who had worked with Theodor Leschetizky, the best-known piano teacher of the nineteenth century. Sophie herself had studied with Puchalsky, who at age sixty-five was a man of total inflexibility. Horowitz said:

> He was good at screaming, not teaching. He made me tense. I hated the endless drudgery he put us through. Even when I played well, he screamed. But we were still impressed because he knew Leschetizky, who had produced people like Paderewski. And Leschetizky had known Russia's pianistic idol, Anton Rubinstein, who, after Liszt, was said to be the greatest of all pianists. We respected him, but stood in terror and awe of Puchalsky, who was still the most important teacher at the conservatory. But maybe he wasn't what I needed.

In 1914, an event occurred which lasted only an hour, but loomed large in Horowitz's life ever after. Horowitz never tired of relating his meeting with Scriabin, arranged by his Uncle Alexander. Scriabin had led a feverish life and died one year after meeting the eleven-year-old Volodya.

Scriabin's music is the summit of high-strung Russian Romanticism. Scriabin was himself a marvelous pianist who played only his own music. He was a messianic and quixotic personality, and would have never suffered to hear the boy if he had not wanted to do a favor for his former pupil.

Volodya was proud that his Uncle Alexander—at that time a successful piano teacher and a critic for the major newspaper in Kharkov—had studied with Scriabin. In our talks, Horowitz reported:

My uncle graduated from the Moscow conservatory. He had received the silver medal, not the gold. The judges giving the awards were anti-Semitic. Scriabin was so angry about this that he left his teaching post at the conservatory. Later, Scriabin and my uncle became the greatest friends, and when I was living in Kiev, my uncle said to Scriabin, "I have a nephew who is very talented and you should hear him if you have time."

Then Scriabin came to Kiev to give a recital. He was staying in a private house, and he made an appointment to hear me there at three o'clock, just four hours before his concert. He was terribly nervous. At that time, I didn't understand why, but he was to play for the first time premieres of his Seventh, Eighth, and Ninth Sonatas, works of the most incredible detail and technical difficulty. Only later did I understand why he was nervous. Yet he was good enough to see a child. It must have been the last thing he wanted to do that day.

Well, I came there, naturally with my mother. I played for him maybe ten minutes of music. The *Melody* of Paderewski, a little bit of Chopin, and I think something of Borodin and Dohnányi. He listened and was very fidgety. He was a very elegant man with a beard perfectly neat and trimmed.

So after I played, he took my mother outside and he told her, "Your son will be a pianist. He has real talent. I don't know, of course, how far he will go, but please make of him an overall cultured man and make him understand not only music, but other important aspects of life. There are the arts of painting, of philosophy, of literature. Only then will he be an all-around musician." Then Scriabin said to my mother, "But a pianist he can definitely be." Scriabin's verdict on my talent was very important to us.

He was a deep man, a very intellectual person. In a way, he looked like his music. Scriabin, as you know, is a mystic composer. His music is supersensuous, superromantic and supermysterious. Everything is *super*; it is all a little overboard. Anyway, my parents were pleased that I played for him. Everyone was shocked when he suddenly died in 1915 at the age of forty-three. My uncle Alexander was beside himself.

In 1986, when I went back to Russia, I play for his daughter at the Scriabin museum on his own piano the C-sharp minor Etude, Op. 2, No. 1, which he composed when he was fourteen. Imagine, I play for Scriabin at eleven and play for his daughter when I'm eighty-three. He was dead already seventy years, and I'm playing for his daughter.

Scriabin's favorable comments gave extra validation to Volodya's talent.

Along with his musical studies, the boy was sent to a regular school, where he proved to be a poor student. Volodya was too impulsive to sit still for long to read philosophy or Tolstoy. He had a certain intellectual curiosity, but much of it was stifled by his own restlessness. He once told me:

I was a terrible student. For me, to take a book home was a trial. All I wanted to do was play Wagner and Tchaikovsky operas. I even knew Puccini from memory. I was a lot lazy when it came to learning Bach preludes and fugues and Beethoven sonatas. I loved singing. But can you imagine my voice in an opera house? At that time, I already loved Rachmaninoff's music and tried some of the easier things, as well as Grieg's lyric pieces, which I liked. I even knew the American composer MacDowell's charming woodland sketches.

Fortunately, Kiev was a musical city, visited by the best performers of the time. When Volodya had just turned nine, he snuck into a recital by Josef Hofmann, whose annual tours of Russia were celebrations. Hofmann, thirty-six at the time, was one of the world's great musical box office attractions. Earlier in 1912, he had flabbergasted glamorous St. Petersburg by playing 255 works in twenty-one concerts before audiences totaling nearly seventy thousand people. Hofmann had been one of the great child prodigies in history and the pupil of Anton Rubinstein himself. For the young Horowitz, this event produced an overwhelming impression. For the first time he heard and felt the tremendous excitement a great pianist could generate.

These were Hofmann's peak years, and no Slavic pianist of the period could rival his torrential powers. Rachmaninoff, who, at that period, mostly conducted and composed, never stopped extolling Hofmann's glories as a pianist. Hofmann was brilliant, complex, and nervous. Later in life, he succumbed to alcoholism. His interest in mechanical inventions took up much of his time. Some sources credit Hofmann with inventing the automobile windshield wiper, inspired by the movement of his metronome.

During Horowitz's formative years, Hofmann's artistry was in the forefront of any discussions of piano playing. When Horowitz arrived in the United States in 1928, Hofmann, Paderewski, and Rachmaninoff were the towering pianists of the day. Horowitz once told me that although Hofmann was at the top in the United States, he had neglected Europe since World War I and nobody knew him there anymore.

Horowitz, however, understood, as did Rachmaninoff, that Hofmann could do things at the keyboard which were unrivaled, especially his devastating evenness in scale playing and passagework. I think it irked Horowitz, who was basically very competitive, to know that his own idol, Rachmaninoff, continued to rave about Hofmann even in the late thirties. Rachmaninoff said, "The best pianist, probably after all is still Hofmann, but only under one condition, when he is 'in the mood.'"

Only once did I ask Horowitz his opinion of Hofmann, but his answer was rather elusive. "He was my first influence, when I was a boy." And then he whispered, saying almost apologetically, "But he wasn't a very nice man. You know, he was drinking too much. He was a little sourpuss. A little *sourpussy*."

Soon after the encounter with Scriabin, Puchalsky was replaced at the conservatory. With a sigh of relief, Vladimir and Regina went into the class of Sergei Tarnowsky, a twenty-six-year-old pianist. He had studied at the St. Petersburg Conservatory with "the fascinating and feminine" Annette Essipova, who had been the second of Leschetizky's four wives. Essipova's great strength grew out of her ability to teach the secrets of a ravishingly beautiful and singing piano tone. Horowitz was captivated by Tarnowsky, who in turn was mesmerized by the rapidly developing talent of Volodya.

Tarnowsky in many ways was lax as a teacher. Tarnowsky more or less let him practice what he wanted. However, without his skillful psychological insight, Horowitz's pianistic gift might have perished, since neither his temper nor temperament could tolerate the usual straitjacket type of training.

Horowitz told me, "Scriabin slept with Chopin under his pillow, and I slept with Wagner under mine. I could not concentrate on memorizing Bach fugues, but I had all of *Götterdämmerung* in my fingers. I don't think that at that time I liked the piano literature much."

Sophie was furious that her son was practicing Rachmaninoff instead of Bach, Mozart, and Beethoven. Tarnowsky was appalled at the pressure that his family exerted on Volodya and pleaded with them to let the child develop on his own.

Despite everything, Volodya's standing at home remained unchallenged. When in a bad mood, the boy would terrorize the household. Never punished, Horowitz learned early on he could get away with what others wouldn't attempt.

Already unfolding was a particular Horowitz trait, near-hysteria before any performance. Even in his youth, there was a resistance to public performance along with a desperate need to show off his skill. Public playing caused him anguish and suffering, and this dilemma was never totally eradicated. Soon, the youngster developed a reputation at the conservatory for being a moody loner, sometimes given to extreme sulking if criticized.

He could be arrogant, too. Once, when a fellow pupil played Tchaikovsky's Dumka, Tarnowsky asked the students their opinions. Horowitz declared, "She played it well, but I can do better." Tarnowsky angrily showed the youngster to the door. There were many such incidents, and the teenage pianist was forever embroiled with Tarnowsky.

Horowitz worked under Tarnowsky from the ages of twelve to sixteen, the most crucial years for the development of piano technique. Under Tarnowsky, Horowitz's growth proved breathtaking. All who heard him realized that his talent was prodigious. At the conservatory, audiences went wild in their excitement.

By the end of 1920, the relationship with Tarnowsky ended. The last work Volodya studied with him was the Rachmaninoff Third Concerto, which he had recently encountered. The concerto was only ten years old and would become his specialty throughout his life.

By 1919, the sixteen-year-old virtuoso wanted to drop Tarnowsky. But how? Every piano student knows the trauma of changing teachers. Student and teacher develop complex feelings for each other. If a teacher seems to prefer another pupil, the student is tormented. If the student leaves the teacher's roost, the wounded teacher may weep forever and never forgive the pupil.

Horowitz had learned much from Tarnowsky but felt that he was basically a miniaturist, and the youngster now needed to expand his playing horizons. Just then, Tarnowsky, who had been on vacation in the Crimea, took ill and was thought to have died. At this crucial moment, the fifty-six-year-old Felix Blumenfeld arrived in Kiev from St. Petersburg. He was to be Horowitz's last teacher.

Blumenfeld was a formidable musician with a European reputation. He had been on the faculty of the St. Petersburg Conservatory and was conductor at the Maryinsky Theatre. He knew everybody and had been with the great impresario Sergei Diaghilev in Paris for the famous concerts of Russian music in 1908. He was also a good composer and knew the piano intimately.

Horowitz was deeply impressed. Blumenfeld had intimate contact with Anton Rubinstein, the pianist who most exemplified the heroic style and the grand manner. Anton Rubinstein had died a decade before Horowitz's birth, and now, at sixteen, the young Horowitz found this vital spiritual link through Blumenfeld. Sixty-five years later, Horowitz proudly told me:

> I studied with Felix Blumenfeld, who had studied piano with Anton Rubinstein and composition with Tchaikovsky. Felix, my professor, was the right hand of Anton Rubinstein. Blumenfeld knew his playing by heart, from every angle. Unfortunately, when I came to him Blumenfeld was paralyzed on his right side, the victim of syphilis. He was still a vibrant and handsome person, but he had many vices.
>
> His piano class was small, it was the best. Anatole Kitain and Simon Barère were with me there. Barère had a tremendous technique. He played professor Blumenfeld's Etude for the Left Hand like a miracle.
>
> Blumenfeld, even though he could not demonstrate much

anymore, was exactly the teacher I needed because he was creative. It was with Blumenfeld that I started to develop my flat-finger technique. I started to practice in a sort of portamento which made my fingers like steel.

Blumenfeld was the uncle of Heinrich Neuhaus, one of the best men that ever lived. He played lots of Scriabin, and we played Wagner together on two pianos. After Blumenfeld, I learned more from Neuhaus than anyone else. He was, you know, later the greatest teacher of Russia. He taught Gilels and Richter.

The young pianist was happy with his new teacher.

Some months later, Horowitz was shocked to see Tarnowsky at his door. Far from being dead, his former teacher had recovered from a terrible siege of typhus. Tarnowsky, horror-struck to find the Horowitz children now under the charge of Blumenfeld, threw fits of jealousy and never forgave Volodya for not returning to him.

Nor did Horowitz give Tarnowsky his due. The world took it for granted that Horowitz's unique gifts were developed only by Blumenfeld. Indeed, generally a musician's last teacher gets the major credit. Tarnowsky, who later emigrated to the United States, could have had a major career boost as Horowitz's teacher if the great pianist had only acknowledged him properly. But Horowitz wanted nothing to do with him anymore. Tarnowsky remained bitter.

When Horowitz, already famous, played in Chicago, Tarnowsky, who taught there, could not resist going backstage to give advice to his former pupil. Horowitz shouted, "Leave me alone! I don't need you anymore."

Tarnowsky made a recording in his eighties which shows he had once been a stylish pianist, but probably never a virtuoso. He died in 1976.

At this period Horowitz needed to throw off all restraint. A budding virtuoso instinctively knows that in order to project in the grand style, he must have a big sound which reaches to the farthest end of a hall. Liszt, Rubinstein, Tausig, and Paderewski, when young, were constantly told they were "bangers."

Heinrich Neuhaus noted, "I have found that every great virtuoso, I mean particularly the virtuosos who play in large halls with very large audiences, at some time or other in his youth, was extremely fond of banging and thumping. The future great virtuoso sowing his wild oats, as it were... Vladimir Horowitz, when he was seventeen or eighteen, used to bang so mercilessly that it was almost impossible to listen to him in a room."

Horowitz graduated from the Kiev Conservatory in 1920. He had dreamed of being a composer like Rachmaninoff, his hero, with the piano second in importance. Through his teen years, Horowitz produced a respectable number of compositions, including a few songs set to poems by Anna Akhmatova and other poets. He completed a couple of chamber pieces, a ballade for violin and piano, and several small works for the piano. In 1930 he recorded the best of these trifles, the *Danse Excentrique*.

Blumenfeld encouraged his creative efforts, but by the time Horowitz was ready to graduate, it was clear that his true calling was piano playing. Although at the conservatory he barely got by in his theoretical studies, Horowitz's original image of himself as a composer stayed with him. He publicly lamented that the Russian Revolution prevented him from continuing on his chosen path.

His composing outlets continued sporadically throughout his life through his dozen or so brilliant piano transcriptions. Some of these were "touch-ups" and amplifications of Liszt pieces such as the second, fifteenth, and nineteenth Rhapsodies or Mussorgsky's *Pictures at an Exhibition*, which was electrifying in performance.

Several critics attacked the Mussorgsky transcription as sacrilegious: "How dare Horowitz tamper with Mussorgsky's original masterpiece?" Horowitz reported to me:

> They said I put graffiti on Mussorgsky, but I don't give a damn. I worked hard on that transcription, I'm not ashamed of it. I am proud of the transcription. I did a good job, and I think perhaps I played it very well.
>
> You see, I felt the *Pictures* had to be brought forward. They were too introverted, and this was possibly because Mussorgsky was a little bit of a dilettante, and he was not really a pianist. Ravel orchestrated the work, and I "pianostrated" it. When I change anything, it is only to make a better piano sound. And Mussorgsky did not know how. I'm sorry but that is true, and the score is also much more awkward to play in the original. But

you see, I am cagey, and I never published my version, and so it is only for me. And others will then not be criticized for my sins, as the critics say.

Now and then, Horowitz played for me a few of his teenage compositions. All were skillfully crafted but derivative. Horowitz well knew he had little original compositional gift and no concentration whatever for sustained creative effort.

While Volodya practiced, great events were unfolding in the world. During the Great War and the opening stages of the October Revolution of 1917, there was German occupation within the Ukraine and devastation within Russia. Although Kiev itself was unharmed, St. Petersburg and Moscow suffered. However, by 1918 the Ukraine decided to become a sovereign state, and soon Bolshevik troops occupied Kiev. The following two years produced tumultuous confusion, culminating in civil war.

During the freezing winter of 1919–1920, the conservatory fell into financial difficulties. The streets were dangerous. Coming home from school one day, Horowitz just missed having a bomb land on him. The tragedy became more personal when the Bolsheviks took over his father's business. Horowitz told me:

In twenty-four hours, we lost everything. *Everything!* We still don't understand how big was that revolution. It shook the whole world. Everything was different as a result of the Russian Revolution. After the revolution, we lost our home and all possessions. We moved to a bad part of the city. We were no longer affluent. My piano was stolen by the Communists and even our clothes were taken. There were curfews. It was terrible. You never knew when bullets would be fired.

My father was a broken man. Like a squirrel, he foraged for food. It was much more horrible than I am able to say now. I felt, even though I was only sixteen or seventeen, that I had to concentrate on the piano. I had to give up my dreams of composing. My main burden in my mind was to help my parents. We were almost starving. And now, all our relatives were living in our home, too, including my Uncle Alexander.

In the early 1920s, Horowitz possessed a driving desire to succeed; his motto at this time was "Success above all." Uncle Alexander was convinced of his nephew's great talent and became his first manager, arranging recitals in Kharkov, Kiev, Odessa, Tiflis, and Moscow.

Late in 1921, Horowitz met the young violinist Nathan Milstein, who became a lifelong friend and valued colleague with whom he would give duo recitals. Milstein was born in Odessa and studied with the legendary Leopold Auer, the teacher of Elman and Heifetz.

Volodya and Nathan were considered "Children of the Revolution" and made to appear at various Communist state functions. By 1922, their budding careers were taken over by the state. Horowitz's uncle was replaced by an official named Paul Kogan, who booked Horowitz, his sister, and Milstein in concerts.

The Soviet desire for music for the masses brought audiences that Horowitz described as "unthinkable, a real horror, eating, talking, smoking. Brahms for the workers of the world. But I did a good job. I played many solo recitals, too. I stormed the piano and they yelled, and we ate. Milstein was a good friend, very funny and sarcastic. And my sister was always good-hearted."

Many years later, Kogan said, "Horowitz was completely in love with music, as faithful to his piano as a medieval knight to his lady." His self-esteem at the time seemed high and he was proud of his position in the family as its prime breadwinner. Just as important, the young firebrand virtuoso acquired quite a reputation as an "audience pleaser"; wherever he performed, he was hailed as a "miracle." It seemed that the power and passion of this youngster had no parallel even in Russia, which possessed an immense pianistic heritage.

In 1923, at the age of twenty, Horowitz caused a sensation in Leningrad, where, with indomitable strength, he gave twenty-two recitals with eleven different programs. He said, "Times were different. You could fill a hall with much more adventurous repertoire. It was a less commercial time."

One of those recitals was attended by the great pianist Artur Schnabel, a dour, no-nonsense man who had been a student of Leschetizky and was an uncompromising musician. He had become the revered guardian of the German classics. In the 1930s Schnabel was the first pianist in history to record all thirty-two Beethoven sonatas.

Horowitz desperately wanted to impress Schnabel. The young pianist already felt he had to escape his homeland and thought perhaps a visa could be arranged for a period of time to study in Berlin with Schnabel.

Schnabel described the mood of Russia after the revolution: "It was absolutely different now from the Russia I had known in czarist times. Then the wealthy classes were amiable, gay, very elegant, and attractive. Now you did not see anybody anymore who was elegant or amiable." After Schnabel's recital in Leningrad, a reviewer said that "[his] rhythm was expressive of the labor battalions marching against the bulwark of capitalism."

Schnabel wrote:

A young Russian pianist who was very successful there at the time was Vladimir Horowitz, then nineteen years old. He played for me privately and I was very impressed. I was, later, instrumental in getting him out of Russia. [Schnabel may have written a letter to the authorities on Horowitz's behalf, asking that he be allowed to study abroad.] He even wanted a lesson with me, but I decided that he was not in need of any. I also asked him whether he was composing and he said, very shyly, "Yes." He had an enormous success, was rather spoiled, and tired. He was really the hero at that time. I thought it was absolutely necessary for him physically and mentally to leave Russia.

However, this was easier said than done. At the moment, Horowitz was enjoying his success in Leningrad, where young female piano students formed a fan club for the elegant, long-haired, slender, and pale pianist who people thought looked like Chopin.

From the start of his career, Horowitz's recitals were frenzied events. The Leningrad citizens even packed the thirty-two-hundred-seat Great Hall of the philharmonic, and these were years plagued by shortages of food and fuel. After one concert, the crowd lifted him bodily and brought him to his hotel, reminiscent of the Lisztomania created in 1842 in St. Petersburg when Liszt first played in Russia. By the time he was twenty-one, Horowitz had performed Rachmaninoff's Third Concerto the length and breadth of Russia. He was the pride and joy of the Soviet world of music.

During the twenties, tensions with the West eased, and many European musicians and pianists appeared in Russia. The first pianist to play in the Soviet Union after the revolution was Egon Petri, who was stunned by Horowitz's octaves. Horowitz in turn said Petri had a good technique but was too German and dry for his taste. It was the first time Horowitz had heard pianists from the outside world, and he felt confident that he could compete with the best of them.

This contact made him yearn for larger horizons. Russia, however, remained secluded from Europe. Much later Horowitz recounted, "My Russian success was nothing at all in Europe. Germany was the citadel of music, and until the time of Hitler, everyone was there."

Horowitz wondered how he could leave his homeland. In 1924 the answer came from Alexander Merovitch, a concert manager who had heard Horowitz play the Rachmaninoff Third Concerto. The impresario invited the pianist to a meeting.

Merovitch had been hampered by the Soviet bureaucracy in many of his projects and he was fed up with life in Russia. For a manager with imagination and ambition, the state-controlled artistic life was a dead end. Merovitch was determined to have Horowitz and Milstein in his managerial stable.

Early in 1925, an arrangement was made with Simeon's approval. Merovitch undertook to get Horowitz out of Russia. He would travel with him everywhere and arrange a city-by-city tour of Europe. For three years Merovitch was to receive twenty percent of their earnings, then fifteen percent "for life," an arrangement Horowitz would later resent. Of course, at the time, there were no concerts in sight.

To contemplate leaving Russia was the most courageous decision of Horowitz's life. He was celebrated in his homeland. His musical relationships with Blumenfeld and Neuhaus were important to him, and he had already made many musical contacts. He had deep ties to his parents and was totally dependent on his father and his Soviet manager, Kogan, who loved him and developed his career through the arduous times of the postrevolutionary years. He was deeply attached to his mother. To leave her and his sister would prove traumatic.

From adolescence on, Horowitz was alarmingly vain: combing his hair was a serious and time-consuming procedure, and he developed a taste for dandified clothes.

Whether the teenage Horowitz had any interest or feelings of intensity for any girl, or sexual desire toward women at all, is unknown. Rumors were fairly persistent, however, that he preferred the company of men. If anything sexual occurred, there is no record of it.

His relationship with Merovitch—who relieved him of all mundane matters, which he could never tolerate—was purely business. His friendships with Milstein and later with the cellist Piatigorsky, whom Merovitch was also to launch in a solo career, were musical only.

Horowitz's sexuality was possibly suppressed or sublimated to his career even as late as his departure from Russia in 1925. In the Soviet Union during that time, sex had none of the permissiveness of Europe or the decadence of Berlin that titillated Horowitz after his arrival there.

Horowitz grew up knowing that in Russia homosexuality was a crime, punishable even by death. He knew of Tchaikovsky's homosexuality, and he had doubtless heard it was rampant in the ballet world. Certainly it would have been shocking for a Jewish boy to show any signs of what was then considered a perversion and taboo. However, many who knew him believed he was overtly homosexual, and throughout his life, rumors of his homosexuality surrounded and tortured him, as they later did his wife.

During the years I knew him, there were no signs of any sex life and very little talk on the subject. I personally doubt that he was capable of loving a man emotionally, but there was no doubt that he was powerfully attracted to the male body and was most likely often sexually frustrated throughout his life.

The important point is that Horowitz as a person was polymorphously erotic. His very being was permeated by a powerful sexual instinct. His art was born unconsciously from his quivering erotic nature. Here was the chief source of his audience appeal, the piano being his sexual organ, the audience, his lover. I once asked him what he thought of when playing Scriabin's Fifth Sonata for an audience. He loudly responded, "I want to *fock* them."

Horowitz made almost everything he played sound sexy. Liszt,

Rachmaninoff, and Scriabin are, of course, intrinsically erotic, even orgiastic, composers. But Horowitz could take the slow movement of Haydn's F Major Sonata and make it a siren's song. His Chopin mazurkas possessed an overwhelming sexual flirtatiousness.

This erotic undercurrent developed even further as he aged. It is almost symbolic that the last music he recorded was Liszt's transcription of Wagner's *Liebestod*.

Horowitz hated any playing that sounded academic to him. "It's too dry," he would proclaim. Someone asked him how playing could be wet. Yet with Horowitz, "the art of tone turned lubricous," in Mencken's inspired phrase. At his best, Horowitz presented a magnificent alignment of feminine delicacy and masculine power. His playing was never effete, nor is there a fear of climaxes.

★   ★   ★

Although the move from Russia terrified Horowitz, it had to be accomplished.

Leaving Russia did not mean to the young Horowitz what it had to Rachmaninoff. Rachmaninoff would miss his homeland desperately. Horowitz was only fourteen when the revolution began and never experienced the intense nostalgia for Russia that Rachmaninoff felt. But with the passing years, Horowitz became more conscious of his Russian roots and always felt homeless. For him, being uprooted at twenty-two was too early to separate emotionally from his country and parents.

Later, he had complex feelings about the United States, his adopted country. While he told people to call him "Horowitz, the American pianist," he often told me how uncomfortable and alien he felt in America.

Horowitz prepared for his Russian departure by becoming as thrifty as possible. He laboriously saved nearly five thousand dollars for living expenses as well as hall rentals in Europe, although by law he could take with him only five-hundred rubles. Merovitch secured visas, and the government gave them a six-month leave, ostensibly to study with Schnabel as well as to have Europe hear one of their talented "Peoples' Artists."

After leaving Russia, he never saw his mother again. She died in 1929 after an appendix operation. His brother Jacob, drafted into the army, died during the revolution; his brother George, who had shown signs of insanity, killed himself in 1922. His sister Regina's failed marriage produced a child she had to raise alone; she desperately hoped to escape Russia with her brother's help, but Horowitz never saw her again, either.

Horowitz did see his father late in 1934. After the revolution, Simeon's life became drudgery. He had a poorly paid state job and had remarried. For nine years, Simeon was refused a visa to visit his now famous son, but then, in typical Soviet fashion, he was granted a few weeks' travel time abroad, but his wife was not allowed to join him.

Simeon had the pleasure of hearing his son's recitals in Western Europe. Horowitz's friend, the composer Alexander Steinert, saw him backstage after a Horowitz concert: "He was a magnificent man, six feet tall, with the saddest face you've ever seen but with great nobility." But Simeon, ecstatic outside the cesspool of life in his homeland, had no choice but to return to Stalinist Russia. Shortly after he returned, he was arrested and sent to a prison camp. As with countless Soviet citizens, no reasons were given. He was never released, and the year of his death is unknown.

Horowitz, whose physical health was always a barometer of emotional events, tried to block out the litany of tragedy that surrounded his family. He was guilt-ridden that he had survived, prospered, and become famous. Was it any wonder that a part of him harbored fear and hatred for Russia? As late as 1980, he told me, "I have no desire to return. I don't like the Russian approach to music, to art, to anything. I lost all my family there. I never want to go back, and I never will."

2

HOROWITZ CONQUERS THE WORLD

In May of 1925, Merovitch booked nine recitals for Horowitz, three each in Moscow, Kiev, and Leningrad. Later that year, Horowitz, the young hero of Soviet pianism, found himself at the Russian border trembling with fear. Would the guards discover his precious savings tightly wrapped in his shoes? They did not check. He looked back once, then made his way to freedom and fame. The world would soon love his art beyond his wildest expectations.

Merovitch chose Berlin as Horowitz's first stop in his conquest of Europe. In 1925 Berlin was the center of European music. To convince a Berlin audience was quite another matter than storming the keyboard throughout Russia. Germany was musically sophisticated in a way that Horowitz had not encountered in the repressed Communist world.

Berliners were familiar with large chunks of the classical repertoire. Bach, Mozart, Haydn, Beethoven, Schubert, Schumann, and Brahms constituted their musical diet. Indeed, Horowitz had little experience with these masters and even felt a temperamental antipathy toward Beethoven. Before his departure from Russia, according to his mentor, Heinrich Neuhaus, he described "how alien Beethoven was to him. Beethoven did not move him in the slightest."

Culturally, Horowitz was enchanted with Berlin and immediately realized how dreary Russian life had become. Berlin's open-mindedness about music and art deeply impressed the young pianist. Horowitz, who had been content to dazzle an audience, now realized that in many ways he was artistically provincial.

In Berlin, he heard opera under Furtwängler and Richard Strauss, and Alban Berg's *Wozzeck* was soon to have its premiere. Arnold Schoenberg taught composition there. Schnabel had taken the place of Ferruccio Busoni, who had died in 1924, as Berlin's intellectual force among pianists. In science, Einstein reigned supreme. In literature, Thomas Mann was beloved. Kandinsky's paintings were already appreciated. It was a parade of intellect and talent which would vanish all too soon under Hitler's hands.

Horowitz looked, listened, and learned. He also practiced. Merovitch was a fearless and uninhibited manager who cleverly extolled his protégé's virtues throughout the city.

In Russia, Horowitz had had to make do with one bad piano after another. In Berlin, he was delighted with the many fine pianos he heard. Piano firms were competitive, and Merovitch made it known that Vladimir Horowitz would soon be a name to reckon with.

Horowitz told me, "In Russia, there was no piano industry. When I arrived in Berlin in 1925, I didn't know which piano to play. There were then maybe eight or nine important piano makers. So I went to Weber, to Bluethner, Bösendorfer, Steinweg, to Bechstein, everywhere, and then to Steinway. And when I played the Steinway in Berlin, I said, 'That's my piano.' And I play the Steinway exclusively all the rest of my life. It has been my inseparable friend."

Horowitz's Berlin debut was scheduled for January 2, 1926, with a second recital to follow two days later. Before the concert, the young pianist's nerves were almost uncontrollable. During the sparsely attended recital, he banged away unmercifully, even breaking a string. Horowitz admitted, "I didn't play well. No critic attended, which was just as well."

Horowitz performed better at the second recital. The hall was half full, and a critic from a major newspaper wrote a favorable review: "This Russian plays with precision and elasticity and the most finely differentiated colors." The writer went on to say that his conceptual powers failed in the Schumann Fantasy. "But it is no wonder that a sense of Romantic poetry and equanimity could not have evolved on the bloody soil of Soviet Russia."

Horowitz felt better after the second recital. He recalled: "I played the *Fantasy of Figaro* of Liszt-Busoni in my second recital in Berlin. Schnabel was at the concert. Afterward, he came backstage and said, 'Oh, very good.' I said, 'Maestro, you never play pieces like the Liszt-Busoni transcription.' 'My God,'Schnabel said, 'I have only so much time to learn Bach. I don't have time for *that* kind of music.' I looked at him and said, 'You know, Maestro, I do the opposite. I play this music, but I still have time for Bach.' I was at that time around twenty-three."

However, Horowitz soon learned the meaning of time because his money was fast running out and his survival was at stake.

His luck changed after the recital on the strength of the fine review and Merovitch's aggressiveness. Horowitz was engaged to play the Tchaikovsky First Concerto with the Berlin Symphony (not the Philharmonic) on January 8. Fortunately, his war-horse, the Tchaikovsky Concerto, rescued him from oblivion. Sixty years later, Horowitz told me, "The German public was not overly fond of 'the hysterical Tchaikovsky,' and I played down the piece's bravura, although one of the critics noticed I had good octaves." Although Horowitz may not have conquered Berlin, he had made a good beginning.

In the book *Conversations with Arrau*, Joseph Horowitz asked pianist Claudio Arrau, who was exactly the same age as Vladimir, if he had heard Horowitz's first concerts. Arrau replied: "Oh, yes, I was tremendously impressed by him. It was some of the most volcanic playing I've ever heard. I remember I was sitting with my mother in the first row of the Beethovensaal, and I was *amazed* by the things he could do in spite of this incredible stiffness of the arms. The first movement of the *Funeral March* Sonata I'll never forget...My mother, who was very musical, and was never pleased with any-body—that night she was carried away. On our way home she said, 'You better get to the piano and practice because he plays better than you!'"

At that time, Merovitch brought Gregor Piatigorsky into his fold, hoping a virtuoso cellist could bolster his finances. The three young musicians got along splendidly. Merovitch now took Vladimir to Hamburg, where he was to play two recitals. The press lauded his Liszt Sonata but found him generally immature. It had been a month since the Berlin debut and Horowitz was becoming depressed. Accustomed to unconditional love in Russia, he was discovering many obstacles to overcome in Germany. To begin with, Germany supported many pianists with a larger reputation than his. Horowitz, however, had almost blind faith in Merovitch, who in turn fanatically admired the pianists' musical genius.

The day after the Hamburg recital, Horowitz and Merovtich explored the city's sights, including its famous zoo. The day was bleak and cold, and it was already dark when they returned to their hotel. In the lobby, they were confronted by a local manager, screaming and begging Horowitz to prepare to play a concerto in forty-five minutes with the Hamburg Philharmonic. The scheduled pianist had fainted and no replacement was at hand.

Horowitz looked terrified. "I cannot do it," he cried.

Merovitch screamed, "You can, you will, you have to. It's the chance of your life."

Horowitz looked like a ghost. "All right, get the librarian to bring the orchestra parts of the Tchaikovsky Concerto."

As he shaved, he gulped a glass of milk. He had not touched the concerto since appearing in Berlin a month earlier. His hands were stiff from being in the cold all day. Manager and pianist dashed to the concert hall, arriving just as intermission had begun.

The conductor, Eugen Pabst, ran to the green room wondering if a soloist had been found and was handed the score of the Tchaikovsky. He barely looked at Horowitz, of whom he had never heard. They spoke in French, since Horowitz then knew no German.

"Look here," Pabst said rudely, "I conduct the Tchaikovsky *just* like this. Here is my tempo. Here, I do this, here I do that."

Horowitz remembered: "The man treated me like a fool. As we walked out, he finally looked at me. 'Just you watch my baton, and nothing too horrid will happen, let's hope.' The man by then had forgotten my name."

As Pabst proceeded with the concerto's celebrated opening, he heard a piano sonority unlike any he had ever experienced. He looked startled as Horowitz crashed through the work's mighty chordal entrance. Pabst, as if hypnotized, found himself walking toward the keyboard to watch Horowitz's hands. All he could do was follow the unknown pianist's tempi. He looked on incredulously as Horowitz's whirlwind octaves concluded the concerto.

Pandemonium surged through the hall. Pabst grabbed Horowitz, hugging him over and over.

Horowitz said, "He devoured me. The man wanted to eat me

alive. My shoulders ached for days. The newspapers went crazy. Not since Caruso had Hamburg gone so wild. That was my big break. I was so scared that I almost didn't do it. Thank God I knew the Tchaikovsky like I did, because nobody could take such a chance. But the outcome was like a fairy tale."

Merovitch quickly changed halls for the second recital, originally booked at a hotel ballroom. Now he rented a hall holding three thousand, and within a few hours, the tickets were sold out. This success was the beginning of Horowitz's fabulously successful German career. He said to me, "They may not have liked much Russian music in Germany, but they liked me." For the next season, he was engaged for ten important appearances in profoundly snobbish Germany.

The little musical troupe of Horowitz, Milstein, and Piatigorsky now traveled to pleasure-loving Paris, arriving at the French capital early in March 1926. Horowitz felt more comfortable in Paris since he had studied French at school and was fairly fluent.

Merovitch had been to Paris in the early twenties and had established some contacts. He knew that success in Paris depended on word-of-mouth beginning with the higher echelons of Parisian society. In 1926 it was in the Parisian salons that reputations were made, just as it was for Chopin and Liszt in 1830. Horowitz was presented in a proper salon before his debut, and soon musical Paris was raving about the virtuosity of the elegant Russian.

The Salle Gaveau was filled for Horowitz's first two recitals, which were public and critical successes. These concerts were quickly followed by three more, the fifth taking place at the Paris Opéra. By the last concert, Paris was undergoing Horowitz-mania. Never had a pianist created such commotion; the audience would not stop clamoring for more. After his recently-composed *Carmen* Variations, the audience became so unruly that the police had to be summoned to bring order to the hall.

That very night, Horowitz boarded the train to Rome for his Italian debut. Merovitch and Horowitz still had barely enough money for third-class tickets and food.

For the 1926–27 season, Merovitch had engaged Horowitz to play sixty-nine concerts in nine European countries. Wherever he appeared, the public loved him, although critics gave him mixed reviews, praising his unsurpassed virtuosity but often condemning his undeveloped musicianship.

After constant success, the spell was broken in England, where Horowitz failed to make an impression. He vowed never to return.

At about this time, he was introduced to the pianist Rudolf Serkin. Serkin, born in 1903, was an exact contemporary of Horowitz. He played the Germanic-Austrian repertory, which made Horowitz feel inferior. Serkin played for Horowitz some Schubert sonatas. Horowitz listened carefully and admired the depth that Serkin attained. Then Horowitz played Chopin's G minor Ballade.

"I nearly fell off my chair," Serkin exclaimed. "It was so amazing. The 'white heat' of his playing, the fire and passion were incredible, and my hair stood on end. And never in all my life had I heard a performance like that."

Next on the Horowitz agenda was the United States. Merovitch had pursued Arthur Judson, America's foremost concert impresario. Judson signed Horowitz for an American tour early in 1928. On January 6, 1928, the twenty-four-year-old Horowitz arrived with Merovitch in the port of New York. Judson had billed Horowitz as "The Tornado from the Steppes," "a superhuman combination of Rosenthal, Paderewski, Busoni, Rachmaninoff, and Hofmann." Horowitz was embarrassed by the magnitude of the publicity.

Horowitz, who spoke no English, was to tour the United States playing thirty-six concerts in the next twelve weeks, no fewer than sixteen of them with major orchestras. Such was the managerial power of Arthur Judson.

Days after his arrival, the young pianist met his idol, Sergei Rachmaninoff, whom many considered the world's greatest piano virtuoso. In the Steinway basement, he played Rachmaninoff's Third Piano Concerto accompanied by the composer himself on a second piano. It was a dream come true. Rachmaninoff was very pleased with Horowitz's conception of the concerto, and the two became friends. It was a relationship that deepened in the years to come.

On January 12, the evening of the debut, Merovitch looked out happily at the audience. The house was full and the entire world of piano playing seemed to be in attendance. In his dressing room, Horowitz felt as though he were freezing as he paced back and forth, his hands shaking.

He was to play the Tchaikovsky Concerto with the New York Philharmonic. However, it was to be a double debut, since the difficult and brilliant conductor Sir Thomas Beecham was also making his American debut. No one was happy with the flamboyant Beecham as an accompanist.

During rehearsal, it was apparent that the two artists totally disagreed in their interpretation of the work. Beecham, who often conducted from memory, had frequently been called a dilettante, even an amateur conductor. Gossip had it that Beecham—heir to the fortune of Beecham's Little Liver Pills—had bought his career. In reality, Beecham was a tremendous musician, but he had never been a good concerto accompanist, nor did he like soloists. And in this case, he was not about to let Horowitz steal the limelight from his *own* American debut.

From the opening bars, nothing worked. Beecham began more slowly than he had promised Horowitz at rehearsal. Instantly, Horowitz tried to quicken the pace, but Beecham denied him his soloist's rights. Horowitz's mouth hung open in disbelief as Beecham went his own way. By the third movement, the Russian knew that the conductor was about to destroy his New York debut. Regarding his American debut, Horowitz told me: "I knew that in the Tchaikovsky, I could make such a wild sound, and I could play it with such speed and noise. I very much wanted to have a big success in the United States. I wanted to eat the public alive, to drive them completely crazy. Subconsciously, it was in order not to go back to Russia.

"But now, I knew I was in trouble, I knew I had to go ahead. So in my mind I said, 'Well, my Englishman, my Lord, I am from Kiev, and I'll give you something,' and I started to make the octaves faster and very wild."

Horowitz was not to be thwarted. By concerto's end, the audience was shocked. One critic wrote, "The keyboard smoked." During the intermission, most of the audience would not leave, calling him back for what seemed like endless curtain calls.

The next day, Olin Downes reported in the *New York Times*, "A mob is a mob, blood is blood; the call of the wild is heard whether it is a savage beating a drum or a young Russian, mad with excitement and physical speed and powers, pounding on a keyboard."

Horowitz was thrilled. He said, "It was wonderful! Everybody here was playing to sold-out houses: Rachmaninoff, Paderewski, Hofmann, Iturbi, Schnabel, Lhévinne, Myra Hess, Gieseking, Friedman, Rosenthal, Backhaus. It was an amazing time, and they were all there at my debut.

"But Rachmaninoff was not happy. He said to me, 'Your octaves are the fastest and loudest, but I must tell you, it was *not* musical. It was not necessary.' So I explained to him why I did it. So I could have success in order not to go back to Russia. That he understood, and he began laughing and laughing.

"You see, I had success after success, overwhelming success in Europe, but we could still barely make ends meet. I was very poor and the United States was the only place I could make money.

"You know that in two months, I would be recording for RCA my *Carmen* Variations. It took three times to get what I wanted. I was very impressed with the electrical records, much better than the piano rolls I had made."

Days later, Horowitz followed the Concerto debut with a jammed Carnegie Hall recital in which the Liszt Sonata was the pièce de résistance. As an encore, he played his *Carmen* Variations. He was delighted as, with each variation, row after row of the audience stood up in amazement at his virtuosity.

A week later, in Boston, one of America's foremost critics, Philip Hale, wrote of Horowitz's Rachmaninoff Third, "There was a sense of enthusiasm such as has not been aroused by any performance of a pianist in Symphony Hall since its opening."

City after city succumbed to Horowitz's pianistic witchcraft. Later Horowitz said, "In the United States, Chicago was to my success what Hamburg was in Germany."

The United States and Horowitz clicked. America's innocence and materialism appealed to his own nature. Horowitz's pianistic dynamism seemed to be a projection of the country's own brash, optimistic, and simplistic views of art and life. With his newfound wealth, Horowitz bought a large Studebaker automobile, and retained his elitism by hiring a chauffeur.

During the next five years, the pianist played tirelessly. During one American tour, he performed forty-two concerts in eighty-one days. In the 1929–30 American season, he played seventy-three concerts in one hundred eighty days.

Judson's firm, Columbia Concerts Corporation, hired Merovitch as the personal representative for Milstein, Piatigorsky, and Horowitz. Merovitch still had almost total domination over Horowitz, who lacked all business acumen. The manager never showed him contracts and even signed his name for him. Occasionally, Merovitch used Horowitz in chamber concerts, accompanying either Milstein or Piatigorsky, or in trio performances.

Even during the first years of the Depression, Horowitz received the considerable fee of fifteen hundred dollars per concert.

By the early 1930s, English audiences had warmed to the young Russian. After Horowitz had been engaged to play with Beecham once again, in April 1933 in London, the witty conductor acknowledged his earlier transgression: "Mr. Horowitz, this time I have the score with me." At rehearsal, Beecham exclaimed in wonder. "Really, Mr. Horowitz, you can't play like that. It shows the orchestra up."

By now, Horowitz had performed with most of the world's great conductors other than Toscanini, the most famous conductor of all time. So Horowitz was particularly excited to receive a telegram from the Maestro in October 1932, inviting him to play the *Emperor* Concerto with the New York Philharmonic in a Beethoven cycle that Toscanini would conduct in the spring of 1933.

But Horowitz was frightened on two counts. Would he fulfill Toscanini's expectation, and could he overcome his sense of intimidation over Beethoven's music?

He did not know the concerto and began to work with all speed, having six months to learn it while pursuing his difficult schedule. This would be the first Classical concerto he had ever played in public. However, Horowitz was a tremendous worker and practiced every spare moment available, including travel time on trains, when he used his portable dumb (silent) keyboard. The French pianist Alfred Cortot once said, "Horowitz has great genius for getting things ready for performance."

Toscanini was by far the most feared conductor in the world. His disdain of "star" soloists was legendary. He was the ultimate musician, a despot who drove his players relentlessly in his quest for perfection. In his long musical career, Toscanini, who was never satisfied, could actually say that he had never yet had five minutes of musical fulfillment. Horowitz had a fanatical respect for him.

By 1932, Toscanini had become a symbol for human freedom. In Italy, he consistently antagonized Mussolini by refusing to play the Fascist hymn "Giovinezza" before his performances at La Scala. He had criticized anti-Semitic policy and refused to conduct Wagner at Bayreuth.

Ten days before performing with Toscanini, Horowitz played the Beethoven concerto in Chicago. The reviews were awful.

Between his insecurity over Beethoven and his fear of Toscanini, the thirty-year-old virtuoso felt panic as he was ushered in to meet with the Maestro at the conductor's hotel. At the piano rehearsal,

Horowitz played the concerto nonstop to the end. Toscanini, with his intense and notoriously nearsighted eyes, abruptly looked at the Russian, saying simply, "That is very good. I shall see you at the orchestra rehearsal."

Horowitz recalled, "I left the hotel and jumped in the air. Toscanini, the man who premiered *La Bohème*, liked my Beethoven. I felt like a student who had finally pleased the teacher."

The performance proved a success. Afterward Toscanini said, "I like to play with this boy!" The *New York Times* reported that "Horowitz could stride with Beethoven and Toscanini."

Two years earlier, Horowitz had briefly met Toscanini's youngest daughter, Wanda, at a party. Even before Horowitz's performance with her father, Wanda Toscanini knew Horowitz's playing, when she heard the dashing young pianist perform in Milan. She said, "Already, I knew he was the best." She was not about to miss the party after Horowitz's *Emperor*.

After dinner, the pianist completely bewitched her with his playing of Chopin mazurkas. By the end of the evening, a sympathy had developed between them. Horowitz, who usually felt inhibited around women, found himself opening up to Wanda, and eight months later, on December 21, 1933, they were married in Milan. It was to be a turbulent marriage lasting fifty-six years.

Wanda had been raised in Italy. Her academic studies ended with graduation from high school. She had studied piano and singing, but a musical career was off-limits because she was mediocre and her father let her know it. Like her mother, Wanda played a maternal, helpful role toward her father. By faithfully listening to her father's conducting, her fine musical instincts became acute. She had acquired a sense of quality and understood the nuances of performance. "I fell in love with Volodya's pedaling," she said.

Horowitz, who for years had been deprived of family life, gravitated to Wanda and her family. Some malicious acquaintances said Horowitz could not resist marrying a Toscanini. Certainly the glamour of being Toscanini's son-in-law was greatly attractive to the status-conscious pianist. Toscanini neither encouraged Wanda to marry Horowitz nor stood in the way.

Horowitz was exhausted from the strain of performing since 1920. For years, the wayward pianist had been the man about town. He lived freely and spent lavishly on luxuries such as a valet. At times he seemed carefree and was frequently vivacious. More often, though, he was solitary, moody, and hysterically neurotic. Aside from his piano practice, he was incapable of handling anything mundane. He was terrified by the thought of marriage, but the lure of domestic life had a strong appeal.

The significance of Horowitz's decision to marry Wanda Toscanini was equaled only by his decision to leave Russia. He gave up his freedom to become part of a close-knit Italian family. Inevitably, he was thrown under the shadow of Toscanini, an authoritarian tyrant who was fundamentally a very different kind of musician than Horowitz. The young pianist had few defenses against his father-in-law's vehement musical ideas and unrivaled experience as a musician.

Marriage also meant that Horowitz would be under pressure to produce a grandchild. But worst of all, he would be under constant surveillance. When Wanda could not travel with him, he was chaperoned by her brother-in-law.

Although Toscanini intensely loved his wife and family, he was a well-known philanderer. Women were irresistible to him. Wanda knew that her mother had deeply suffered over her husband's womanizing. If it was true that Horowitz was homosexual, such behavior would have to be eradicated.

Ten months after their wedding, Wanda gave birth to a daughter, Sonia, named after Horowitz's mother Sophie.

Horowitz soon learned that a large Italian clan is similar to a typical, large Russian Jewish family. However, he was not the star in his new family, and Wanda was temperamentally a carbon copy of her father. Horowitz said, "My father-in-law was the law. He was more difficult than me." But he proudly told everyone he was "a pupil of Toscanini."

Horowitz soon became depressed. Being a father and husband and a member of a big enclave took its toll. During the 1934–35 season, his playing was erratic, and the strain of endless concertizing had become unbearable.

During the summers the entire Toscanini family lived at the Maestro's beloved summer home, Isolino San Giovanini on Lake Maggiore. Horowitz must have felt like a prisoner there. In her book *Our Two Lives*, Halina Rodzinski, the wife of the conductor Artur Rodzinski, describes a visit to the island:

"We arrived on a warmish Sunday afternoon in mid-June to find the entire family still at table having coffee. Maestro's children, with their families, were all talking noisily, animatedly, very much in the tradition of an Italian household.... Toscanini's youngest daughter, Wanda, sat dangling Maestro's favorite grandchild, little Sonia Horowitz, while Vladimir stood around shy and out of place in the midst of such Latinate family doings. The two daughters were haranguing Maestro for not demanding greater royalties for his recordings."

It was about this time, under Wanda's influence and business acumen, that Horowitz was able to break free from the financial stranglehold Merovitch held him in.

Late in 1935, Horowitz's behavior became increasingly neurotic, and he began to cancel concerts. In London, in 1936, he made his last recordings until 1940.

He now feared he would die as his mother had, of appendicitis: although nothing was medically wrong, he had his appendix removed. The operation caused complications. His health deteriorated, and he developed colitis and other stomach ailments that would plague him throughout his life. Horowitz and Wanda spent practically the next two years in Switzerland, with the pianist more or less immobile as he suffered from phlebitis and took various cures.

In Switzerland, he resumed his friendship with Rachmaninoff, who kept encouraging him to play again. His disappearance from the concert stage even elicited an obituary from *Figaro*, the Parisian newspaper.

Late in December 1938, he started performing once again after nearly three seasons of inactivity. He had a fresh outlook and seemed, for the first time in years, to be well adjusted.

By the summer of 1939, Toscanini, who had continued to attack Mussolini, now realized that staying in Italy was too dangerous. That summer would be the last they would spend in Europe. Not until the war had been over for six years did Horowitz again play in Europe. Henceforth, New York City was to be his home, and the United States would be the beneficiary of Horowitz's piano virtuosity.

The thirteen years from 1939 until his voluntary retirement in 1953 were of little event, except for coast-to-coast concertizing. He continued to play his well-worn programs, including the Tchaikovsky and Rachmaninoff concertos, which never failed to bring him acclaim. Soon after returning to the United States, he recorded the Brahms Second Concerto with his father-in-law. During the 1940s, he made many recordings, all of them interesting, some among the great recordings of the century.

On March 23, 1943, Horowitz received the crushing news that Rachmaninoff had died at the age of seventy. He felt isolated and lonely. It had always irked him that Toscanini didn't like his idol's music and never performed any of his compositions.

Horowitz proudly became an American citizen and displayed his patriotism musically in many ways, the most important being the War Bond Concert at Carnegie Hall on Easter Sunday, April 25, 1943. At the time, it was the greatest fund-raising concert in history, bringing to the United States Treasury Department over 10 million dollars.

Horowitz was also learning the so-called *War* Sonatas of Prokofiev. Horowitz told me, "The Sixth Sonata was composed just before World War II. I was the first to play it here. The Seventh and Eighth Sonatas I played at the Russian consulate during the war. Many musicians came to the consulate. They all wanted to hear the new sonatas. In the first rows were Stokowski, Bruno Walter, Toscanini, the young Bernstein, all the critics, and many American composers like Barber and Copland."

Late in 1944, Horowitz's patriotic fervor propelled him to create his most sensational transcription, Sousa's march *The Stars and Stripes Forever*. It was sheer dynamite. At war's end, Mayor La Guardia invited him to play it on "I Am an American Day" in Central Park for over one hundred thousand people. For the next eight years, until his retirement in 1953, the march haunted him. Audiences would not let him go until they heard the irresistible tunes.

Beginning in 1944, Horowitz experimented with teaching. He took on one pupil, sixteen-year-old Byron Janis, whom he had heard in Pittsburgh playing the Rachmaninoff Second Concerto with the fifteen-year-old Lorin Maazel conducting.

Since the age of ten, Janis had been working with Josef Lhévinne's assistant, Adele Marcus. For Janis, the new relationship was a mixed blessing because Horowitz's overpowering personality made for confusion and imitation. It took Janis years to sort out the experience. He enjoyed an early success and displayed all the traits of great talent, but in later life, severe arthritis drastically curtailed his concert career.

In an interview, Janis discussed his three years with Horowitz:

His concert tours were endless and it was all train travel then. But one cannot imagine the kind of commitment Horowitz had to me. I would often travel with him and Mrs. Horowitz so the lessons went uninterrupted. I became like a son, a part of the family. We all went on vacations together. Sometimes I had lessons at his father-in-law's house in Riverdale. This was not just a father-in-law. It was Toscanini himself.

Horowitz certainly had no "method." There was tremendous experimentation, trial and error. Indeed, he had never taught before and he was learning himself. Horowitz was a great cataloguer of ideas. In a sense, he needed me creatively. Through these sessions, he was himself spurred on to new ideas musically. One cannot properly imagine the creative imagination of an artist like Horowitz. He understands the instrument's insides, and at certain times in his life, he needed a pupil to bring out things he needed to articulate. You know, the endless concert schedule can leave you dry, and teaching is a unique form of giving.

The lessons ended in 1948. Horowitz would teach again after his retirement in 1953, but he acknowledged only two pupils other than Janis: Ronald Turini and Gary Graffman. However, over the years, many others played for him on various occasions.

Horowitz, now in his late forties, found the strain of travel had become more and more difficult. He despised trains, hotels, and bad food. Besides stomach ailments, an assortment of illnesses caused him to cancel many concerts.

And Horowitz's personal life became increasingly difficult. His daughter Sonia was morose and unhappy, suffering not only the usual adolescent pangs, but the severe hardship of growing up in a famous household. Sonia was deeply troubled, but Horowitz, instead of trying to help, only withdrew from her. Although it is not publicly acknowledged, she committed suicide in 1975.

The Horowitz marriage also became a hell of hysterical bickering. Horowitz's analyst thought that he needed time alone. Late in 1949, he moved to a hotel with a valet. However, Wanda was indispensable to every Horowitz whim and decision, so the couple still traveled together for many concert dates.

In 1953, Horowitz celebrated the twenty-fifth anniversary of his American debut. The Silver Jubilee season, heavily booked with major events, began with the Tchaikovsky Concerto at Carnegie Hall on January 12, twenty-five years to the day after his American debut.

Early in March, Wanda joined her husband for a concert in Minneapolis. Emotionally incapacitated and physically exhausted, suffering terribly from colitis, Horowitz totally collapsed. Although he was terrified of flying, Wanda hired a plane and brought him home. They were never to be separated again, and over the next years she patiently nursed him back to health. His days as a traveling virtuoso were over. He had spent his American years since 1940 in an endless procession of triumphs and applause. He had conquered the world, but he had lost himself.

3

AN EARLY RETIREMENT

In 1953, not yet fifty years old, Horowitz was at the height of his technical prowess. When he performed, the instrument seemed to possess an added dimension. He sounded like a force of nature.

For nerve-racking excitement, listen to the pirated recording of the Tchaikovsky Concerto performed live with George Szell conducting the New York Philharmonic for the January 1953 Carnegie Hall concert celebrating the Silver Jubilee of his American debut.

No longer was the concerto the tight, well-harnessed performances recorded twice a decade earlier with Toscanini. This evening, Horowitz was there to slay the dragon, and he hurled thunderbolts at the audience. He relentlessly pushed the disciplined Szell to compete with him. No mere orchestra would best Horowitz. Such playing caused dire ensemble problems and the massive ending turned into chaos. It was the wildest performance in the grandest manner—never has there been such playing before or since.

For Horowitz, a concert was always a life-and-death struggle. And nothing is more physically grueling and mentally exhausting than endless concertizing. But worse still, many of Horowitz's audiences began wanting merely to be entertained and exhilarated by the physical miracles he accomplished. The crowds wanted blood and thunder; they shouted and stamped until he gave them his sizzling encores.

Horowitz, who wanted desperately to please, could not resist "wowing" his customers. This aspect of his musical personality, although a very legitimate part, became his albatross. He felt the public was causing the stuntman in him to strangle the artist, and every season he waged an artistic war with himself.

While each concert brought triumph and endless ovations, it inevitably drained him. Every tour became more exhausting, and each new audience more difficult to conquer. He found he no longer had the strength or the will to outdo himself, and finally, he shut his piano to his adoring public.

It was a cruel time to retire; the world was at that moment sadly lacking in star pianists. By 1953, most of the great virtuosi of the Golden Age of piano playing had died. Of the old guard, Josef Hofmann had retired in 1947, and Alfred Cortot and Edwin Fischer were in ill health. In 1950, music lovers wept bitterly over the death of the thirty-three-year-old Romanian master, Dinu Lipatti. In 1951, Artur Schnabel passed away, and so did Simon Barère. The idol of American pianists, William Kapell, was killed in an air crash in 1953 at the age of thirty-one. And the greatest of Italian pianists, Arturo Benedetti Michelangeli, had already become notorious for canceling concerts.

Romantic piano playing continued to shine with the irrepressible Arthur Rubinstein, and Horowitz's pupil, Byron Janis, attempted to uphold his master's ideals. There was great excitement when Emil Gilels and Sviatoslav Richter surfaced in the West during the late fifties, but they were generally locked away under the Soviet system. In 1958, a young man from Texas, Van Cliburn, helped ease the Cold War when his victory at the first Tchaikovsky Competition in Moscow took the musical world by storm.

But where was Horowitz? The years were rushing by. Piano connoisseurs were somewhat relieved when the pianist released albums of rather unsalable composers: a recording of Clementi sonatas and an all-Scriabin record.

Muzio Clementi, who is buried in Westminster Abbey, was born in 1752, four years before Mozart. But aside from a few of his piano etudes, the prolific Clementi—frequently called "the Father of the Pianoforte"—has been a neglected composer.

Horowitz had shown some interest in Clementi in the 1940s, but his curiosity was piqued after his wife brought back from Italy many volumes of first editions of Clementi's nearly sixty sonatas. The more Horowitz studied him, the more important he felt Clementi to be. After a long dilemma, he chose three sonatas to record.

Since his voluntary exile, he had lived the life of a recluse. He was seldom seen in public and felt uncomfortable if he was ever recognized. RCA naturally wanted him to record again, but he refused even to venture as far as their recording studios. His record producer, Jack Pfeiffer, compromised. After much acoustical juggling, the Clementi album (and later the Scriabin) was recorded in Horowitz's own living room.

Although Horowitz had recorded Haydn and Mozart years before, his Clementi album reveals a deeper feeling for Classical style. The pianist seemed to be saying he no longer wanted to be typecast as a performer of the Romantic or bravura repertoire. The Clementi disc was not a best-seller, but it is a landmark in the pianist's development.

He had also been studying Scriabin's music. The Russian master had suffered an eclipse in performance after his death in 1915. This sensuous and esoteric branch of the piano literature was ideal for Horowitz's temperament. He recorded Scriabin's dark Third Sonata, a composition which in most performances sounds incoherent. In Horowitz's hands, however, it became charged with Romantic drama and tension. For the flip side of the disc, he chose sixteen of Scriabin's ninety-five preludes, most of which were unknown. The performances are exquisitely refined, showing Horowitz's uncanny ability to mix subtle tonal colorings.

Clearly, Horowitz was winning his artistic battle as well as championing an unhackneyed repertoire. While his withdrawal from the world's concert stages had deprived his public, he had saved himself. Now he had the necessary leisure for artistic growth. If he was not prolific, he wasn't idle. By the early 1960s, Goddard Lieberson, president of Columbia Records, lured Horowitz to his company. The recordings he made there of Scarlatti, Schumann, and Beethoven exhibited new depths in his playing.

During the early sixties, he remained tense about performing in concert, yet at the same time, he was feeling the urge to return to the stage. He often asked friends, "Do you think the people will still love me?"

The public, after all, is fickle. Twelve years is a long time in the life of a performer. A whole new generation had never heard him. Horowitz had become a legend, and he had much to lose by returning to concert life.

By 1965, however, his desire to perform a recital became irresist-

ible. He had to find out if, once again, he could create the magic of
yesteryear. Could he fuse twelve years of artistic development with
the frightening pressures of the stage?

He took the plunge and announced a Carnegie Hall recital, "just to
see what would happen." He promised only one recital, making no
further commitments. The media immediately gobbled up the
announcement, calling it "the comeback of the century." The great
event was scheduled for Sunday afternoon, May 9, 1965, at three-
thirty.

4

THE TRIUMPHANT RETURN

I had heard about the recital late, and from that moment I was struck with anxiety. People had stood through the night and the tickets were sold out in two hours. However, on the night before the concert, reports said that some extra tickets would be made available.

"I'll never get in," I said dejectedly.

My wife at the time, Greta, who was not a musician but a great Horowitz fan, replied, "We must stand on line. We have to try."

"Of course, you're right." And off we went.

Hour after hour, we guarded our position waiting for the box office to open. Soon came the cruel announcement that the only tickets available were an unspecified number for standees in the upper balcony.

Our anxiety mounted. I began to hate everyone in front of us, convinced that tickets would run out just before we received the privilege of standing at Horowitz's recital. My heart began to pound.

Minutes later, another announcement indicated that the line would be cut off at one hundred standees. I madly counted the people ahead of us. Thankfully, we would just make it within the charmed number. As we purchased our tickets, I sighed with relief. I would hear the master after all.

It seemed like I had been on my feet for days. My lower back felt broken. I was cold and my head ached. We had barely two hours to rest before the concert. I wondered if I could even concentrate on the playing, but it didn't matter—we would be part of the excitement.

Never had I seen such a glamorous audience: Stokowski, Bernstein, Nureyev, Stern, Cliburn, all were waiting for the return of the sixty-two-year-old pianist.

From the moment the houselights dimmed until he appeared on stage seemed like an eternity. The audience sat motionless. Carnegie Hall itself seemed alive to Horowitz's agony. On the vast stage, the piano looked like a sinister coffin.

Suddenly, the stage door opened. Horowitz, looking like a ghost, walked slowly out to greet the thunderous applause. His look of helplessness was heartbreaking.

Only later, after knowing him well, did I fully appreciate what he must have gone through to undertake such an ordeal. Horowitz himself was by no means certain he could play in public again. He said, "I thought maybe I would collapse on stage."

After acknowledging his welcome, he sat down to play. For the opening work, Horowitz had chosen an eighteen-minute trial by fire, the *Toccata, Adagio, and Fugue* of Bach-Busoni. Within seconds, his fingers hit a devastating clinker. The audience prayed. Horowitz breathed deeply. He had performed this music for forty years, and his experience and mastery saved him.

He bravely continued, missing a number of notes, but with a grandiose sweep. Never had this arrangement from Bach's great organ work seemed more fervent. The Adagio was penetrating in its churchlike atmosphere, and Horowitz sounded glorious as he threaded his way through the strands of the complex Fugue. The audience literally lived through a collaboration with the pianist. They were gripped with fear, faith, and the spirit of Bach.

The relief Horowitz felt as he left the stage must have been enormous. Later he told me, "At that moment, life began again."

Horowitz continued his demanding program with the monumental Schumann Fantasy, a work written during the composer's passionate courtship of the pianist Clara Wieck. The middle movement, a daring march, mingles the chivalry of the tournament with wedding bells for Schumann's marriage to Clara, thwarted by her father.

Toward the end of the march occur some of the most dangerous leaps in the piano literature. They are seldom hit squarely by any pianist. Horowitz, in the heat of battle, with perspiration dripping from his eyelashes, made a mess of the passage. Later, he blamed the perspiration and the humidity in the hall for missing the dreaded skips. Nonetheless, it was a gorgeous performance full of color and emotion.

During intermission, I noticed that my back was still in severe pain from the hours of standing and the high tension of the recital itself. Yet I also realized I had never listened so attentively to anyone before.

The second half of the recital resembled the procession of a conqueror. The Scriabin Poem was played with a quivering intensity, and the Ninth Sonata, *The Black Mass*, reeked of the odor of decay.

In the Chopin group, Horowitz displayed breathtaking finger control with the F Major Etude. His performance of the Mazurka in C-sharp minor possessed a bitter nostalgia, Chopin yearning for his vanquished homeland. The final work of the recital, the G minor Ballade, was played in a bardic mood, its epic poetry flooding the great hall.

Horowitz had surpassed my expectations, and the encores ending his historic return were delightful. He had carefully chosen four delectable morsels: Debussy's *Serenade for the Doll*, played with at least five layers of color; the passionate C-sharp minor Scriabin Etude; an Etude in A-flat by Moszkowski, rippling across the keyboard; and *Träumerei* of Schumann, sounding like a concluding benediction.

I staggered home from the concert and slept for sixteen hours, filled with music from the recital. The next day, I awoke content. I was one of the few of my generation who had actually heard Horowitz live, and my friends, many of whom were now teaching in universities across the country, were filled with envy.

5

THE SECOND COMING

I thought Horowitz was back to concert life, and that I would have the chance to hear and learn from him on a continuing basis. But with the elusive and unpredictable Horowitz, such was not the case. During the remaining 1960s, his concertizing was meager.

In 1966, he seemed to be back in full swing, performing in major cities such as Washington, Boston, and Chicago, as well as at Yale and Rutgers. However, in 1967, the number of recitals dwindled to five, and in 1968, to four. In 1969, he peaked with ten concerts. Then boom! After a Boston recital, he caught cold. This triggered a depression, and once again he halted his concert career, the silence this time lasting for five years. Not until May of 1974 did he find the courage to perform again in public.

His second comeback took place in Cleveland's elegant Severance Hall, the home of the Cleveland Orchestra. Again, there was a hail of publicity. Clevelanders had not heard him in years. Tickets for the best seats were twenty-five dollars, an outlandish price at the time.

The Cleveland concert was a triumph and it gave Horowitz confidence. Schuyler Chapin, the new general manager of the Met, invited him to give the first piano recital in the Metropolitan Opera House at Lincoln Center, which was then eight years old. Chapin had known Horowitz for years and was sensitive to his many demands.

Horowitz liked the idea of making a New York comeback at the Met—the largest opera house and stage in the world, with nearly thirty-seven hundred seats—if the acoustics were acceptable to him.

43

Horowitz was pleased with his tryouts and announced that on November 17, 1974, he would play at the Met. Once again, there was the usual clamor for tickets.

At that time, I was in a state of bleak depression. Since 1967, I had been music and program director of radio station WNCN, but I had recently lost my job. The powers at Starr Broadcasting were convinced that classical music could not be a commercially viable format. The owners, headed by chairman of the board William F. Buckley, decided to change WNCN into a hard rock station, WQIV. The affair caused a scandal; New York City was outraged that WNCN, which had become a cult station over the years, was in jeopardy.

During my seven years at WNCN, I had made many innovations in classical music programming, and much to my satisfaction, the station was greatly appreciated and listened to. The change of format to rock-and-roll elicited an outburst; nearly half a million signatures protested the change to the FCC. Listener groups formed, attempting to save a valuable cultural format from the ever-increasing junk music that was fast making radio into a wasteland. It was the largest such protest in broadcast history.

WNCN's plight achieved national media coverage, and I was interviewed on the news several times. Although a court battle raged on, WQIV, as planned, arrogantly superseded WNCN with a rendition of "Roll Over Beethoven." The last composition I programmed was the Mozart Requiem. At the time of Horowitz's Met recital, I was on the unemployment line feeling that my years at WNCN had been wasted.

I had been, it seemed, defeated fighting the Philistines for the survival of WNCN, and now, to my dismay, here I was, freezing in a line for a pianist who continually deprived his public, a public who would come to hear him ten times a year if he would let them.

I was irritated that Horowitz had decided to titillate New Yorkers with one concert in five years. Yet I wanted to hear him. At seven in the morning, I went to the Metropolitan Opera, where I encountered a staggeringly long line.

Instead of gathering in the basement, as was usual for purchasing tickets at the Met, the line stretched outside, where it was cold and windy. TV cameras circulated. It looked like a well-calculated public relations gimmick.

Noticing my agitation, a reporter whom I recognized from ABC News came over to interview me. I belligerently cried, "Who in the hell does this Horowitz think he is?! Why can't he play the piano every season like any normal pianist instead of making us line up like fools?" That outburst calmed me somewhat.

After standing for nearly seven hours, I heard the dread announcement: "Sold out." I shook my head in frustration and went home angry.

The next day, I was reading Camus. And although I was not contemplating suicide, my mood was no better.

Suddenly, the phone rang. It was Francis Robinson, the assistant manager of the Metropolitan Opera, whom I had once hired to do a weekly opera series on WNCN. I gulped. I was certain Francis had seen me on "Eyewitness News" and was upset with me.

"David," he said, "I know how you love Horowitz and I have my two press tickets. Unfortunately, I'm on duty that day in the press room, so I won't be in the hall. I have to give one to the Milan critic, and I'd like to offer you the other one."

My mood brightened. "Francis," I said, "I accept with all my might."

"And David, if you'd like, let me introduce you to Volodya after the concert."

The late Francis Robinson was one of the finest gentlemen in the world of music. I was touched by his invitation.

On the Sunday afternoon of the concert, the usual celebrities who came to hear Horowitz were in attendance. Most eyes were riveted on Jackie and Aristotle Onassis; somehow, I had not seen either of them standing in the ticket line outdoors with me. However, I was content sitting in one of the best seats in the house. I was also curious to hear how a piano sounded in this vast space.

Horowitz exerted his usual magic. The hall's acoustics are excellent for a piano. Horowitz played Clementi's F-sharp minor Sonata very differently from his recording of 1954. Today, it was rhythmically less severe, a highly flexible, relaxed rendering. For me, the best part of the recital was a volatile performance of Scriabin's Fifth

Sonata. It was the first time he had played it in public, and the audience was captivated by this ecstatic and unfamiliar work.

For an encore, Horowitz performed Chopin's C-sharp minor Waltz with a heartbreaking throb of sorrow. The Milan journalist seated next to me was quietly sobbing.

During the applause, he took my arm and apologized, saying, "The playing so stabbed my heart that it took me back to my childhood when on summer nights my sister was practicing that divine lyric. She is long dead from tuberculosis and Horowitz's playing reminded me of how deeply I miss her."

After the concert, I located Francis in the press room. After a glass of champagne, he led me on the trek through the labyrinth of the most complex of any opera house.

The pianist was wearing a light blue cashmere sweater, lounging languidly on a sofa. Francis, who had long known Horowitz, introduced me as the music director of WNCN, the classical station fighting for its life.

To my amazement, Horowitz, who had seemed very sedate, leaped from the couch, grasped my hand, and exclaimed, "How is the battle going? We must not lose a classical music station."

I was surprised that he knew anything about such matters. I responded, "Mr. Horowitz, who knows, perhaps we will win," adding, "may I say that your recital was inspiring, and that you have the most wonderful nervous system in the world."

Horowitz almost screeched, "I'm a nervous system? I'm a nervous system?" And with that, I let the next well-wishers congratulate him.

After thanking Francis, I left and walked home. I was no longer depressed; that evening, I found myself happily practicing the music of Scriabin.

After a furious ten-month-long court battle, WNCN regained its status as a classical music radio station. Its victorious return on August 6, 1975, was cause for celebration among thousands of classical music lovers. I would continue my duties as its music director.

•

6

MY FIRST VISIT WITH
THE MAESTRO

It was early November 1979, five years since meeting the Maestro after his Metropolitan Opera recital. Sedgwick Clark, editor of WNCN's *Keynote* magazine, asked, "Isn't it about time you interviewed Horowitz?"

I said, "I'd love to, but how?"

Sedgwick said, "Let me phone Jack Pfeiffer at RCA and put the bug in his ear." Pfeiffer had been Horowitz's record producer for many years.

Horowitz had just released a new recording, and Jack thought an interview would be good publicity. Horowitz agreed, and the interview was set for November 16 at his home. Jack was to be there, and I was to bring WNCN's engineer, Richard Koziol.

Jack warned, "Be there exactly at nine-thirty. Not a minute late, God forbid! You are in for a fragile evening. Horowitz is as finicky as a cat, and Wanda will be there, too. Good luck. You'll need it."

Pfeiffer also gave me the dress code, "Now remember, you *must* wear a jacket and tie."

I said nothing. I hated ties. For years, I had been in the habit of wearing a scarf instead and felt this would suffice. Why should I wear a tie? I thought. Let's see if the Horowitzes would really throw me out as I heard they had done if someone appeared at their home without this sign of respect.

The weather had been abnormally warm for days, and I was sweating as Richard and I arrived at the house at least fifteen minutes early. We killed time by walking around the block. Richard speculated on how we would be treated. He fussed with his tie, and we both wondered if I would be booted out at the sight of my silk scarf.

The Horowitzes were famous for being temperamental. Richard, too, was aware that they were the royal couple of music and that Mrs. Horowitz was the high-strung daughter of Toscanini.

From the street corner, we spied Jack. As he rang the doorbell, he prepared his appearance with a thorough combing of his hair and was soon let in. This was surely a signal for us to proceed.

Curiously, I was not as nervous as I thought I would be. In fact, I felt quite composed as we were ushered upstairs. I was ready for whatever would happen. Although I deeply admired Horowitz's art, I was not there to genuflect. My questions were prepared, and I was hoping for a good interview.

As we entered the living room, Jack, sitting alone, got up to receive us. The Horowitzes had not yet made their entrance. He appeared anxious but told us not to be nervous. Richard plugged in his tape recorder.

Meanwhile, I looked around the room and was disappointed to find that the marvelously lithe Picasso *Acrobate* was not hanging above the couch, as I had seen in photographs of the Horowitz home. I later learned that the painting, which Horowitz bought in the 1940s for a mere eighteen thousand dollars, had been sold. In its place hung a large Japanese panel.

The room was rich and spacious. Everywhere were figurines and small sculptures of animals, especially cats. Two chairs surrounded the long couch, before which stood a table with a small low seat in front of it. On the table were a few magazines and various books about music. The ceilings were high, and a large mirror hung on the opposite wall.

Next to the windows facing the street was Horowitz's concert grand Steinway, with neatly piled stacks of music on top. Signed photographs of Rachmaninoff, Paderewski, Puccini, and Toscanini hung on the wall behind the piano.

This room had personality and warmth. There was no ostentation in its furnishings, no aspect of vanity, showing signs of the Maestro's career, no masses of memorabilia. The atmosphere smacked of wealth, yet was extremely livable. I was surprised that there was only one piano, but I reasoned that since Horowitz seldom played a concerto, he did not need a second piano. But what most impressed me about the room was the simple yet fascinating fact that Vladimir Horowitz practiced the piano here.

Soon, Mrs. Horowitz entered, a handsome woman, sturdy, small, very pale, and richly dressed. Her brown hair was straight, thick, sleek, and immaculately coiffured. Her dark eyes were piercing. She looked astonishingly like her father.

Although she had "no talent," as she often said, Wanda Toscanini Horowitz was a star in her own right. She was feared and fearless, a woman who lived for Horowitz's career. She had watched him, guarded him, and supported him, through good times and bad, in sickness and in health.

Many people in the music business called her "Wanda the witch" for her fiery temper and uncanny ability to produce "scandals," a word that I was later to learn she used with relish. In short, Mrs. Horowitz was considered a formidable and dramatic woman.

Jack greeted her with enormous deference and respect. She held out her hand as Jack made the introductions.

Mrs. Horowitz made some nice comments about WNCN and reported that Mr. Horowitz would be down shortly. Jack seated himself to the right of the couch and Mrs. Horowitz sat on the left. Richard and I sat awkwardly together on the ottoman in front of the empty couch.

Mrs. Horowitz began lambasting her servants, bewailing the fact that getting good help had become practically impossible. When she spoke of her derelict cook, her nostrils flared in disdain. Jack sympathized with her plight.

Mrs. Horowitz looked at me sternly and said, "We shall have coffee and cookies later."

Suddenly, as if from nowhere, Horowitz himself appeared. At that time, the great pianist was seventy-six years old. He looked taller than I had remembered. He was snazzily dressed, sporting a brightly-colored bow tie and a striped jacket. He smiled as he walked toward me with his hand outstretched and grasped my hand with considerable pressure. Unlike many pianists, he obviously had no fear that somebody would crush his powerful fingers.

He said, "I was listening to your station today and it sounds good.

I listen more to WQXR because they have more news. But everybody tells me that yours is the better station."

"I will have to agree with everyone, Mr. Horowitz. I can't tell you how pleased I am to be with you and Mrs. Horowitz. May I introduce WNCN's chief engineer, Richard Koziol."

Horowitz shrugged as he looked at the tape recorder, saying, "I don't like or understand machines. Could we have it so I don't see it?"

Koziol quickly found a hiding place.

Horowitz sat on the couch and we began talking. I noticed that he constantly made a most unpleasant noise—*tchi, tchi*—with his tongue and lips and realized that all of those ugly sounds would have to be edited out of the tape.

At first, Horowitz seemed insecure while answering my questions. After each comment, he would ask Jack, "Am I right? Do you agree?" Each time, Jack answered with exaggerated distinctness, "Of course."

As we talked, I found Mrs. Horowitz could not resist interjecting something just as Horowitz was about to make a point.

I complimented the Maestro on his new recording of Schumann's monumental Humoreske. I said, "It is wonderful that you are learning such major works."

"I know." Horowitz smiled and congratulated himself. "Not bad, you know, for an old man. It's not so easy, you know."

Whereupon, Mrs. Horowitz said, "Volodya, you know very well that you learned the Schumann Humoreske in 1933."

Horowitz looked sullen as his eyes fell to the floor. All this, I thought, would have to be edited out, too.

It was obvious that Mrs. Horowitz was making a show of power. By now, I was pretty sure that I was not going to be reprimanded or thrown out of the Horowitz home for lack of a tie. However, I realized that as an interviewer, I was fast losing control, the first and last principle of the interviewer's art.

Richard Koziol and I looked at each other as if to say, "We are in trouble."

The celebrated couple appeared childish and spoiled. In midsentence, Horowitz stopped to complain about his air-conditioning breaking down in the hot weather. It certainly was hot.

I needed to gain control. I took a deep breath, stood up, and calmly but firmly told them that I was not getting anything to use on the program and that I needed Mr. Horowitz to answer my questions without interruptions. It seemed that my tone of voice and newfound authority worked wonders, because information began to flow.

However, we were now to experience a unique example of the Wanda Horowitz brand of drama. Just as Horowitz began concentrating, I heard her sniff the air several times. We continued talking, but her sniffing continued as well.

Soon, she interrupted, saying, "Volodya, on your walk today, did you step in dog doodoo?"

This was the last thing in the world I expected to hear when I asked Horowitz about his thoughts on Chopin. Horowitz looked at Wanda and sniffed the room's oppressively hot air. He shrugged his shoulders and lifted his leg to inspect the soles of his shoes. Neither I, Richard, nor Jack apparently possessed Mrs. Horowitz's acute sense of smell.

The Maestro slowly lifted his feet and looked. "No, Wanda, I stepped in nothing," as he clamped down his doodoo-free shoes with a thud.

There was no doubt in our minds that we were all in for an inspection. A long moment of silence occurred. Then, with trepidation, Jack lifted his feet. "*Not me!* They're clean," he exclaimed loudly.

I didn't have the strength to look at the bottom of my shoes. I beseechingly peered at Richard, who decided he would be next. With an audible sigh of relief, Richard gratefully said, "Not me either!"

There was no way out. What damn luck, I thought. I'll have to leave the room to clean my shoes and the mood will be ruined. I lifted my feet to see if the cursed crud had lodged itself on my sole. "NO, NO! Not me!" I uttered in disbelief. I had thought, surely it must be me!

All of this absurdity seemed to take forever. It was now Mrs. Horowitz's turn. As she brought her high heels up for inspection, she said coyly and blithely, "Oh, it's *me!* Gentlemen, will you excuse me."

Once she left the room, I continued interviewing the great master of the pianoforte in peace. In ten minutes, Mrs. Horowitz returned. But now, a more democratic atmosphere reigned in the room. She did not interrupt and all went smoothly. Mrs. Horowitz realized that Mr. Horowitz felt at ease with me and was giving a good interview.

We talked of various composers. At the time, Horowitz was practicing Mendelssohn's *Scherzo a Capriccio*, a neglected but important work of about six minutes long.

Horowitz said to me, "Nobody ever plays this work. *Nobody*! I discovered it."

I gently replied that although the piece was seldom played, a few pianists in each generation appreciated it.

"Who?" Horowitz practically yelled.

"Well, none other than Anton Rubinstein played it on his famous series of 'historical recitals' [in which he programmed a survey of the piano literature until his time]."

This information excited Horowitz and intrigued Wanda. Anton Rubinstein was the greatest Russian pianist of the nineteenth century, and his name was still magic to Horowitz.

Wanda rushed from the room and shortly returned with a biography of Rubinstein which included the historical programs. "Here it is, Volodya."

At first, I thought she was validating my knowledge, but then I realized that she considered this book a kind of authority symbol. If the great Anton played and sanctioned the Mendelssohn, then it must be a good piece. Or, at least, he added to the status of the composition.

Horowitz seemed delighted. Yet I also sensed that this bit of information lessened Horowitz's pleasure that the Mendelssohn was his own private discovery. He did not appear pleased when I mentioned several recordings of it, most notably by Anton Kuerti.

"He's a good pianist," Horowitz remarked of Kuerti, "but a little dry."

I began to understand that every composition Horowitz performed or recorded came out of an agonizing selective process. Horowitz wanted to own these pieces, and I believe he secretly resented anyone playing "his" repertoire. If he played them, they should be his property.

Unfortunately, our interview was interrupted by a maid bringing us coffee and cookies. This put an end to any more productive talk.

I feared that after coffee we would be dismissed. Although I dared not ask, I was hoping to hear the Maestro play in his own living room.

As if he read my thoughts, Horowitz grabbed the Mendelssohn score and pointed to me. "Mr. Dubal, look here at the music. I will show you how I fixed up and improved some passages." My longing was to be fulfilled as Horowitz launched into Mendelssohn's *Scherzo a Capriccio*. "See, I have added octaves here for a fuller effect, and listen, I make these into double notes. Watch, I take these notes out. It makes for a much more fluid effect."

He played with a disarming casualness, all the while talking and looking up at me. He was entirely unselfconscious and was spattering wrong notes by the bushel. Horowitz appeared to be getting a kick out of showing me his tricks. As he played, I felt very natural being with him.

He exclaimed loudly, "You know, this is not my good piano. My beauty [as he called it] is in our place in Connecticut, and this was brought over by Steinway as a loan. The humidity tonight is making the piano slow."

It amazed me that on this strange piano, the mighty Horowitz sounded just as thunderous as ever. Many people thought that to get such a sound, Horowitz must have had a special instrument. This was nonsense: being only inches away from the piano, one understood more than ever the uniqueness of his sonority.

Now that he had warmed up, Horowitz decided to give me a special treat and played the Rachmaninoff Second Sonata. Horowitz loved this work. Rachmaninoff had published it in 1913, but felt it was too long and years later condensed it.

Horowitz said, "I told Rachmaninoff, 'I think it is now too condensed.' He said, 'Mr. Horowitz, you are a good musician. Put what you think best of both versions together.' So I did, and Rachmaninoff approved."

It was now past one in the morning, and Horowitz played the earsplitting composition as if he were in a concert hall. During the evening, Horowitz said he was impressed by my knowledge of the piano literature. He said to Jack, "Mr. Dubal knows everything and he plays piano, too." He repeated this statement twice again.

I was flattered that I had made a good impression and would have blissfully listened to him all night. But the ever-watchful Wanda, who had left the room an hour before, reappeared and graciously said to Jack, "Volodya must get some sleep. He should practice tomorrow."

We said our farewells. As I thanked Mrs. Horowitz for her hospitality, I realized that I liked her. On the street, I thanked Jack for making the interview possible.

Being so close to Horowitz's playing had bowled me over. I was completely under its spell. As I took a taxi home, my ears were still ringing with the clangorous basses of the Rachmaninoff sonata.

7

THE GREATEST PAWS IN THE WORLD

The next day I listened to the tape of the evening's proceedings. It was a mess.

The editing was difficult because of that weird smacking sound Horowitz made with his mouth. However, with the steady hands of my production engineer, Charles Pitts, we created miracles on the cutting block and made Horowitz sound intelligible. Charles was so good that he could take a word from an unused sentence and insert it in place of the unintelligible word Horowitz spoke while retaining the exact breath. For twenty-five minutes of material, we removed over two hundred of Horowitz's peculiar *tchi* sounds.

The program was advertised in the *New York Times*. When broadcast, it caused a flood of mail to the station.

A few days later, David Rubin, then head of the Concert and Artist Department of Steinway & Sons, called to ask if I would do a series of interviews with Horowitz, sponsored by Steinway & Sons.

I agreed to do six programs in prime time, Monday through Saturday.

Actually, I put my foot in my mouth with this rather grandiose project. After the first program, I had barely enough Horowitz talk for even half of a second show. I nervously called Jack Pfeiffer of RCA and explained the predicament.

"Can you convince Horowitz to see me again? I need more material."

Jack was cautious. "David, you now have a good idea of how tricky they can be. With the Horowitzes, everything is difficult, and the usual answer to most things is *no*—*no*—and more *no*s. But I will try. It would be a great coup for all involved. Let me get back to you as soon as possible. You understand that he will probably say, 'They are exploiting me.' So don't count on even my effectiveness."

After I dejectedly hung up, I tried to convince myself that it would be too much work anyway. Charlie and I had already slaved for thirteen hours to create one program.

Two days later, Jack called. "David, good news! Horowitz likes you a great deal and although he hasn't been feeling well, he will see you and agrees to the series. But it will have to be accomplished in one evening. Can you come tomorrow night at nine-thirty sharp? I'll be there. By the way, Wanda left for Milan."

The weather had turned cooler and it was a comfortable night. I hoped Horowitz was feeling well.

I arrived at nine-thirty on the dot, this time with a tie. Jack and I were talking when I spied a lovely gray cat near the living room doors. I bent down to pet it.

Just as I was caressing the animal, I heard Horowitz descending from the floor above. He called for Jack in an irritated voice. Jack went to the stairway where I heard the capricious pianist growl, "Cancel the interview. I'm in a bad mood."

Jack said slowly, "Oh, Volodya, what a shame. Dubal is here and ready to go."

At that moment, Horowitz peered into the room and saw me on my knees with the cat. The scene seemed to kindle some emotion in him. All of a sudden, the mercurial Horowitz smiled and extended his hand.

"That is Madame's cat. He doesn't like my piano playing, you know. I heard our program together. I didn't know I talked so good. I was terrible on the Mike Wallace Show. I sounded like a clown. But he doesn't know what to ask me." Then he added, "But I'm in a bad mood today."

"But why is that, Mr. Horowitz?"

"Because I'm old and I'm not a good pianist anymore. I can't play the Chopin *Black Key* Etude anymore. And today, the piano is good. There is no humidity."

Horowitz's sensitivity to the piano was so acute that the most minute change in humidity could effect his performance.

"My fingers don't move. I'm old." He looked sad.

At that moment, I felt a flood of sympathy for him. How difficult it must be for him to accept the fact that his perfect reflexes and the once split-second mechanism was subject to the vicissitudes of life. Horowitz showed no sign of arthritis, but it was inevitable that even he had to slow down eventually. Yet in his case, his technical powers remained the envy of everyone.

I said, "But Mr. Horowitz, the *Black Key* Etude is a trifle compared to your ability to plunge the depths of Schumann's Humoreske. What's the big deal about the *Black Key* Etude?"

At that, he went directly to the piano and played it through.

I said, "But it sounds wonderful. It's so clean and crisp. What do you want?"

"No, no, it's sluggish, I can't make it talk. It doesn't go. There's no zip. No *jeu perlé*. No—I'm old. I'm no good."

I continued, "Chopin, you know, didn't think that much of the piece."

Horowitz looked up from the piano, like an astonished child. "What you mean?"

I said, "Oh, yes. Chopin chided Clara Schumann for playing that etude. He told her, 'Play my other things which are better than that etude.'"

"Really! I didn't know that," Horowitz replied. "So *Chopin* didn't think it very important."

Jack watched us silently, recognizing that we were developing a rapport.

I then said, "Mr. Horowitz, why don't you play the *Black Key* once more before we talk?"

"Okay. I'll do as you say. Maybe it will improve now." And indeed it was the best *Black Key* Etude I had ever heard. "Oh, now it goes. Maybe I got young again," Horowitz looked at me gleefully.

"You *are* young, Mr. Horowitz. In fact, nobody at any age can play it as well as you do."

I was learning how to use strategic flattery. But it was an honest kind of flattery that he needed, and which possessed no strain of hypocrisy or falsehood.

Horowitz smiled. "Phew, I'm tired today," he said and walked the few steps from the piano to the couch.

Jack reported that RCA would love for Horowitz to record a concerto, which would naturally be a huge commercial success.

"But what can I do?" Horowitz went on, "There is no concerto I want to play. Maybe Liszt A Major. I used to do it good. But you know, the ending is not so good. I have to change some things and maybe fix up the ending. And the critics would be mad. They'll say I'm a bad man. Also, Mr. Dubal, there is no conductor I want to play with. They are all bad."

I mentioned several conductors. Horowitz screeched, "He can't count!" Of another, he said maliciously, "No. I cannot look at him. He's so ugly." And of yet another, Horowitz retorted, "He has no respect. He once came to visit me without a tie. You know, Wanda makes a big thing about such things."

He continued, "She was mad when I went to the White House before I play for President Carter. He came out of his office without a tie."

"Well," I said, "I'm glad Mrs. Horowitz wasn't upset at me for not wearing a tie last time."

"No, she likes you."

"Mr. Horowitz," I continued, naively trying to help Jack out, "what about recording the Grieg Concerto? It's an easy concerto to conduct. Perhaps you wouldn't need a conductor," I said jokingly.

"But the Grieg, it's a little cheap. Don't you think?" Horowitz replied.

Jack said, "But it's not played much these days, and it would be a big seller."

Horowitz shouted, "Money, money, that's all the record hooligans think of. Money!"

Jack mildly protested, "Come, now. You know you record more or less what you want."

Horowitz countered, "RCA doesn't want Medtner. I'll do a Medtner concerto!" he exclaimed. "Yes, that I would do, and solo music of Medtner, too."

Nicolai Medtner, a Russian contemporary of Rachmaninoff's, was a composer Horowitz deeply admired. Rachmaninoff also tried to promote his music, but to no avail.

"But Volodya," Jack retorted, "nobody has ever heard a Medtner concerto. Do the Grieg and the whole world will be thrilled."

"If I did the Grieg, that would be only one side of the record," Horowitz said. "What solo music do I put on the other side? I cannot do two concertos, you know."

Jack said, "Of course not," knowing very well that Horowitz was not going to record *any* concerto.

"Mr. Horowitz," I said, "a marvelous work for the other side would be the Grieg Ballade. Do you know the piece? I think it's Grieg's finest work. It's nearly twenty minutes long in the form of variations."

"*My God*, I played that piece in Russia," Horowitz exclaimed. "That's very good music. I have not seen the score in years. Rachmaninoff loved the piece and played it. He liked Grieg in general, you know." Horowitz's eyes grew misty.

I felt that the mention of the Grieg had brought him back to another time and place.

He had been reclining on the long couch with his arm resting on his chin, when suddenly he pushed himself off the couch, looking as if he were in a trance. He seated himself at the piano and began not so much to play, but to feel, his way through the poignant theme which begins the Grieg Ballade. His fingers groped for the right notes. His eyes looked like slits as he brought the recondite and difficult composition back to his conscious memory.

He played through several variations, then suddenly stopped, waving a fist in the air. "I think I still know it," he said triumphantly. "Maybe I look for the music tomorrow."

My attention was totally focused on the scene. I was getting a glimpse of Horowitz's deep knowledge and experience of the piano literature.

It seemed as if he had willed the music back from the depths of his mind, and somehow his hands responded. "I have not played the Grieg since I was still in Russia," he quietly added. He had left Russia fifty-five years before.

Now he left the piano to return to his reclining position on the couch.

I said, "The Grieg Ballade isn't played much these days, and most young pianists don't even know of its existence. It would be wonderful if you recorded it."

Horowitz replied, "Who knows!" He continued, "Do you know Rachmaninoff recorded Grieg's Third Violin Sonata with Kreisler? Rachmaninoff made some beautiful transcriptions of Kreisler's violin pieces, too."

"Oh, yes," I replied, "their performance of the Grieg sonata is the best ever recorded."

Fritz Kreisler was one of the most popular violinists in history. He and Rachmaninoff occasionally appeared together in concert, and his own small compositions endeared him to the public. For years, he had palmed many of them off as the work of obscure composers. When the truth came out that these gems were his own, the revelation caused a sensation.

Horowitz continued, "Kreisler and Rachmaninoff liked each other a lot—just like me and Nathan Milstein. But Rachmaninoff was a perfectionist. Absolutely a perfectionist! He was never satisfied. On that Grieg Sonata, he told me he made Kreisler do it over and over until Rachmaninoff was satisfied. But Kreisler, Rachmaninoff said, was always satisfied. He said, 'Fritz is a great artist and I wouldn't call him lazy, but he wasn't happy about working too hard.'" Horowitz laughed. "Me, too! But I think I *am* lazy."

I thought the time had come to proceed with our interview. I told Mr. Horowitz my plan for the intended series, which would be titled "Conversations with Horowitz." Each program was to have a different theme: Liszt, Chopin, Russian composers, and so forth.

He seemed pleased with the idea, saying, "You know, I never do a long interview on radio. This will show I know something. My friend Mike Wallace filmed me all day, hours and hours. I was exhausted. All for fifteen minutes for the sixty-minute show. Forty-five million saw me. But our programs will be for people that know a little more. You are a good man. You know everything. You will do a good job and people will know I am not stupid."

As the tape recorder was switched on, Horowitz gave the machine a silly grin and continued making those disturbing *tchi* noises with his lips and tongue which I knew would cost Charlie Pitts and myself many extra hours to eliminate them. Interestingly, in subsequent years, Horowitz never made that sound again.

Now that I felt more relaxed with Horowitz, I began to sense the intense magnetism of his personality. He had nothing in common with anyone else I had ever met.

As the evening continued, Horowitz answered my questions carefully. I felt that he wanted to create a good impression through this series. He seemed to trust me, and again, peppered the conversation with "You know everything!"

I was flattered when he asked me, "What are you working on at the piano?"

"I'm studying the *Norma* Fantasy of Liszt," I replied.

"My God," he screamed. "That's too difficult! Almost as horrible as Liszt's *Don Juan* Fantasy."

"Maestro, just because I'm working on it, doesn't mean that I'll ever conquer it."

"But Mr. Dubal, nothing is ever conquered. The piano is the easiest instrument to play in the beginning and the hardest to master in the end."

"I agree with you totally, Mr. Horowitz."

Later, when we spoke of Prokofiev, he said, "You know, I sent Prokofiev my recording, I think in '46 or '47, of his Seventh Sonata. Not bad playing. Prokofiev sent me back a copy of the music. I'll show it to you. Do you know what he wrote on it?"

"Yes, I do, Mr. Horowitz. I know exactly what Prokofiev wrote."

"What, then, did he say?" Horowitz inquired suspiciously.

"The inscription says, 'To the miraculous pianist. From the composer.'"

Horowitz screeched. "How do you know such a thing? You know everything!" He looked at Jack, "He knows *everything!*"

Jack responded with his usual, "*Of course,* that's why he's here with us."

I responded, "Mr. Horowitz, I read it somewhere, and since everything about you is interesting to me, and since I have a good memory, I remembered it."

At that, Horowitz started looking into the stacks of music on his piano and found the treasure. "Look, it's Prokofiev's writing. Here it is." Horowitz proudly showed me the inscription.

I said, "Do you still have the Seventh Sonata in your fingers?"

"No!" the pianist cried. "I can't play even a note." But within seconds, he was again at the piano, showing me how most pianists play the last movement of the sonata far too fast.

Horowitz talked more candidly than I had expected. I was satisfied with our night's work, convinced that I now had enough conversation to create the necessary programs.

It was nearly one in the morning, but the evening wasn't finished.

"I'm glad you like Clementi," Horowitz commented. "Look. This is a first edition of Clementi sonatas. Some of them are amazing. *Believe me!* Beethoven was influenced by him for good reason." Horowitz placed the large volume on the piano rack. "Listen to this slow movement. When we hear Clementi, we know why Beethoven admired him."

I realized Horowitz was far from the unknowledgeable and silly buffoon that he himself had often portrayed. He simply had to feel comfortable and needed to know he was appreciated.

I was blissfully happy turning pages for him as he went through one Clementi sonata after another, playing and talking simultaneously.

"I must tell you," Horowitz said. "Mozart hated Clementi ever since they had the contest in front of the emperor."

Horowitz was speaking of the 1781 piano duel between Clementi and Mozart before Joseph II in Vienna. Each displayed their skills at improvisation, sight-reading, fugue playing, and so forth. The Emperor called it a draw. Mozart was peeved by the decision, while Clementi had nothing but praise for Mozart's singing tone, his exquisite taste and style.

"Yes," I answered. "I think Mozart resented Clementi because he was a more powerful virtuoso."

Horowitz continued, "I think you are right. Mozart wasn't a good colleague. He wrote to his sister that Clementi was a mere *mechanicus*."

Horowitz was clearly pleased with our conversation. The great composers were his companions, and he loved talking about their thoughts and lives. "Mr. Dubal, you should come and visit me often. Wanda said so, too. She likes you."

"I would like that, Maestro."

"By the way," Horowitz continued, "do you know that Mozart warned his sister not to play the Clementi sonatas because all the octaves and passages in thirds would make her stiff?"

"Oh, definitely. Mr. Horowitz, there is no doubt that Clementi deeply bothered Mozart. Actually, it's Clementi's expanded piano style that was to influence the future of piano music, not Mozart's. Mozart once said, 'Clementi is Italian and all Italians are charlatans.'"

"Oh my God!" Horowitz laughed. "Don't tell that to Wanda. But Mr. Dubal, I can assure you that Toscanini was no charlatan, and Clementi was none either. Oh, yes, Mozart was a bad man."

"Mr. Horowitz, Clementi, as you know, lived most of his life in London, where he became rich and famous. When he was eighty, he said, 'I am an old Englishman, but a young Italian.'"

Horowitz replied, "Ah, I am only old. But you heard, I can still play the *Black Key* Etude like a young man."

"Oh, absolutely, Maestro. And you should stop calling yourself old."

Before I left, I took Horowitz's hand and said, "Maestro, these are the greatest paws since Anton Rubinstein and Rachmaninoff."

Horowitz looked at me and softly replied, "Do you really think so?" I nodded. "I know so, Maestro."

As I was putting on my coat, I looked up at Horowitz, standing on the second floor. He looked sad. I felt that he was a very lonely man. His look seemed to say "I think I will not see Dubal again." Our gaze was long.

The series "Conversations with Horowitz" was broadcast the last week of January 1980. Hearing Horowitz speak on music thrilled the radio audience and brought the beloved artist closer to them. Although I could have tried to see Horowitz again, I felt there was no professional reason to enter his life.

Later that year, he performed at Lincoln Center's Avery Fisher Hall. I was included on the list of visitors allowed into the greenroom after the concert.

Horowitz seemed pleased to see me again. I said, "Maestro, I only wish that Schumann could have been here this afternoon to hear his *Nachtstücke* played so exquisitely."

Beaming, he turned to Wanda, saying, "Mr. Dubal would have liked if Mr. Schumann could have been here today. I wish he was here, too. Believe me, I would ask him plenty of things."

At that comment, I disappeared from his life until I phoned him in May of 1981. Much to my satisfaction, our radio series was given the George Foster Peabody Award, and I called to invite the Maestro to the awards ceremony and luncheon at the Hotel Pierre.

"I know that award," Horowitz shouted through the phone. "That's a good award."

I said, "Maestro, how would you like to attend and accept the award with me?"

"What time will it be?" he asked.

"At one p.m.," I answered.

"But I'm sleeping then. Have them move it till four o'clock. Maybe I go then."

"Ah, Maestro, I would if I could." I well knew that Horowitz would not attend, but I had wanted to let him know about the award.

"Mr. Dubal," he said, "please call me. It's already been a long time since you visited me."

8

HOROWITZ DECIDES TO
VISIT JUILLIARD

When Horowitz left RCA after thirty-four years, Tom Frost became his record producer for several years at Columbia. However, in 1975, Horowitz returned to RCA and Jack Pfeiffer resumed his work as the pianist's producer.

Early in 1985, Deutsche Grammophon wooed Horowitz to their company with an irresistible contract. Relations with Pfeiffer had unfortunately deteriorated, and Horowitz asked Frost to be his producer.

It was now September 1985, almost five years after I had seen Horowitz. Tom and his wife Lynne were now frequent guests of the Horowitzes. Tom Frost, a fine musician with years of experience as a recording producer, had worked with Ormandy, Glenn Gould, Casals, Rudolf Serkin, and a host of greats. Tom treated Horowitz in a straightforward manner, yet with an uncommon warmth and gentleness. Tom stood in awe of Horowitz's art, and as a producer, he showed never-ending patience with the fidgety pianist. Whatever Horowitz wanted, Tom spared no effort to make him happy.

Lynne Frost, a singer and an executive at CBS, was deeply sensitive to the Horowitzes. Mrs. Horowitz liked and admired Lynne, and Lynne's ever-ready smile, diplomacy, and cheerful good-will were an asset to their evenings together. Tom and Lynne had kept me up to date on the Maestro's activities. One day, Tom unexpectedly told me that Horowitz had asked about me several times. Horowitz knew I was now teaching piano literature at the Juilliard School and had said, "Maybe I will do something at Juilliard with Dubal."

Tom thought it a great idea. He asked, "How would you like to see Horowitz again and do something at the school with him?"

"Absolutely! What an exciting prospect. But Tom, will it really happen?"

"God knows," Tom responded. "But in the meantime, it would be great for Horowitz to see you. He wants to go out to dinner a lot lately, and he is not at all depressed. He appears to be more outgoing since about the time he made the film *The Last Romantic* [an intimate documentary showing the Horowitzes at home, with both of them speaking and the Maestro at the piano].

Tom continued, "Deutsche Grammophon is holding a press conference on September thirtieth to announce Horowitz's new recording of the music from *The Last Romantic*. Why don't you come and say hello to him?"

At the press conference, Horowitz was ebullient and treated everyone to a Scriabin etude. A few minutes later, I walked over to say hello.

"Where have you been in my life?" he cried enthusiastically.

"Maestro, I've been around."

To my surprise, he said, "Mr. Dubal, you know, *you* are a good pianist. I heard you play a piece by Hofmann on WQXR. Very good! Was that by Josef Hofmann?"

"No, Mr. Horowitz, it's a work by a nineteenth-century American composer, Richard Hoffman."

"Well, you are a good pianist."

"Maestro, I am overwhelmed that you say that, but it makes me blush."

"How did you like my Scriabin etude?" he asked. "It's different than before."

"I like it very much. I love your opening, which is much softer than is usually played."

"Yes, you know what you hear. Scriabin put no dynamic markings at the beginning, and everybody plays it loud."

Just at that moment, Alison Ames, a Deutsche Grammophon

executive, came over and said something in the pianist's ear which made him get up. He waved to me and said, "Have Mr. Frost bring you over the house."

"I shall."

On October 26, the Maestro played in Paris at the Théâtre des Champs-Elysées. It was an important concert, intended to prepare him for 1986, a year of world-wide travel at the age of eighty-two.

Early in December I joined the Horowitzes and the Frosts for an evening of conversation. Mr. Horowitz greeted me with evident pleasure. Mrs. Horowitz looked marvelous and was particularly charming. Tom brought up the possibility of Horowitz doing a program at Juilliard with me late in January.

"Do they still know who I am, the young people?" Horowitz asked. "I don't think so."

"Come now, Maestro. You are the most famous musician in the world."

"What about von Karajan?"

"You are more famous and more loved than von Karajan," Tom said.

"I don't know," Horowitz said. "Maybe to the old, but the young may not know or care for me."

"Mr. Horowitz," I said rather loudly, "I teach all the pianists at the Juilliard School, and one thing I know for a fact in this sad world is that you are a hero and a god to them."

"Is that true?"

"You know it's true," Tom replied.

On one level, Horowitz knew it was true, but on another, deeper level, he was insecure about everything, including his standing with young pianists. "Maybe I'm too old. They think I can't play, maybe."

I interjected, "Mr. Horowitz, believe me, even if a pianist does not feel sympathy with your music making, each has to come to terms with you. No pianist can ignore you. You have set new standards in so many works you have played."

"Do you think so?" he asked softly, with a touching naïveté.

We continued speaking about the project at Juilliard. Tom said he had already discussed the idea with the president of the school, Joseph Polisi, and that Polisi would attempt to get funding to film the event.

I said that not only pianists, but the whole school should be able to

hear Horowitz. Dancers and actors, too. We all agreed that the event
would have to be held at the Juilliard Theater, which seats nearly one
thousand.

"How are the pianos at Juilliard?" Horowitz asked.

Tom responded, "We can bring your own piano if you want."

"I don't want students to see what my piano is like."

Horowitz was intensely secretive. He jealously guarded many
things, such as his piano, as if it had magical qualities which might
be discovered by others.

Tom continued, "We'll go over to the school to try out their
concert grands. If you don't like them, I'm sure Richard Probst at
Steinway will send to Juilliard a piano that will be to your liking."

Horowitz went on, "I want most of all to shatter this overly-slow
playing that everybody does today. I will play examples, and tell the
students that exaggerated slow playing is harmful. Yes, it is! People
today think that slow playing means profound."

"I agree with you, Mr. Horowitz," I said. "Slow seems to be
equated with profundity. Even when the music isn't profound at all."

Horowitz screamed, "Yes, this ponderousness is terrible. There is
very little music that is only serious." Horowitz propelled himself
toward the piano. "Here is how they play the Mozart Rondo in A
minor. It goes on for eleven minutes with some pianists. They think
because it is in minor key, that it must be Mozart at his most serious.
But listen to how it needs to move. There are dance elements, too, in
this rondo. It can't be academic. It is not really sad. It is pensive.
Listen to the way I think it should be."

Horowitz played phrases from different parts of the rondo. "Yes," I
said, "the piece is earthbound when played too slowly." In Horowitz's hands, the A minor Rondo was charged with new meaning.
Harmonies that had seemed hidden suddenly sprang forth. It was
extraordinary how three-dimensional Horowitz's playing sounded.

I said, "If only we could hear Mozart play, so many mysteries
would be solved. Perhaps he would have hated the sound of the
modern piano."

Horowitz looked up at Lynne, Tom, and myself huddled around
the piano. "This I know. Mozart was alive. He loved life. I don't
think an eighteenth-century person like Mozart, a man who was
never dull, would play as slowly and stiff as people play him now. We
do not know what *adagio* meant to them. Today, everyone plays
adagio like a funeral. No, no, no, I show you how I play the Adagio

in B minor of Mozart. I *cannot* play it this slow. The music dies. This is a lament, but it is dramatic also. I will demonstrate for the students in these pieces. Maybe it will make them think. I don't know what their teachers will think."

Tom said, "Whatever you say will be valuable for them, believe me."

I enthusiastically agreed. "Mr. Horowitz, this slowness today is a pretentious thing. In the last twenty-five years, it seems tempi have been getting more ponderous, and slower, even in the Romantic composers. Do you remember the scandal when Glenn Gould played the Brahms D minor Concerto with Bernstein conducting? It was so slow that Bernstein actually told the audience he was not responsible for Gould's tempi. Today, there are quite a few recordings of the Brahms D minor that are as slow as the Gould performance."

Horowitz said, "We must go by musical sense. Listen to the middle movement of the Beethoven *Pathétique* Sonata. Does it make sense at the slow tempo that everybody plays it? When too slow, it sounds flat. This is a love duet."

I had played the movement quite slowly myself, but when Horowitz played it, I felt mine was too slow. Horowitz now launched into the *Moonlight* Sonata's first movement. He said, "Everyone plays it like a dirge. My own recording is terrible. I'm too slow. I followed the tradition too much."

Wanda, who was sitting in her chair, said, "My father used to say tradition was only the last bad performance."

"How true that can be," Tom interjected. "Mr. Horowitz, I think we should get a group of musical examples together and talk of different subjects to the students at Juilliard."

"Yes, yes, we will," Horowitz said impatiently. "But now, I must think of the recital at Carnegie Hall on Sunday. You know, Mr. Dubal, I am going to play the *Kreisleriana*. I hope you will come. I think I play it very different from my record I made in 1969."

"He certainly does," Tom said.

"My *Kreisleriana* is much better now, you will see. You know, it's the most glamorous piece of Schumann."

"What do you mean by using such a word to describe it?" I asked.

Horowitz thought for a while. "Each piece is glamorous. It's a big fulfillment. It's Schumann at his fullest, his most meaningful. His heart was beating fast in every bar. All mystery."

"What about the Schumann Fantasy?" I exclaimed.

"Yes, it's glamorous, too, but not as much as *Kreisleriana*. In *Kreisleriana*, every note is part of a great mystery."

"Yes, Maestro, I understand. Schumann said he heard inner voices urging him on to compose it. He wrote to Clara, 'Play my *Kreisleriana* once in a while. In some passages, there is to be found an utterly wild love, and your life and mine.'"

"Oh, yes," Horowitz said, "*Kreisleriana* is Schumann of the highest, the most intense. All eight movements are wonderful. Do you know it's dedicated to Chopin?"

"Yes," I replied. It was Schumann's return gift for the dedication that Chopin gave to him of the F Major Ballade.

Horowitz said, "But Chopin absolutely hated Schumann's music."

"Yes," I replied. "It was Schumann's return gift for the dedication that Chopin gave to him of the F Major Ballade."

Horowitz, what piece of Schumann would you recommend for students who want to get into Schumann's world?"

Horowitz answered instantly, "The work which pupils should study is the *Symphonic Etudes*. This work brings the secrets of Schumann to the pupil, and it is very difficult, very cruel technically. They think they will learn a lot from the Fantasy. No. Learn the *Symphonic Etudes*, and they will have to work hard."

Suddenly, Horowitz declared, "I must lose weight. I'm getting too fat. I had ice cream again tonight. Did I write that down?" He opened a big book where I saw he notated all of the food he ate. "I will lose ten pounds soon, you will see."

"I notice you no longer smoke," I said. "I remember when I first met you, you said that you allowed yourself three cigarettes a day."

"I gave that up years ago. You know, I take good care of myself. I have a lot to do still. We will see each other all the time now. We must give something to the students. Tom, it's a good idea to do it at Juilliard."

"Oh, yes. We will announce it to the school in January. It's a wonderful gift you will be giving them."

"*Okay.* We shall see. You come again, Mr. Dubal, right after the recital. Don't let me down."

"Maestro, I'm so happy to see you again, and it will be an honor to be on stage with you at the Juilliard Theater."

Horowitz smiled. "Afterward, we will all have a good dinner. Mr. Polisi, the president, will come too."

Mrs. Horowitz took us down stairs and grasped my hand warmly at the door. Having Horowitz on stage seemed vague and unreal. Ostensibly, I was back in Horowitz's life to prepare him for this venture. The more I thought of the prospect, however, the more I wanted it to happen. It would surely make me a hero with my students, and how wonderful if it could be filmed.

9

HOROWITZ AND
SCHUMANN MERGE

On Sunday, December 15, 1985, Vladimir Horowitz, at his usual time of four P.M., played at Carnegie Hall. Through the power of his art, he once more brought three thousand people together, each hoping to be lifted to a higher realm than that of their common daily experiences.

It was apparent from the instant his hands touched the keyboard that the eighty-two-year-old master was probing deeper than ever into the music's core. The atmosphere in the hall was rarefied, as if together we were celebrating a mystical, divine rite. The faces in the audience radiated goodwill.

As he played, my eyes fixed on the pianist's luminous hands. What might the great painter Renoir have said of Horowitz's powerfully sculpted and elegant hands? Renoir thought the hands to be the essence of the human body. He would say, "Stupid hands, witty hands, ordinary hands, a prostitute's hands."

Horowitz's hands looked ageless. They had a life of their own but controlled his entire being. To find their fulfillment, he needed only to play the piano.

I once asked him if he ever had the desire to conduct, as so many pianists did.

73

"No, no! Never!" He was emphatic. "I saw Barenboim and I said to him, 'Why are you conducting? You are a pianist.' A true pianist, a real pianist *must* play the piano. He must not divide himself."

The major work on this concert was Schumann's *Kreisleriana*, a work inspired from a weird story by the German writer, E.T.A. Hoffmann. Eight fantasies constitute the sprawling cycle in which Schumann revealed his entire complex soul. It is music that no one before Schumann even vaguely imagined. After completing his vast, convulsed canvas, he wrote, "My music now seems to me so wonderfully complicated for all its simplicity, so eloquently from the heart."

That afternoon, Horowitz captured the elusive work in all of its subtle interplay of light and shadow. He brought out strange, disturbing, hallucinatory feelings. The impression of disembodied threads of mysterious sound hovered in the air. Yet their was also a sense of cohesiveness. It seemed as if Schumann's tortured soul had found release in Horowitz's re-creation.

As the final notes evaporated, the audience fell silent. Horowitz himself looked dazed. Finally, applause broke the enchanted spell. Music making on this level is purer, more elevated, than words have the power to describe.

The remainder of the concert was beautiful and original. But nothing that day could match the Romantic inspiration that had permeated his *Kreisleriana*. I was convinced that Schumann was the German Romantic closest in temperament to Horowitz. He had said to me, "If I go to heaven, and if Schumann is there, too, I hope we can become good friends. I love him. He touches me deeply, and he is always creative."

After the recital, I met Tom and Lynne Frost for a drink at the Parker Meridien Hotel. The Horowitzes had invited them to dine later, and I wished I had been invited, too, as I particularly wanted to note his mood after the concert.

As I left, Tom said, "Let's continue next week on the Juilliard talk."

10

GETTING THE RIGHT TEMPO

Several days after his Carnegie Hall recital, I was asked to Horowitz's home to continue discussing our Juilliard program. When I arrived that evening, the Frosts were already sitting in the living room, chatting with Wanda.

Within minutes, Horowitz bounced into the room. "Good to see you, Mr. Dubal. Let's talk about Juilliard, yes?" He sat at his usual end of the long couch and took a swig from a bottle of Evian water sitting on the table beside him.

"You know," Horowitz said proudly, "I have lost five pounds already. This jacket is starting to fit me." He looked at me. "How much you think I weigh?"

"I'd say one-sixty-five."

"You are crazy! I weigh over two-hundred pounds. I'm fat. I have to lose twenty pounds. When I was young, I weigh a hundred forty pounds. *I was like a boxer.* I was in top shape. But I'm not that for many years. I'm very sluggish now."

Wanda nodded her head in agreement, "He must lose weight. It's no good for his playing. He gets tired easily at this heavy weight."

I said, "Mr. Horowitz, before we go further, I'd like to say how wonderful your concert was last Sunday."

75

"It wasn't too bad, especially *Kreisleriana*. Did you read the stupid review in the *Times* about the concert?" Horowitz clapped his hands in disgust. "The critics are getting worse every year."

"Maestro," I replied, "I didn't read it. It's a waste of time. Why would I want to read somebody's opinion of what I heard myself?"

"I agree, David," Tom said. "But it used to be fun to read all the different opinions when New York had ten daily newspapers."

Lynne said, "The main thing is that Mr. Horowitz was pleased on Sunday."

Tom continued, "With so little interesting criticism, it's a wonder that youngsters even want to play in New York any longer. They spend thousands of dollars renting a hall, and are lucky to get a review. But if you don't mind, Mr. Horowitz, let's talk a little about the program at Juilliard."

"*Tempo*," Horowitz cried, "*tempo*. They must know how I feel about *tempo*. The *Moonlight* Sonata's first movement is in two beats, not four. And I will play E Major Etude of Chopin." Horowitz demonstrated by singing.

He continued, "For the singer, for the violin, for the orchestra, it's the same thing, *for all of them*. You have to establish the tempo, and then you can do what you want. Interpret how you want. Like Chopin and Mozart said, the left hand is your conductor, the right hand is the solo, then there is rubato. Rubato, you know, is robbing the time, making it faster here and slower there. Liszt said rubato was like a tree with the trunk in ground and the breeze going through the branches, with the leaves and branches having their own life.

"By the way, largo is not a tempo. Largo means *broad*. Broad doesn't mean slow. It means play broadly. Those Germanic pianists who play six-eight in six slow beats—*it's impossible*." Horowitz interrupted himself, "By the way, take a drink. In the little room is everything. It stays there. Nobody takes anything. There is all kinds of drinks. Maybe I play slow movement of the *Pathétique* Sonata for the students."

"Would you want the music on the piano at Juilliard?" I asked.

"I don't need to play that much. I can do it from heart. You know, Chopin's four scherzos are also in one beat to the bar. They are all the same tempo. Most pianists play the Third Scherzo three times as fast as the other ones. They all want to show off their octaves in the Third Scherzo. Even Rachmaninoff sins badly on his recording." Horowitz imitated the Rachmaninoff tempo. "It makes no sense. It's technically wonderful, of course."

"Yes," I said, "Rachmaninoff plays it very fast."

Horowitz continued, "I must tell you it's not necessary."

"Yes, Maestro, but somehow, Rachmaninoff makes his own special sense of it, because he was Rachmaninoff."

"But to imitate his way would sound nonsensical." Horowitz continued, "You know, Siloti was an important pianist and Rachmaninoff's cousin. Years ago, he came to me and said, 'Sergei doesn't know how to play the Third Scherzo.'" Horowitz sang bits from all four scherzi in the same tempo.

Tom asked, "What about Chopin's mazurkas? Are they in *one beat* also? I think the Chopin mazurkas are among the most elusive dances ever written."

Horowitz replied, "Sometimes, they are in one beat, but not always. They are like poems, and they are always different. And also, they need much rubato in them. They must be played with great metrical freedom or they sound stiff. Each mazurka is pure gold. One is better than the other."

"Maestro," I interrupted, "in Liszt's 1850 biography of Chopin, he said that you have to harness a major pianist to each Chopin mazurka."

"Oh, that is good," Horowitz replied. "Liszt understood everything. Oh, yes, he did." He continued, "Chopin himself didn't play them in time. Once when Meyerbeer, who was the most famous opera composer of the time, heard him in C Major Mazurka, Op. 33, he accused Chopin of playing it in four-four time, not as written in three-four. Chopin was furious at Meyerbeer because he didn't like him. He screamed, 'You tell *me* how to play my own work? *That I can't play it in time?*' Chopin was bursting a blood vessel.

"Then it so happens some weeks later, Chopin is giving a lesson to his student, Charles Hallé, who, by the way, later became the founder of the Hallé Orchestra. And Hallé plays the same mazurka. Chopin pushed him away and played it for him, and Hallé remarked to Chopin the same thing, that Chopin was not playing his mazurka in time. Chopin said to Hallé, who he *liked*, 'You are right. I can't play in time. It's a national trait.' So you see, Mr. Frost and Mr. Dubal, this story tells a great deal. It tells us about Chopin's playing. His rubato was a new thing in music making."

"Exactly!" I exclaimed. "Chopin's music was exotic. It was the first voice of Slavic music to enter Western Europe. His playing was exotic, too. He said 'I want to emancipate music from the bar line.' Academic pianists of the day had a terrible time interpreting Chopin. It baffled them."

As I talked, Horowitz tried to leave his couch, but each time, he lacked the strength. On his third attempt, huffing and puffing, he pushed himself off and stood wobbling. As he walked to the piano, he said, "The couch is like quicksand. Maybe I play at Juilliard the A minor Mazurka, Op. 17, No. 4." He sat down and treated us to his inimitable Mazurka playing.

Lynne's eyes shone brightly. At the mazurka's conclusion, she shook her head as in disbelief. "Mr. Horowitz," she said, "that was enchanting."

I looked at Wanda, who was smiling wistfully. "I must tell you, Mr. Dubal, that if he didn't play Chopin mazurkas so well, I would not have married this meshuggener."

Horowitz looked up from the piano. "I tell you, they are pure gold, and so intimate. You know, I heard my mother playing a mazurka when I was five years old. I cried. Can you imagine, I know these mazurkas for eighty years, and Chopin himself only lived to be thirty-nine?"

Tom said, "If you play only that, everyone at Juilliard will be happy."

"I know," Horowitz agreed. "I do it. The Carnegie Hall recital tired me out. You will come back Saturday. We have a good dinner and then we will *talk* more about what we say at Juilliard."

11

"I Like to Improvise"

It was December 23, the year 1985 was drawing to a close. I was getting more excited about the prospect of our Juilliard appearance together. If this was really going to happen, I wanted to be at Horowitz's beck and call. We believed the end of January would be a good time for him to come to Juilliard.

I had been with Horowitz nearly every second or third evening. Tonight, I was alone; Tom and Lynne could not come.

Mrs. Horowitz said, "Tom is going to see about the installation of equipment to record Volodya's improvisations."

During the past several months, Horowitz spent a good deal of time improvising.

"Why this sudden surge of inspiration?" I asked. "I don't know why lately I do this," Horowitz said. "I was always a good improviser. You know, I'm at heart a composer, so I do it naturally. It is a part of me that the public knows nothing of. Some of my improvisations are tremendous, some very poor. Today, it was mixed like that. Some good with startling things, then twenty minutes bad."

Wanda joined in, "I'd like Tom to be able to preserve the good parts. But we are losing it every day the equipment is not installed."

"I want to capture it on tape, too," Horowitz continued. "But I must be able to press a button. I can't work complicated machines."

"No, Maestro, it will be easy to work. You must, however, remember to push the button when you begin improvising."

"Mr. Horowitz, would you recommend the students to improvise?"

"No!" Horowitz cried. "Only if they are composers, too."

"Why do you say that?"

"Then it is a creative outlet, and maybe it will help them to compose. But if they have no direction in that way, it will be a waste of time. Better to practice what they are working on."

I disagreed. "I think that every student should improvise, and they will *become* more creative."

"Maybe that is true," Horowitz said. "Everyone in this world is a specialist today, and we are losing the spirit of creativity."

"Yes, I think so. I think that pianists especially are creatively lonely without composing. The acts of playing music and composing were not separated until recently."

"You are right," Horowitz said. "Bach could not have been a composer only. And to compose those organ works, he must have been a tremendous organist. To hear him must have been to die."

"Oh, yes. But to hear Bach play the organ must have been to *live*. When Liszt heard César Franck improvise at the organ, he exclaimed, '*Bach lives!*'"

"Goodness," Horowitz said, "I'd like to have heard Bach, who was a practical keyboard player, you know. Bach said, 'People ask me how I play so well, and I tell them I put my fingers on the right keys, and I play.' Bach says this. Imagine! That's all you do." Horowitz, after delivering this quote, sent out gales of laughter. "I love *that!*"

"Well, Maestro, that's a very un-German method, I must say."

"*I know, I know,* the Germans like to write books on how the muscles work," Horowitz went on.

"Yes, do you know the ultimate book on such claptrap on piano playing, a tome called *The Physiology of Piano Playing*, by Otto Ortmann?"

"Oh, I know. I couldn't read one paragraph!" Horowitz screamed. "After reading it, one could never play again. It's like the man who tried to analyze how to swallow, and choked."

"And worse, the Germans ruined this century with those two wars," Mrs. Horowitz said vehemently.

"Yes, those wars were cataclysmic. But do you know what the Germans invented that is the worst invention of all time?"

"What is that?" Horowitz looked interested.

"Maestro, the Germans invented the *footnote!*"

We all laughed heartily. Horowitz said, "You bet!"

I proceeded to give them my theory of how the division in composition and performance occurred. For instance, Mozart and Beethoven played very little music other than their own. The repertoire was much smaller. They were marvelous improvisers; but improvisation demands skill: it is composing on the spot.

The tradition of improvisation started dying out by the 1840s. By the time the modern piano was perfected, the great composers had written an astonishing number of masterpieces for the instrument. Piano music by Mozart, Beethoven, Chopin, Schumann, and others was of such high quality that talented musicians, instead of composing their own works, spent their lives learning this large literature. To compose took time, but to perfect Beethoven sonatas was a never-ending process.

As more musicians played in public music of established quality, they were called *performers*. But more importantly, the word *interpreter* came to be used. A discriminating public came to prefer one interpretation to another. Many celebrated pianists still composed, such as Rosenthal, Paderewski, Sauer, Scharwenka, and Friedman. But their own music was weak in comparison with their powers as interpreters. The world wanted to hear Paderewski play Chopin, not hear his own symphonies and sonatas.

On the other hand, great composers such as Debussy and Ravel composed masterpieces for the piano, but others played them better than they could. In the twentieth century, many composers don't play any instrument adequately, and most performers cannot compose at all.

Horowitz said, "You are right. This is exactly what happened. But what about Rachmaninoff? He was a composer and a pianist."

"Yes, Maestro. Rachmaninoff is the reverse of this trend. By adulthood, he had settled on a career as a composer. He had to earn a living when he left Russia after the revolution, and his life was to become an endless succession of concerts. He worked feverishly on his piano playing at the cost of his creative work. From 1917 until his death in 1943, Rachmaninoff composed very little compared to his earlier years. Piano playing and composing don't mix. One will destroy the other."

Horowitz said, "Rachmaninoff was always practicing. Once I asked him if the acoustic was good at some hall somewhere. He said, 'I don't remember the acoustic, but the money was good.'"

Horowitz laughed. "These things are now clear to me. I never looked at it this way. You know, I don't even have time to write down my own transcriptions."

Wanda interjected, "I think he is too lazy to write them down. Schirmer's wants to publish them, but he won't write them down."

"What a pity," I said. "So many pianists would have a terrific time learning your transcriptions, that is, if they can."

"Let them make their own," Horowitz shouted, irritated at the thought either of having the works published or having to concentrate on actually notating them.

"But Maestro, that is the point. Modern pianists only learn the music of other people. They do not have time to make their own."

"Too bad!" Horowitz bellowed.

At that moment, Horowitz rose from the couch, "I'll improvise for you a little. I'm in the mood. Let's see what comes out."

The old master sat at the piano, and with tremendous fury, he began with a mountain of arpeggiation. Soon, I was hearing a potpourri of styles, interspersed with glittering scales in thirds and sixths, with all sorts of pianistic lollipops tossed off for high effect. Here and there, a tune would emerge only to be smothered by another one. Some melodies were insipid, others sounded à la Russe, and one was quite sophisticated and sentimental, in the manner of Poulenc.

It was all dazzling, provocative, vulgar, and derivative. I wondered if he knew how bad it was.

As this burst of inspiration concluded, he peered at me with a disappointed, sour-looking expression. "Ah, terrible. It was ghastly! You see, Mr. Dubal, how bad it can be. Not one good minute."

"Well, I'd like to hear you when you are really on. How I wish I could fly around the keyboard like that," I said. "Do you want to talk about or do some improvising at our Juilliard discussion next month?"

"*No!*" he said loudly. "But I will tell them that when you can improvise well, a lot of fear about memory slips disappears. Because then, you just improvise until you get back on track."

"Maestro, have *you* had memory problems, too?" I asked.

"Of course I have memory slips. Many people think I have an infallible memory, but it's not true. But if something happens, I am a good improviser. I keep going in the style of the composer until I find myself. I will tell this to the Juilliard students, but I won't improvise. Maybe it would be terrible like I just did. You never know what will happen."

It was getting late. "Maestro, I have a big day tomorrow."

Horowitz said, "But you come again tomorrow night. And we continue talking about Juilliard. Maybe I improvise better tomorrow."

12

THE COCKTAIL PIANIST

It was December 27, a freezing and starry Sunday night. Even the Manhattan skies could not dull the stars. The Frosts and I arrived simultaneously at the Horowitzes'. As we entered the spacious living room, Wanda said, "Sal the chauffeur is already here. Tonight, we'll dine at the Stanhope Hotel. It's not too bad."

Horowitz, sitting quietly on the couch, pointed to his jacket and said, "How do you like it? I never wore it before. I was too fat."

We complimented him on his weight loss and the new jacket.

As we drove to the restaurant, Sal told Horowitz that during the afternoon he had taken a girl to the airport. "Did she look weird!" the chauffeur reported. "Strange clothes and purple hair. She was reading last Sunday's *Times*, and in the mirror I spotted your photo, the one next to the review of last week's concert which she was reading. I said to her, 'Do you know that tonight, I will be driving Vladimir Horowitz to dinner?'"

Horowitz listened with interest. "She knew me?" he said exuberantly.

"Maestro, she was so excited, I can't tell you. She gasped, 'Do you mean I am sitting in the same car that Vladimir Horowitz will be in? I grew up listening to his records. My dad has a passion for him. I'm into heavy metal, but I like Horowitz better.'"

Horowitz said, "You see, all kinds of people love me. Even the heavy metal."

In minutes, we were at the Stanhope, on Eighty-third Street and

Fifth Avenue across from the Metropolitan Museum of Art. Horo-witz's arrival at a restaurant was always known ahead of time, and his reception by the staff was never less than royal. Naturally, we were given the best table, and Wanda calmly conversed with Lynne.

Tom and I talked to Horowitz about the repertory for his next recording, a topic of endless concern. Each day, the selection would change and the discussion would start again with the pros and cons of which pieces will sound best together.

During our talk, I was distracted by the ever-present cocktail piano music. Live or recorded, music in a restaurant is a gross violation of conversation. Its effect on intimacy is disastrous. The finest wine and the most ardent lovers have little chance against the never-ending din of musical patter.

Unfortunately, the Stanhope's restaurant offered the ritual of light piano banter. I kept glancing at the entertainer, hoping that her break would come soon. The playing continued. However, it was seasoned with tidbits of classical music, Bach and Chopin interspersed be-tween "Gigi" and "All the Things You Are."

Lynne said, "I think you have a fan, Mr. Horowitz."

He responded, "I wish she would stop. I hate music when I am eating."

But Maestro, you must be nice to her if she comes over," Tom said.

"I will be nice. I'm always nice." Horowitz proceeded to take out his wallet and pulled out a five-dollar bill. "Should I give her this if she comes here?"

"No, no, Maestro," I said. "I think just meeting you will be her reward." Horowitz shrugged and put the money away.

During my years with him, I came to realize he had almost no sense of diplomacy.

Eventually the pianist, a well-dressed, genteel-looking, late-mid-dle-aged woman, took her break. She beckoned me to her, saying she had recently seen me at a party in Soho where she had been engaged to play. In fact, I now remembered her. She had played a solo version of Gershwin's *Rhapsody in Blue* and I had complimented her.

She said, "Would it be inappropriate if I came to pay my respects to the Maestro? I worship him, but, of course, I wouldn't want to disturb his dinner."

She added, "I was beside myself when the maître d' told me he would be here tonight. And damn it, just before I was told, I had a drink. I'm afraid my playing was lousy."

I assured her that her playing was fine and brought her to our table. She was quite overcome with pleasure at meeting the Maestro and gushed forth her admiration. Horowitz sat fidgeting. She told him that she had long ago studied with Josef Lhévinne, a pianist Horowitz always spoke well of. "How sorry I am," she continued, "that I wasn't able to attend your last Carnegie Hall recital."

"I will play there again, I hope," Horowitz said.

Horowitz was bored with the encounter and wanted to return to his filet of sole. Just as he lifted his fork, she impulsively tore a large, heavy, and valuable-looking necklace from her neck. "Please, Maestro, accept this as a mere token of my admiration. For years, I lived in India, where I amassed a valuable collection of Indian necklaces."

Horowitz gulped, "It is very nice. But *please*, I cannot accept this gift."

"Oh, but you must. It would make me feel so good."

Horowitz looked helpless and, raising his voice, said, "But I cannot wear such a thing."

I desperately wanted to laugh.

Horowitz continued, "Then you must give it to Madame Horowitz."

Wanda looked upon the scene with amusement.

"Oh, forgive me, Madame Horowitz. Of course, this gift is for you. Won't you please accept it?"

"But please," Wanda replied, "you *must* not give me this from your collection."

"I insist," the entertainer said.

With Lynne's help, Mrs. Horowitz fastened the heavy necklace around her neck. "It looks wonderful," we all said at the same time. Mrs. Horowitz looked embarrassed but was gracious to the pianist, who now seemed satisfied. After bidding farewell, she left for the back of the restaurant to calm down. But soon she returned to the keyboard and we smiled at each other. By now, we had finished our dinner and were contemplating dessert. Horowitz had to be persuaded by Tom that he was allowed to have some ice cream.

"But not too much," the Maestro said as he slowly consumed his dessert. "Ah, it's good. I'm still doing good today on my diet. But maybe I can have one cookie when I get home. Maybe. We'll see."

As our dessert progressed, the Stanhope pianist seized an opportunity that must have been irresistible. The pop music stopped.

There was a moment of silence, then she launched into Ravel's iridescent Jeux d'eau.

Horowitz said, "Not bad! You know, I played that piece for Ravel in Paris. Ravel said to me, 'I think you play the work too Lisztian and not impressionistic enough.' I said back to Ravel, 'But I think it *is* Lisztian,' and Ravel thought for a second, 'I think you are right after all.'"

Ravel—who had been dead for sixty years—composed the piece in 1903, the year Horowitz was born. I was certain that the pianist at the Stanhope was feeling her moment intensely. I only hoped that she would not regret her impulsive generosity. I never saw Mrs. Horowitz wear the necklace. It wasn't her style.

It was getting late and Horowitz announced that he wanted to go home to finish reading the *New York Times*. "Come to dinner tomorrow night and we talk more about the Juilliard event."

The evening had swept by so quickly that I hadn't realized we'd made no progress on our presentation to the students.

As we left, I waved to the hotel pianist, who smiled back. Horowitz, following suit, waved too.

13

HOROWITZ TALKS
MUSIC

Tom Frost met me at the corner of Madison Avenue and Ninety-fourth Street. The evening was to be spent with just the three of us.

Tom said, "We must try to get Horowitz to concentrate on the Juilliard project."

We found Horowitz alone on the couch. He called us in with a wide circular wave of his hand.

"My dinner didn't agree with me," he said, patting his belly. His stomach was where all of Horowitz's anxieties centered. "I have lots of gas tonight. The weather is too cold to walk. I feel dull."

After a long silence, Horowitz looked earnestly at Tom, "You know, I have to go to Russia probably. Should I go?"

"Maestro, you've got to go," Tom replied. "You know you will go. It's very important for you to go. And why think so much about it now? This is December 30, and you won't go to Moscow until April."

Tom's words seemed to calm him, and Horowitz suddenly looked noticeably better. He pushed himself back into the couch. "Last night on WQXR, I hear that horrible woman announcer I hate so much. She's on all night. She put on the Chopin F-sharp minor Polonaise. I miss the pianist's name, but I say, 'Not bad playing. Big

89

sound, big technique. I wouldn't play it that way. Too severe, too cold. But this is a good pianist.' "

Horowitz asked, "Do you know who the announcer said the pianist is? It was me!" he screamed, smiling broadly.

Tom reminded him, "That was your 1968 record from the CBS TV special."

Horowitz's beady eyes danced. "I not know who it was." He enjoyed saying he didn't know the identity of the pianist. I believe that in fact he did.

Horowitz had often talked to me about the art of the interpreter. He said the greater the music, the more ways it can be illuminated. Every phrase has countless alternatives of touch and tempo. The artist must be convinced that his choices are the best, the only way. But down deep, he must also be aware that interpretation is a matter of choice that sacrifices other ways.

Horowitz preferred staying away from certain compositions for years at a time, and upon returning to them, he often found that his conception changed drastically.

Horowitz continued. "Records are terrible things. You change, but they stay the same. The recordings live on to haunt you. Even worse are these videos. Last week, I look at TV. What do I see? *Me!* Playing the *Polonaise-Fantaisie*, my favorite Chopin polonaise. It was the film made of my recital in London in '82 when I play for the Prince Charles. It is terrible playing, ugly sound and so affected."

"Mr. Horowitz," I said, "at Juilliard, I think I should ask you a few questions about Chopin. Are there any points you want to make?"

"Yes, I want to tell the students what Chopin says in a letter. He says that students come to him and they try to imitate him. Chopin said, 'I want to throw them out. Why do they want to imitate me? I never play the same way twice.' And I can say the same as Mr. Chopin. Forgive me, I don't presume to be Mr. Chopin, but I *never*, never play the same way twice. *NEVER!*"

Tom joined in. "What else do you want to tell the students about Chopin?"

"I tell them that Chopin must not be played like a weakling. He may have been ninety pounds because of the TB, but in the music, he could be a lion. Chopin's music is virile, not sweet and sickly. He was not a sissy. You know, the photo of Chopin in London at the end of his life? It shows the saddest man in the world, dying of consumption, away from his home, no money left. This is no dandy. This picture shows a man of great strength."

"That is wonderful, Maestro," Tom said. "A real lesson. Do you want to talk to the students about Liszt?"

"Liszt I understand very well, I think. He was very prolific, so pupils must choose what to play of Liszt very carefully because there is a lot that is not so good. But there are so many good things that are never played. By the way, do you know my recording of the Liszt Ballade in B minor? Now *that* is a good work, an epic. It is hardly known.

"I must tell you that Liszt was the greatest of them all in the piano. We cannot even estimate how high he is. When he was very young, he made an arrangement for piano of his friend Berlioz's *Symphonie Fantastique*, which was just played for the first time in Paris. That, of course, was the most brilliant symphony of the time. At one concert, the orchestra played the movement, 'March to the Scaffold.' Right after, Liszt came out to play his solo version. The audience couldn't believe it. Liszt's playing on the piano was more effective than the original. You see, that was nerve. One man could outdo all the colors of the orchestra. Liszt said, 'I orchestrate on the piano,' and that is my motto, too."

"Maestro," I asked, "did you know anyone who knew Liszt?"

"Yes, the most important was the composer Glazunov who Liszt helped. I say to Glazunov, I was about seventeen, 'Tell me about Liszt.' He said, 'Liszt was a brilliant conversationalist. Brilliant, but more, much more.' He said that every word was like an apparition. And Glazunov was a great, great musician."

Horowitz continued, "Liszt helped everybody. But lots of people were jealous of him. In Berlin, there was a critic who loved to tear him down, every chance he could. He said, 'Liszt was a bad pianist, a terrible conductor, and the worst composer.' He tried to destroy him. So Liszt's students begged him to write a letter, and he did. He said, 'I am sorry you don't like my playing and my music. You are right, and I make no protest at all. I am very happy that through my name I could help you to be noticed.' I think this is a beautiful story," Horowitz said, clapping and laughing.

Tom said, "Mr. Horowitz, these are such interesting stories. The students will be delighted."

"But how do I remember them?" he asked with a worried look.

"Mr. Horowitz, I will be interviewing you. Believe me, I shall carry you through it like a baby."

"Okay. I trust you," he said.

"We should also speak about Schumann in our interview."

Horowitz replied, "I love Schumann's Toccata. People try to make it too fast. I remember Simon Barère. He loved to play fast. Once I hear him do the toccata so fast"—Horowitz made a sour face—"like a blur. I go backstage. I say, 'Simon, isn't your toccata too fast?' You know what he answered? 'Volodya, I can do it even faster.' You know, maybe Simon was a little stupid. I don't say he was. Maybe. He made a big splash when he died. I don't know what year. I think '51. Imagine, he is playing Grieg Concerto at Carnegie Hall with Ormandy conducting, and right in the big climax, he dies of a heart attack on stage. This is the way to go, tremendous! In middle of Grieg Concerto, terrific, eh?"

"Returning to Schumann," I said, "you made two recordings of the Schumann Toccata, both very different."

"Both not so good, by the way," Horowitz added.

Tom said, "The one we did together, I think in '63, I think is wonderful."

"I agree with Tom. It's very strong and humorous, too. You made the other one in London in the thirties."

"Oh, yeah," Horowitz said. "Maybe it was there that I made my recording of the Schumann Fantasy on 78s. I should have recorded the fantasy again."

Tom asked, "Didn't you do the Fantasy at your '65 comeback recital?"

Horowitz hotly retorted, "*No!* I only recorded it once, on 78s. That is the oldest record I ever did."

Tom and I stared at each other. We said nothing more. All three of us knew that he had played the Schumann Fantasy in 1965, and that the recording made from the concert has been one of the best-selling classical albums of all time. But for some reason, Horowitz didn't want to acknowledge the existence of this recording. Perhaps, at that moment, the thought of the "comeback" recital was painful, or he was again thinking of his return to Russia in the spring.

There was no reason to pursue the topic. If Horowitz wanted to change his personal history, so be it. The strange thing is that what he had denied was the existence of one of the greatest performances of Schumann ever recorded.

Tom continued, "I hope you play a little Mozart for the students. David, don't you think that Mozart is one of the composers young musicians play miserably?"

"Absolutely yes. I agree entirely."

Horowitz said, lifting his eyebrows, "Oh, Mozart is one of the best composers for piano. Everything is pianistic. He is always clear and beautiful. And the last movements are never weak, like so many composers. Arthur Rubinstein was playing lots of Mozart concertos when he was old. He told me, 'Only now can I play him. He is for old children like me.' You know who I think played Mozart very good? A real master of Mozart. That is Edwin Fischer, the Swiss pianist."

"Oh, yes. Many people admire Fischer. I've played his records for my class at Juilliard."

Tom continued, "I think the students are afraid to play Mozart. They fear making a real forte. They make him prissy and so thin-sounding."

Horowitz asked, "Why do they think Mozart has no red blood? His blood was just like ours."

"They're confused," Tom said. "They don't know his operas, which are the key to Mozart. If the pupils only understood that the piano sonatas and concerti are operas. And they are confused about Mozart's pedaling. So many old books say don't play Mozart with pedal. The result is that he sounds so dry, so arid. They make him so sterile, with no sensuousness of sound."

Horowitz said, "I must tell the students that Mozart, Chopin, Schumann, Bach, and Haydn have the same blood, veins, pulse, the same heart, the same brain as we have today. There may be changes in the environment, but the human being is the same. From the first time humans hear the birds sing, they love music. Nothing changes. Why are we today so afraid to express our feelings in music? Mozart had the same faults we have. Mozart died because he was drinking too much, but in his music, he was flying. He was singing like the birds. The great composers were people, and I enjoy them as people."

"Well, Tom," I said, "I think we had a good musical talk. Believe me, Maestro, the Juilliard students will love you."

"How many people will come? You know, it must be at four P.M."

I blurted out, "Of course, it will be at your usual time. There will be nearly a thousand students to hear you. The whole school. You are an idol, an icon to them."

Horowitz looked frightened. "One thousand people to hear me talk and play a little. That's too many. I can't do it." Horowitz waved his hand in the air, dismissing the entire idea. "I can accommodate a dozen here in the living room. We choose the twelve best pianists. They come to my home."

Tom said, "Maestro, there is nothing to worry about. I want to film it so your thoughts can be heard by music lovers in the future. David will have the whole thing outlined, and it will be great. Then we all go to have a good dinner."

Horowitz looked encouraged. "Come again tomorrow. Oh, yes, it's New Year's Eve. We go out and have a good time. I see you tomorrow."

In the taxi, Tom said, "I think this can come off. We must keep him interested. Just imagine if we could have on film the voice, the thoughts, the playing of Mozart, Chopin, Liszt, Paderewski, Paganini, or Rachmaninoff."

"Of course," I said. "Let's make good use of this technological stuff. But Tom, you know me. I'm always a little skeptical until it happens. And he is *so* mercurial."

"I know," Tom said, his voice filled with sympathy. "But David, let's have a little faith."

"All right," I replied as Tom was getting out of the taxi. "But as Verdi once said, 'To have faith is good, but to have no faith is better.'"

14

FROM DARKNESS TO LIGHT

Occasionally, Horowitz stared off in space, looking bewildered, as if he wanted to climb out of a cage. I was convinced that Horowitz in his old age was bravely attempting to try to feel contact with the world. The Juilliard program was one example.

At this stage of life, Horowitz was extremely cautious. His life had been in shambles in the early 1980s. The pianist had been under the influence of a psychiatrist—an "evil doctor," Wanda called him. Horowitz had long sought the help of psychiatrists in his fight against depression and lethargy. But under the care of this doctor, he had been relying on antidepressant drugs and was drinking heavily. Much of the time, Mrs. Horowitz told me, he was stupefied.

Horowitz, who could be monumentally stubborn, was convinced of his doctor's worth. Mrs. Horowitz was equally certain that this doctor was killing her husband. There was a daily clash of wills. Wanda, ever watchful of Horowitz's art and health, realized that his playing had deteriorated sadly.

Wanda told me that his playing during this period was strangely erratic as well. "He practiced works, such as Schumann's *Carnaval*, which he had never found sympathetic. I would listen to him practicing and scream, 'Volodya, don't you hear your playing?' He didn't." Soon she refused to attend his recitals.

In 1982, Peter Gelb, a young and brilliantly effective impresario with unswerving dedication to Horowitz, became his manager. Gelb quickly opened new avenues for Horowitz's career. He started filming Horowitz in concert and making advantageous financial contracts for television rights, which brought Horowitz the largest fees ever received by a classical artist.

On May 22, 1982, Horowitz performed his first European recital in thirty years, at London's Royal Festival Hall, at the request of his Royal Highness, Prince Charles. The concert was telecast live in Europe and beamed via satellite to the United States. Some of Horowitz's playing was ghastly, and the artist himself looked as if a vampire had sucked him dry.

For this recital, Horowitz traveled to London with his piano, entourage, and doctor. Wanda was beside herself with anxiety. She could not bear the awful reviews he was receiving. His recent American performances had been terrible. I was embarrassed for him when I heard him at his New York recital.

When Gelb signed Horowitz for a series of Japanese concerts, Mrs. Horowitz beseeched them not to undertake such folly. But Horowitz, who had never been there, wanted to conquer the Japanese. Tickets were immediately sold out at astronomical prices.

The Japanese recitals were a disaster. Horowitz, predictably, played miserably. The press was respectful but cutting. One review called him "a beautiful antique vase, unfortunately broken in many places."

The young Yugoslavian pianist, Ivo Pogorelich, who at the time was creating a furor in Japan, heard Horowitz for the first time in his life. He was shocked. Pogorelich said, "I only wish he had not gone to play in Japan. I had grown up with his records. He was white-hot, his passion and volcanic power, his ability to excite, the fire of his temperament dominated the piano playing world."

The Horowitz legend was becoming badly tarnished. Was he to end his career in defeat?

If Wanda could not make him aware that his playing had deteriorated, the adverse criticism from the press began to seep in, and fortunately, he became disenchanted with his doctor. The psychiatrist was banished. Later, the pain of this experience was so great that he avoided even passing the doctor's office on Park Avenue.

When I had entered his life at the end of 1985, the resilient Horowitz had recovered from those dark days, and had begun the final victorious chapters of his long life. His love for the piano was rekindled by Mozart, as it had been with Clementi thirty years earlier. His playing now possessed a mellow glow, and a new simplicity and relaxation emerged in his art.

Earlier in 1985, he had been the subject of the film *The Last Romantic*. Although he told me that in the film he looked and sounded like a clown and a fool, he was accommodating and entertaining. The film was a commercial success and contains large amounts of his playing.

The year 1986 proved to be one of the most eventful of his life. Although he had trepidations about returning to Russia for the first time in sixty years, he was nevertheless excited by the idea. His Moscow recital was to be televised everywhere in the world.

In one concert, Horowitz would play to more people than any other concert pianist in history. He was indisputably the most famous living pianist. Even his two great contemporaries, Claudio Arrau and Rudolf Serkin, could not claim his celebrity.

15

NEW YEAR'S EVE

The Horowitzes had invited me and the Frosts to spend New Year's Eve with them.

On this last night of 1985, Horowitz was in an amiable mood, chatting about his daily foray into piano improvisation.

"I'm having a good time with it," he said. "I'm too lazy to practice, but my improvising keeps my fingers busy and in good shape."

"Maestro, do you really need to practice more than an hour or two?" I asked.

Horowitz replied, "I need to, but I don't want to. But you know, I know how to work."

Wanda overheard us and said, "He is lucky. Nobody can get away with so little practicing. Even after a long time away, he gets in shape immediately."

"This is truly a wonderful thing," I replied. "I think it was Paderewski who said, 'One day away from the piano, I and my wife know it. Two days away, the critics know it, and three days of not practicing, the world knows it.'"

"Ah, that is good" Wanda said, "but that gives the critics the benefit of the doubt."

Another guest, a close friend of Mrs. Horowitz, Sally Horwich, asked if I knew the work of James Gibbons Huneker. Neither Wanda nor Horowitz had heard of him. Huneker was a writer on all the arts, and in a culturally virginal America, he wrote about every European artist of note. His books remain vividly perceptive and invigorating.

I told them I adored the florid style of Huneker, who was one of the great piano lovers.

Horowitz asked, "Did Huneker ever hear me?"

"No, Maestro. He died in 1921 at age sixty-one. You didn't play in America until 1928."

Tom and Lynne were curious and asked me more about him.

I continued, "Huneker was a lusty, ironic, and witty man who hated cant and hypocrisy and prohibition. His only novel, *Painted Veils*, was banned in Boston. It was too sexy for 1920. He had studied piano and knew personally every pianist of his time. In his last letter, he wrote, 'I'm dying of diabetes—such a sweet death. Vita sexualis very low indeed. Guts are going. And what with one's teeth, hair, testicles on the wane, what is there to live for? Pardon the pessimism. You no doubt suffer more in an hour than I do in a month.'"

Horowitz was delighted with Huneker.

"Maybe I read something of his," he said.

We were in high spirits as we left for a festive New Year's dinner at Salta in Bocca, an Italian restaurant on Madison Avenue.

It was close to the enchanted hour of midnight when our little group arrived back at the Horowitz home. The Maestro asked Tom to turn on the television to see the ball drop in Times Square. I smiled to myself; even Horowitz likes to partake in such rituals.

Horowitz looked serious, "I hope that I live through 1986."

Tom and Lynne responded that it would be a good year for him.

Wanda humorously said, "I hope he won't kill me in '86."

At the stroke of midnight, a bottle of champagne was uncorked and we offered toasts. Horowitz had water.

As we sipped our champagne, Horowitz pushed himself off the couch, saying, "I think I play a little New Year's music for good luck." The Maestro sat down at the piano and played the Schubert-Liszt Serenade. The first hour of the new year exuded warmth and goodwill.

Horowitz said, "Come tomorrow night. We try a new restaurant. Come early, at seven o'clock, and we'll continue work on our Juilliard program."

16

HANGING BY A THREAD

It was New Year's Day. I arrived at East Ninety-fourth Street promptly at seven p.m. The Frosts had not yet arrived and Wanda was sitting alone. We briefly talked about the night before.

Shortly, the Maestro appeared, looking rested and rosy-cheeked. He began by reporting all the bad news he had just heard on the radio. "Who is Ricky Nelson? He was killed last night in a crash."

I answered, "He was a rock star. Do you remember the Nelson family—Ozzie, Harriet, David, and Ricky? For years, they had a TV show portraying an ideal family life. They were practically an American institution."

"I don't know. I never heard of them," Horowitz muttered. "But there is at least one good piece of news."

"And what is that, Mr. Horowitz?"

"Rudolf Firkušný can play Schubert, that's for sure. I heard him on radio this afternoon, I think on your station, playing the three Klavierstücke. *Beautiful!*" Horowitz beamed. When Horowitz liked a colleague's work, he always showed appreciation.

As soon as Tom and Lynne arrived, we departed for Mortimer's, a trendy, crowded, noisy restaurant on Lexington Avenue.

Horowitz, who was basically shy and uncomfortable with strangers, acted like a silly child in the restaurant, pointing and making stupid comments and weird faces. In the next month, I was to see this kind of behavior frequently. Interestingly, in the next few years, however, he never again acted so awkwardly in public.

101

I saw Horowitz almost every night that January. The Frosts joined us whenever possible. To Horowitz, food was more engrossing than working on our Juilliard program. Every morsel of his risotto was fully appreciated. If on a particular night he denied himself a scoop of ice cream, he would allow himself a baked apple. Tom and I acted like his children, hoping Papa was enjoying his repast.

Once the date of our Juilliard appearance had been settled, Horowitz shied away from discussing any subject matter. I gently prodded him, but any kind of planning bored him. There was little I could do.

Around the fifteenth of January, he went to Juilliard with Tom to choose a piano and look over the nine-hundred-seat Juilliard Theater. I was teaching and could not join them.

The following week, the students were offered free tickets. A huge line formed the moment it was announced; the students stood for hours. The Horowitzes had stipulated that each pupil had to sign a release stating that the ticket would be used only by a Juilliard student. No outsiders could attend.

Nobody could afford to miss Vladimir Horowitz speaking and demonstrating at the piano. I had become a hero to my pupils.

I proudly reported to the Maestro that all the tickets were swiftly gobbled up. He didn't seem to care for my enthusiasm and made a sour face. Horowitz at Juilliard started to become unreal.

A few days later, I was told that filming the occasion was being thwarted by the Horowitz management. I smelled a rat, and now suspected that the great event would never take place. The Frosts were still convinced that he would appear. Wanda seemed noncommittal.

On Monday and Tuesday, at least officially, all was still "go," although I was becoming ill from anxiety and strain. My outline was complete, my questions were ready. I didn't see Horowitz Wednesday night, but he assured me that on Thursday we would go though our material before dinner. He wasn't worried, so why should I be?

Early on Thursday, the phone rang. It was Tom. "David, I have bad news."

My heart was pounding. "How bad, Tom?" I asked.

"Horowitz has a cold. He's canceling the Juilliard. I feel terrible for you. I really thought he would go through with it."

"Damn it!" I screamed. "He has a cold, what a joke. I've been sick

The twenty-three-year old Horowitz in the Berlin offices of Steinway, with two of their representatives. (Photo courtesy Steinway and Sons)

Horowitz with his early manager, Alexander Merovitch, and Steinway's Director of Concerts and Artists, Alexander Greiner, Paris 1930. (Photo courtesy Steinway and Sons)

The Philharmonic Society of New York

FOUNDED 1842

| 1927 | - | **EIGHTY-SIXTH SEASON** | - | 1928 |

CARNEGIE HALL
Thursday Evening, January 12, 1928
AT EIGHT-THIRTY
Friday Afternoon, January 13, 1928
AT TWO-THIRTY

2248TH AND 2249TH CONCERTS OF THE PHILHARMONIC SOCIETY

Under the Direction of
SIR THOMAS BEECHAM
GUEST CONDUCTOR
(First appearance in America)

Assisting Artist:
VLADIMIR HOROWITZ, Pianist
(First appearance in America)

PROGRAM

1. HANDEL..Overture to "Teseo"
   (First time by the Philharmonic)
2. HANDEL...Musette from "Il Pastor Fido"
   (First time by the Philharmonic)
3. HANDEL...Bourrée from "Rodrigo"
   (First time by the Philharmonic)
4. DELIUS....................Intermezzo, "The Walk to the Paradise Garden"
   (from the opera, "A Village Romeo and Juliet")
   (First time in New York)
5. TCHAIKOVSKY............Piano Concerto No. 1, in B-flat minor, Op. 23
   I.   Allegro non troppo e molto maestoso; Allegro con spirito
   II. Andantino semplice
   III. Allegro con fucco
   VLADIMIR HOROWITZ, Pianist

   INTERMISSION

6. MOZART................Symphony No. 34, in C major, (Köchel No. 338)
   I.   Allegro vivace
   II. Andante di molto
   III. Finale: Allegro vivace
7. BERLIOZ...................."Chasse Royale et l'Orage" ["Royal Hunt and
   Tempest"], from "Les Troyens"
   (First time by the Philharmonic)
8. WAGNER..Prelude to "Die Meistersinger"

ARTHUR JUDSON, Manager
EDWARD ERVIN, Associate Manager

THE STEINWAY is the Official Piano of The Philharmonic Society
MR. HOROWITZ USES THE STEINWAY PIANO

The program of the celebrated concert of Horowitz's American debut, January 12, 1928. It was also Sir Thomas Beecham's debut in the United States.

The young Josef Hofmann with Anton Rubinstein's portrait. During Horowitz's childhood, Hofmann was one of the greatest box office attractions of any pianist.

Anton Rubinstein, the greatest Russian pianist of the nineteenth century, died a decade before Horowitz was born. But Rubinstein's name was magic to young Horowitz, who studied with Felix Blumenfeld, a Rubinstein student.

An extraordinary photograph of Anton Rubinstein (center) in December 1893, in front of the Imperial Conservatory in St. Petersburg, which he founded in 1862.

Horowitz in his mid-twenties.　　　　　Horowitz just before his first American
concert tour in 1928.

The hands of Vladimir Horowitz in 1937. Oscar Levant called Horowitz's
hands "supple, strong, flexible, and magnetic." (Photo courtesy
Steinway and Sons)

A 1931 program from a concert with Jascha Heifitz and Horowitz. The two young musical giants were playing together at the home of a wealthy patron.

Returning to New York in 1934 from Italy on the Italian liner *Rex* are Vladimir Horowitz, Nathan Milstein, Gregor Piatigorsky, Arturo Toscanini, and Bernardo Molinari.

Left to right: Therese Milstein, Alexander Greiner, Vladimir Horowitz, Fyodor Chaliapin, Nathan Milstein, and John Steinway. (Photo courtesy Steinway and Sons)

Horowitz was one of Rachmaninoff's great interpreters. This 1931 photo shows Rachmaninoff leaving his apartment on West End Avenue in New York City.

Sergei Rachmaninoff in 1936 with the electric muff he used to keep his hands warm before concerts. (Photo courtesy Steinway and Sons)

Toscanini and Horowitz around 1940. (Photo courtesy Steinway and Sons)

A rare photo of Franz Liszt around 1854, when he composed his Sonata in B minor—one of the staples of Horowitz's repertoire.

Ignacy Jan Paderewsky around 1920. Horowitz had Paderewsky's signed photo on the wall in his living room. (Photo courtesy Peter Rosen Productions, Inc.)

Horowitz wires Alexander Greiner, of Steinway and Sons, about a cancellation.

Greiner sends a telegram to Horowitz about the difficulty of getting tickets to Horowitz's recitals. (Courtesy Steinway and Sons)

Oscar Levant with Horowitz. Levant was no mean pianist, but the body language in the photo proclaims Horowitz as the owner of the piano bench. Levant wrote, "Horowitz gave me lessons in canceling concerts. I used to cancel as far ahead as two weeks when I was ill. 'Never do that,' Horowitz explained. 'Always cancel at the last minute.'" (Photo by Adrian Siegel, courtesy Steinway and Sons)

Franz Liszt at age twenty-four, from an oil painting by Henri Lehmann. Horowitz called Liszt "the greatest in the world for the piano."

A rare photograph of Horowitz with Rachmaninoff. (Photo courtesy Ruth Laredo)

all week in anticipation that he would do this. How selfish, all those kids standing in line for hours. They'll be so disappointed and I could cry. Do you think his appearance will be rescheduled after his cold?"

Tom replied, "He may have a little cold, but I'm sure the Juilliard show will never happen."

"I know it won't," I answered. "I don't even want to know the real reason for this."

"But, David, cold or not, Horowitz wants us to join them for dinner Friday night. He certainly doesn't want you out of his life."

"Yeah," I said, "another meal, big deal. What a pity this didn't happen. Tom, I'm very angry, and I feel exploited."

Throughout the day I felt sorry for myself. Yet deep down, I had always known that Horowitz would "cop out." He was like a cat, untrustworthy. A little cold was certainly not the reason he canceled. The real reason was probably not clear even to himself. Perhaps he was told he should not be so generous; after all, there was no money in it for him.

But most likely, he was simply too scared. He was just not secure enough to speak in public. I remembered an old Horowitz story I had heard years before, when he was so nervous before a concert he refused to go on stage and play.

"I can't do it tonight," he told his manager. "Tell them I'm sick."

"Oh, no, I won't. You go out there yourself and tell them" came the manager's furious reply.

"Okay, I will," and Horowitz stormed out. As he stood at the apron of the stage, he was tongue-tied. His mouth hung open, but nothing came out. Flustered, he meekly went to his piano and began playing.

I finally realized Horowitz really did not have it in him to survive such an ordeal.

He might have been becoming more outgoing, but visiting a restaurant is not the same thing as appearing at the world's most glamorous performing arts school, where a thousand eager students are expecting gems of wisdom to inspire them.

On Friday, my students clearly showed their disappointment and indignation at Horowitz's cancellation. I was the one now with a bad cold, and I was angry.

Between classes, I impulsively went to the phone and called the Horowitzes. It was noon. Horowitz of course was still sleeping.

Giuliana, their indispensable housekeeper and "lady-in-waiting," answered with her always cheerful voice: "Mr. Dubal, how are you?"

"Giuliana, I am not happy. Will you please tell Mr. and Mrs. Horowitz that I am *canceling* dinner tonight?"

"Oh, no," Giuliana cried, "Maestro and Madame will be disappointed."

"Giuliana, do you understand that I and one thousand others today are more disappointed?"

"I understand, Mr. Dubal. I understand."

I came away from the phone with a little sigh of relief. At that moment, I had had my fill of Horowitz and felt unnecessarily used. "Good-bye, Maestro," I mumbled as I walked back to Room 549, where my next class of disappointed pianists was waiting.

17

RECONCILIATION

It had been nearly a month since I had dropped the Horowitzes. Lynne Frost said it was a pity I was no longer seeing them and that the Maestro had made comments showing that he was hurt.

According to Lynne, Horowitz pouted, "Now that Mr. Dubal does not visit, I shall *never* go to Juilliard with him."

Lynne had retorted, "But Mr. Horowitz, David is David and not Juilliard. You should see each other for the enjoyment it brings to both of you."

"Well, I want to see him if he wants to see me." However, their pride would never permit them to call.

Tom declared, "David, forget the Juilliard fiasco. You two are made for each other. Horowitz misses you. His musical friends are few enough. Call him."

As the month passed, I realized that I missed both of them, and I certainly missed his piano playing. After all, he was the *great* Horowitz. Obviously, I could not have twenty dinners a month, but visiting perhaps once a week, that might work.

I thought, how shall I go about this? I don't want to apologize and ask to come back to the fold, nor do I want to mention the Juilliard debacle. I decided to broadcast several old programs—not the interviews—I had done on Horowitz and his recordings on my radio show.

I phoned while sitting in my office at WNCN. Mrs. Horowitz answered. I told her about the programs, which would be aired weekly for a month. "I thought you and Mr. Horowitz might like to tune in," I said.

Her voice was pleasant. "Oh, yes, we would love to hear them," she replied. Wanda, who never beat about the bush, said, "Mr. Dubal, you know that Mr. Horowitz never went to Juilliard because we found out that a certain piano teacher whom we detest disregarded our rules and was going to bring as a guest a certain music critic."

I thought this was incredible. She had apparently forgotten the "cold" which Horowitz had used as an excuse to cancel. I replied, "Mrs. Horowitz, what does it matter?! I never understood why Mr. Horowitz wanted to put himself through such an ordeal."

With those words, Wanda's voice brightened. It seemed that I had uttered a blazing truth, and with that she asked, "When can you come for dinner? You know we go to Russia soon."

"Yes, I know. Let's make it next week."

"Giuliana will call you."

"Say hello to Mr. Horowitz, and try to listen to my programs if you remember."

Early Monday morning, I answered the phone to Giuliana's cheery voice asking me when I would be able to join Maestro and Madame for dinner.

Our little reunion took place on Wednesday. Horowitz was happy to see me again and acted as though nothing had happened. Juilliard was never mentioned, then or ever. We had dinner at the well-known La Caravelle, where Mr. and Mrs. Horowitz were treated like potentates.

Afterward, we returned to their home and talked about the recitals in Moscow and Leningrad in April.

It sounded like the Russian concerts were not quite real to him yet. He did not seem convinced that he was really going back to Russia. After all, he had declared countless times that he would never return to his homeland, that nothing there appealed to him.

Later in the evening, he played bits and pieces of his recital program for me, but his playing seemed somewhat tentative and a little sloppy. He told me, "I rather improvise these days than practice my program."

It was getting late, and I was anxious. Once again, I myself had not found time to practice; for a pianist, not practicing always brings the uneasy feeling that the day has been squandered. I was leaving the next week for my own concerts in Detroit, followed immediately by two more in Arizona and a talk at the University of Arizona in Tucson.

Horowitz said, "You come again next Wednesday."

I replied, "Maestro, I'm sorry. I leave for about a week to give lecture-recitals on American music in Arizona."

"Ah, then I see you when you get back. Why are you going there?"

I explained that Ozan Marsh, a pianist who teaches at the university, invited me. Horowitz said, "I think I know of him."

"Yes, Ozan is an excellent pianist. He plays the hell out of the Kabalevsky Second Concerto," I said.

"I know Kabalevsky well. A good composer. His music is very pianistic. A little like Prokofiev, perhaps."

"You're right," I said. "I think Kabalevsky is one of the best of the Soviet composers. By the way, your recording of his Third Sonata is fantastic."

Horowitz replied, "Yes, it's good. Kabalevsky thinks so, too. You know, I gave the American premiere of the Third Sonata, I think in '47. The last movement is very amusing. I performed his Second Sonata also, but never recorded it."

"I wish you had. I've looked at the score, and it sounds like a serious and fine work."

Horowitz continued, "Why go to Arizona? Stay here. We go to dinner."

Was he joking? I couldn't really tell.

I told him I had always been interested in lesser-known branches of the piano literature and considered myself something of a missionary for American music. I had devised a lecture-recital I called *The Piano in America*, which showed the development of piano music in the United States.

Horowitz rumbled, "I see you when you get back. You know, when I go to Russia soon, maybe you come."

"Oh, Maestro, I would love to be with you. What a thrill it would be. But I have obligations here. The programming deadlines at WNCN, my own radio show, my classes at Juilliard, and on May 2, I leave to give concerts and master classes in Korea."

"Oh my God!" Horowitz shouted. "How do you do it all?"

"Mr. Horowitz, I'm used to it. But believe me, I'm often pretty tired. But I will be thinking of you a great deal when you are gone, and you will have plenty of people with you. Gelb, Frost, Giuliana,

Probst, Franz Mohr [Steinway's master technician], and most important of all, Mrs. Horowitz will be with you."

Wanda smiled. "He will have lots of company with him. We will stay at the American embassy. He will have anything he wants and the best gray sole in the world. He won't even know he has left his living room."

Besides a fee of half a million dollars per concert and most of the receipts from the gross, Horowitz was notorious for his demands for comfort. Not for Horowitz the usual plights of concert life: bad restaurants and hotels, strange beds, imperfect pianos, noisy streets, and the hundred horrors of travel. It had to be ascertained that a local fish market could provide gray sole. If not, Horowitz would not play in a city unless the local impresario could manage to fly in his staple fish.

His requirements concerning living quarters were specific. During the 1970s, when Harold Shaw managed Horowitz, the impresario sent out a questionnaire to prospective concert presenters, detailing what Horowitz needed—water purifiers, special cooking utensils and cutlery, thick black drapes, certain types of chairs, special clothes hangers, and many other specifications as to a proper bed, perfect silence, total privacy, and a well-equipped bathroom. The living room, of course, had to be big enough for a nine-foot Steinway.

Finally, wherever he stayed had to be close to the concert hall and in a secure enough area that Horowitz could take his daily walks.

"In Moscow, everything will be perfect for you," I continued. "It will be a grand time. And I think the Russians deserve to see you after sixty years."

"I don't know," Horowitz responded. "Maybe they don't even know me anymore. The whole century has passed by."

"Maestro, I assure you, they know you." At that, I said good night. "I'll see you when I return."

I looked fondly at Horowitz. He was reaching out to the world. The tension and resistance regarding the Juilliard appearance was over, and the entire evening was relaxed and pleasant. I no longer felt any anxiety about being drained. And I was delighted that our relationship would continue.

18

THE PERFECT ENCORE

Almost the first thing I did upon returning from Tucson was to phone Horowitz. He seemed anxious to talk to me.

"I want to discuss my Russian repertory with you," he said. "I'm not sure of the order of the pieces yet. Can you come April 1? That's Tuesday."

"Maestro," I replied, "I can't on that day. I'm flying to Cleveland for a lecture-recital."

"What? You are just back and you are leaving me again? Come then Friday the twenty-eighth."

"That I can do," I replied. "I'll see you then." I was amused that Horowitz had not asked about my trip to Arizona.

On Friday evening, I arrived at seven-thirty. After chatting a while, Horowitz took a deep breath and headed for the piano. "I play for you a little from my program."

Horowitz's playing sounded sluggish again. He simply was not in the best pianistic shape. I wanted to say "Maestro, the Mozart lacks your usual verve and sparkle," but my courage faltered.

An hour later Wanda announced that she was dying of hunger. In the backseat of the car, Mrs. Horowitz and I talked about their forthcoming trip.

"I've never been there," she said. "The American ambassador, Mr. Hartman, assures us that everything will be to our liking."

I followed the Horowitzes as we were ushered to a secluded table. Mr. Horowitz said, "Have your Stolichnaya vodka. I have my juice."

109

The mood was quiet and relaxed. Possibly the vodka had made me bold, and to my surprise I blurted out, "Maestro, you *are* going to play wonderfully in Russia, aren't you?"

Horowitz looked at me almost in alarm. Wanda, surprised, watched us intensely. The great Vladimir Horowitz was not asked such questions. But the tone of my voice spelled a certain urgency and sincerity.

I only wanted him to triumph when he returned to Russia. Success frightened Horowitz. But so did failure. This conflict was always with him.

It appeared I had hit a sensitive spot. "What do you mean, *play well*? I don't play for the audience or for critics. I play for *me!*"

"But, Maestro, that's exactly what I mean. Are you going to play well for *yourself?*" As I said this, I put my hand gently on his arm. This gesture seemed to calm him. "You know, Mr. Horowitz, I want them to go mad over you on your return to Russia."

Horowitz looked at me. "I know what you say. I understand. I'm an old trouper. I'll do well. I still have the time to work." He shrugged his shoulders. "But now it's time for a little dessert."

Mrs. Horowitz, sitting opposite us, bent over and whispered in my ear, "Good! Volodya needs to hear this. The *Shtunk* doesn't practice."

After dinner, Horowitz said, "Let's go back home. I want to talk more about the program for Russia."

Horowitz was helped on with his black coat and looked in the mirror for several seconds, adjusting his hat to its proper angle.

I felt better that I had been direct with the Maestro. In fact, he had not spent much time practicing since his Carnegie Hall recital three months earlier.

He told me that most nights he was staying up late, watching three movies. On his daily walks with Giuliana, he enjoyed renting films from the video store. His recent choices were one Clint Eastwood movie, one current "hit," and one that was X-rated.

"You know," he said, "they call the X-rated ones *pornos*. What an ugly name. Don't tell Wanda about the porno," he added with a wink.

"Believe me, Maestro, it's our secret."

"You know, they have amazing things on cable TV these days."

"Such as?"

"Have you ever seen this woman called Byrd? I forget the first name. She calls herself a Byrd-watcher."

"Of course I've seen her, Maestro. Her name is Robin Byrd."

Horowitz was laughing. "She sounds crazy. You know this program is pure pornography. It's on all the time."

"Oh, yes," I replied. "She's been on for years. She has almost acquired the status of a campy New York cult. One doesn't know if one should laugh or cry."

"I think cry," Horowitz said. "It's unbelievable. She laughs and dances, and has women taking clothes off, and now she has men doing it, too. It's a little disgusting, you know."

"Maestro, whatever the show is, it certainly isn't sexy."

During our talk, Wanda had been out of the room. As she returned, Horowitz said, "Mr. Dubal, you are right. I'm improvising too much. It's easy, and I am preferring it to the practice."

"I well understand," I said. "Improvising is great fun, and one can waste hours entertaining oneself."

Horowitz continued, "As you know, I play *Kreisleriana* in Leningrad. But I can't play it in Moscow, unfortunately, because it will be too long for the television. In Moscow, I play three Scarlatti sonatas, then the Mozart C Major, K. 330, sonata. I do two Scriabin etudes before intermission. But before them, I think I play two Rachmaninoff preludes. You know, I must give them enough Russian music, too."

"Of course you must. But which preludes do you intend to perform?"

Horowitz answered, "I think I do G minor and G-sharp minor."

I abruptly cried, "No! Mr. Horowitz, please don't play the G minor Prelude. It's played to death."

This is certainly true, but what I did not tell the Maestro was that I never liked the way he played that particular prelude. His performance could not match the subtlety of Rachmaninoff's and Hofmann's interpretations.

Mrs. Horowitz joined in, "Absolutely, Volodya. Listen to Mr. Dubal. I can't stand that prelude."

"Maestro, instead of the G minor Prelude, why not play the G Major Prelude, which you do with exquisite fluidity?"

"I don't know," he said. "We will see. Then maybe I do G minor for encore."

"Naturally, it's up to you. But in my opinion, it would be best to leave it out completely. It's so hackneyed."

"The second half of the program is okay," Horowitz went on. "But I must have a good encore. Encores are very important. I need one that is very short, about two minutes. I play the Rachmaninoff Polka for last encore, that's more than four minutes. My first encore will be *Träumerei*. That I have to play. Audiences expect that. But in the middle, I need something brilliant and short."

Horowitz scratched his head. "I don't know what can work. It must be exactly right."

Here was another indication of how important good programming was to Horowitz. He had said to me, "I want a program to have contrast, contrast, and more contrast." We shared in common our love of programming, and we spoke of this art often and in many contexts.

Suddenly, my programming light bulb switched on. "Maestro, I *have* it! I have the perfect encore for Russia," I almost shouted.

"What? What then is it?" he asked impatiently.

"Maestro," I said, "you must play Moszkowski's *Etincelles* [Sparks]. Your old recording is fabulous!"

"*No, no,*" Horowitz exclaimed. "I don't know it anymore. No, I don't even have the music. I don't know where the music is."

"I guarantee you success with it," I said. "You will play it as smooth as silk. Every time I program your recording of the *Etincelles* on WNCN, calls come in immediately asking for the title of the piece. *Etincelles* is brilliant and fits the hand like a glove."

"Ach, I don't like it. *No!*" Horowitz said. "I don't have it in my fingers."

"Mr. Horowitz, I talked to Frost today, and he told me that he is coming to see you tomorrow. If you don't have the score to the Moskowski, I'm sure he would go over to Patelson's music store and get you a copy."

Horowitz said nothing more. The subject was closed. He rejected several other suggestions for encores, but I was convinced the *Etincelles* was exactly what was needed. It would be the perfect encore.

19

OFF TO RUSSIA

The cultural doors between the United States and the Soviet Union had been locked since the Carter administration. In spring 1986, signs of *glasnost* were clearly on the horizon, but it was still early.

Horowitz had not received an official invitation from the Soviet government. His appearances had been arranged by his manager, Peter Gelb, and the American ambassador, Arthur Hartman.

Horowitz's recitals were officially viewed as "nonevents," and no mention was made of them by the Russian news agency. The absence of fanfare or official Soviet recognition bothered him, but there was no way to change the situation.

I saw the Horowitzes once more, on April 8, 1986, before their departure. The journey was now a reality to him and the Maestro was pianistically prepared.

Horowitz told me, "I'm an unofficial goodwill ambassador." I think he rather liked the undercurrent of semisecrecy.

He went on, "I will be the first artist to go back and open the doors for peace between the two countries. Not a bad role, eh?" He smiled. "But it's typical of them, that I'm there but not there. We see how it goes. Maybe nobody will care if I'm there."

I said, "Believe me, Mr. Horowitz. They will know you are there. But it is a shame that you are to give only one concert each in Moscow and Leningrad."

"This part is bad," Horowitz agreed, "because only the bigwig bureaucrats can get to hear me, which means the real people and the

113

students can't go. The Moscow Conservatory's hall is called the
Great Hall, but it's not nearly as big as Carnegie. In the old times,
when Anton Rubinstein played, he knew the students could not
afford to hear him, and he played for them for free in the afternoon at
the conservatory. I'm hoping to be able to go through the recital at
the rehearsal on Saturday for only students and people who really
love music. They are the ones that count. Maybe this can be
arranged. Nothing is easy there. I still remember that nothing goes
smoothly."

Mrs. Horowitz sat erect, listening carefully. During the last weeks,
she had bolstered her husband's fragile ego. She knew it was time for
him to do something "big" again.

Wanda herself had no fear. She loved adventure and liked to travel.
Although often plagued by various aches and pains, basically she was
as strong as an Italian peasant.

One had to admire them. They had been through thick and thin
together. Once more, the old trouper was doing what concert
pianists have done since the days when Liszt traveled from concert to
concert in an elaborate carriage.

The piano had been invented in 1709 by the Italian instrument
maker Bartolomeo Cristofori, who wanted to create an instrument
capable of producing an emotional reaction in the listener instead of
the "plucked," crisp sound the harpsichord makes. Cristofori invented a hammer mechanism which enabled the pianist, through various
touches, to create a soft (piano) and loud (forte) sound, with many
gradations in between.

After Cristofori died in 1731, nobody in Italy cared about his
invention. The Italians loved the voice, and violin making was at its
apogee.

By the 1730s the Germans had begun building pianos based on
Cristofori's model. By the 1750s the pianoforte had traveled to
London, where the "instrument of expression" became the rage. The
first piano performance in history was given in 1768, when J. S.
Bach's youngest son, Johann Christian Bach, played a solo at a
concert in London.

Concerts then were variety shows. The other performers at that
concert included a harpist, a violinist, and a singer. It was unthinkable to devote a whole evening to a single instrument: it would have
been considered tedious to the ear.

However, by the 1830s, Liszt's fame was so great that he had no need to share the stage with anyone else. Liszt had created the idea of the performer as "Romantic hero." In Milan in 1839, in a daring step, Liszt finally gave the first solo piano concerts proclaiming, "Le concert, c'est moi." He soon coined the word *recital*. People laughed: "How does one recite at the piano?"

After Liszt retired from the concert stage in 1847, it took years for most pianists to think they, too, could interest the public in two hours of solo music without the relief of other instrumentalists and singers.

By the time Horowitz had begun his career, the solo recital was an established fact of concert life. Horowitz was merely following the path of pianists since Liszt, true musical troubadours wandering the planet, singing on the piano the immortal "songs" of the masters.

On our last night together before he left for Moscow, we spoke about Liszt. Horowitz reminded me of the two photographs of the great Hungarian that he kept with him at all times during his tours.

Horowitz said with gusto, "We owe him everything. He was the greatest."

"I agree," I continued. "Without him, everything would have been different. Because of Liszt, a musical career was no longer a haphazard affair. He had a manager, and everything was arranged in advance. For twelve years until 1847, he never stopped.

"Someone wrote 'Liszt has created a madness. He plays everywhere and for everyone.' He was indefatigable, crossing miles of frozen land through Russian blizzards, pushed forward by dog teams. He even submitted to days of quarantine to be the first major pianist to play in Constantinople."

As I talked, Horowitz's small beady eyes, black as coal, opened to their widest. Horowitz, nearly eighty-three years old, was continuing the great concert ritual.

"Imagine!" he said. "I am living longer than Liszt did. He was seventy-five when he died. And I'm still at it. Nobody had such a life like Liszt's."

"I know, Maestro. Once when someone asked him why he had not written an autobiography like his son-in-law Wagner, Liszt slyly replied, 'It was enough to have lived it.'"

The evening went by quickly. As I got up to leave, I bent over to kiss him on the forehead. I had a lump in my throat.

Horowitz said, "Adieu. I wish you were coming. We would have good time. I may even go to Japan again. We will see."

"I wish I were going, too, Maestro."

At the door, I hugged Wanda. She said, "Let's pray all goes well. It may be a long while till we are back."

And so the great virtuoso returned to the land of his birth after six turbulent decades. For Horowitz, Russia was fraught with emotional perils, but it was also a country with a lofty tradition of great performers and devoted audiences.

Going back to Russia was important for Horowitz. As he had said, "I want to see the country where I was born." When Russia had been forbidden to him, he blocked out a great deal of the pain of his young years and the tragedy of his family. Horowitz was undergoing a rejuvenation, and he had to face Russia. It was an emotional breakthrough for him. His appearance was not a nonevent.

20

THE CONCERT HEARD
AROUND THE WORLD

Several days later, Horowitz, Wanda, Steinway piano CD 503, a film crew, and entourage were in Moscow. Lynne Frost called to say that Tom reported from Moscow that all was going smoothly.

Horowitz was comfortable at the embassy. He was pleased with the amenities, hospitality, and food. When he took walks around town, curious people followed him through the streets. Horowitz was in high spirits, and the musical public of Moscow was undoubtedly aware of his presence.

The concert was to be televised worldwide, for an audience even larger than that of his London recital, which had been broadcast in Europe and on public television in the United States.

The large sum of money he was to earn from this journey served as the financial incentive for his trip to Russia. He said, "I have become a millionaire by playing Mozart, and he dies at thirty-five and is buried in pauper's grave."

Somehow I was unaware of the exact date of his recital and its broadcast. I was asleep Sunday morning, April 20, when, fortunately, my brother called. "You know, your pal Vladimir is playing right now from Moscow."

I screamed, "How can I be missing this?" and scrambled to the TV.

I tuned in during the last of the three Scarlatti sonatas. I was irritated to have missed the first two.

His Mozart sonata went smoothly. The old man, I thought, is in good form. He looked well and seemed calm. He had lost the ten pounds he said he would, and his concert "uniform," as he called it, looked elegant on him.

After the Mozart, he returned to the stage, where, to my delight, he played the Rachmaninoff G Major Prelude, as I had advised. I was still curious to see if he would play the G minor Prelude as an encore.

The two Scriabin etudes ended the first half. I was amused when he missed a chord in the opening of the Scriabin D-sharp minor Etude. The Maestro, however, wasn't amused, and a tiny scowl appeared. Every pianist who has ever played that piece knows the danger of the opening bars. Horowitz had been playing it a lifetime, but disaster is always impending. Piano playing is a perilous profession.

His playing of the Scriabin etudes possessed an ineffable nostalgia. Many in the audience were moved to tears. The writer Boris Pasternak, who had often heard Scriabin perform, wrote, "No sooner do the melodies of his works begin than tears start to your eyes. The melodies, mingling with the tears, run straight along your nerves to your heart."

By the second half of the concert, Horowitz was more relaxed, and the audience was deeply attentive. Horowitz said "For me, silence is the success. I want them so silent that you can hear a pin drop. I don't want them to cough. They should die first before they cough." In Moscow on April 20, 1986, the audience sat spellbound. Horowitz had stolen their hearts.

The concert concluded with Chopin's great A-flat Polonaise. The applause brought Horowitz back to the stage several times. The last time, he patted his piano affectionately and smiled at the audience. His eyes were moist. He was visibly moved.

After raising his hand to stop the applause, Horowitz played his first encore, his signature piece, Schumann's luscious *Träumerei* from *Kinderscenen*. As he played, the cameras lingered on the huge portraits of Anton Rubinstein, Chopin, and Schumann on the wall of the legendary Moscow Conservatory.

I wondered how, with each successive playing, Horowitz managed to make this hackneyed piece sound fresh. Perhaps to play these

"Scenes from Childhood" with awestruck innocence, one had to be very old.

As Horowitz launched into his second encore, I was shocked. What? I thought. That old devil is playing *Etincelles*. Ha! So he knew a good idea when he heard it. Here is my contribution to Horowitz in Moscow.

It may not have been in his fingers when I suggested it, but he had practiced it well. This delightful romp over the keyboard was played spotlessly. Horowitz attached a little ending of his own to the piece which made the "sparks" float off humorously in space. The audience responded with a hushed chuckle.

Horowitz never missed an effect. He was always the consummate performer and subtle showman, yet everything was done without a shade of ostentation. Oscar Levant once wrote, "Horowitz never moves a muscle other than those in his hands when he plays. He's always erect, unexhibitionist, and his stage behavior and pianistic address are faultless."

All through the day, my smile was a mile wide when I thought of Horowitz gruffly complaining of the Moszkowski's *Etincelles*, "No, no, I don't even have the music to it."

The Moszkowski was a terrific success, just as I had predicted. He continued to play it in Europe, Japan, at the White House, and during his 1987 concerts in Amsterdam, Berlin, and in Vienna, where he had not performed for fifty-three years.

On May 2, I went to Korea to perform and to give master classes. I heard nothing more about Horowitz.

Soon after my return two weeks later, the Frosts dropped over to hear about my Korean adventures. I mentioned seeing the Moscow recital and related to them, how I had proposed that he play the *Etincelles* as an encore.

Tom roared with laughter. "That old demon. So that's why I found myself buying that piece. Naturally, he never told me that you recommended the Moszkowski."

"I'm certain that he never remembered it was my idea," I replied. "The main thing is that he found his encore."

Several months later, I was discussing this concert with Richard Probst, Steinway's Director of Concerts and Artists, who had accompanied Horowitz to Russia. He said that the recital seen by millions on television was wonderful. But for him, the concert

Horowitz gave the day before for students and friends of the conservatory was even better. It had begun as a rehearsal, but when the word was out that Horowitz was testing the piano, the place filled rapidly.

Richard said, "There were no Soviet bureaucrats. All were true lovers of the Maestro. He was in top form. From the opening piece there was a special atmosphere in the hall. It was as if, through Horowitz's playing, the yoke of oppression was lifted from their shoulders."

Indeed, this nonevent came at the beginning of a new epoch in Russian history.

21

BACK HOME

One Monday morning, early in July—nearly three months since I had last seen Wanda and the Maestro—Giuliana called, brightly announcing the Horowitz's return. The next evening, I went to visit them.

When I entered the room, Horowitz stood, and I hugged him and kissed Mrs. Horowitz's hand.

I thought the old master would regale me with stories about his adventures. But on the contrary, nothing interesting seemed to have occurred outside the fact that he played his recitals. He casually passed over his triumphs.

Horowitz reported that he was fitted for some expensive suits in London, but he had nothing much to say about Russia, Japan, or anywhere else. "This time, I made a good impression in Japan," he said. "That is important."

The very fact that he was away as long as three months was a remarkable feat. For a man as self-indulgent as Horowitz, who did exactly as he pleased, this long tour displayed an astounding flexibility.

The film *Horowitz in Moscow*, documenting his recital, was an immediate best-seller on video. The recording became a high-status disc, appearing on the *Billboard* charts for more than five years running.

"The old trouper is back," Horowitz laughed buoyantly. "Look at the ribbons and medals they gave me. Quite a haul. Here is the

Legion of Honor from France, the Distinguished Service Cross from Germany. Here is something from Italy. My sorrow is that my sister never got to see me again, but I saw my niece for the first time. I'm not even tired, and my weight is still down. Not bad, eh?"

Mrs. Horowitz asked, "What have you been doing?"

"I, too, have been roaming the world. In May, I went to Korea, where I played and gave master classes, and in June, I judged the Casagrande Piano Competition in Terni, Italy."

"What about Korea?" Mrs. Horowitz asked.

"I gave a lecture, two days of master classes, and a recital of American music in a beautiful hall with fifteen hundred people attending. The piano has big status in Korea, and they have a large piano industry. Like Victorian England or America, every little Korean girl is given piano lessons. It's the proper thing to do. Everything Western is worshipped."

Horowitz continued, "But Orientals can't play Western music. They can only imitate. They are like robots. Of that, I'm sure."

"Mr. Horowitz, I beg to differ with you. Believe me, once the Asian musicians get to know the best in performances, have good teachers, and have some tradition seep in, they play as musically as if they were born in Odessa or Kiev. But enough of me. Tell me, Maestro, what is next for you? What do you want to do now after this succession of triumphs?"

"I don't know what I'll do now. But Deutsche Grammophon wants me to record a concerto, maybe the Liszt E-flat. I don't know if I can do such a piece anymore, but they would like it because the sales, they tell me, will be phenomenal. You know the world associates me with Liszt. But I don't know if I can still have such bravura for a Liszt concerto, so many octaves, so tiring. Maybe I can do it still. It's only an eighteen-minute concerto, the E-flat. But I'm not now interested in the Liszt concerto so much."

"Maestro, if I may venture an opinion, I think it's a good thing for you now to do a concerto. It's something different. It's many years since you have made a studio recording of a concerto, and of course, you shall be able to choose any conductor you want."

"Who has a good recording for the Liszt?" Horowitz asked.

"There have been many good recordings of it. Richter's is justly famous, and one of the best is the Byron Janis, your very own student. It's played like steel.

"But I'll tell you one thing I have against recording the Liszt concerto. You are eighty-three years old. The world will inevitably compare your Liszt concerto with that of other virtuosi, and they will compare you with yourself. The Liszt No. 1 is a young man's concerto. And I know the critics; they will have a field day saying the famous Horowitz octaves are fading. Then they will compare you to the old Liszt pupil, Emil von Sauer, who recorded it when he was seventy-seven. Sauer plays it marvelously—elegantly, but slowly."

I continued, "No, Maestro, believe me, if you choose to record the Liszt No. 1, you won't be happy with the decision. It will be too tiring and to hit all the octaves cleanly will need many takes in the recording studio. I feel you should be playing a concerto by the composer you are now most involved with. I think you should record a Mozart concerto. You can choose from a feast of masterpieces. I know you're already thinking about one, if I know you."

"Mr. Dubal, you are absolutely right. I am falling in love with one of them after another. Mozart is, for me, number one. I start looking through them from now on. Next year, I record a concerto."

Wanda interjected, "Let's hope he gets the right conductor."

Horowitz said, "Maybe von Karajan."

"That would indeed be an all-time best-seller," I said.

"But," Horowitz continued, "I have to take into consideration what the record company wants, too. So who knows, maybe it will be Liszt. We'll see."

22

A PRESIDENTIAL
INVITATION

During the rest of the summer, I visited the Horowitz household weekly. The Maestro seemed rather content and his health was excellent. He practiced a little and seldom improvised anymore. Mrs. Horowitz spent some time in Milan and London.

On Wednesday, October 1, 1986, a small party celebrated his eighty-third birthday. I visited the Horowitzes the following evening as well.

Conversation centered around his forthcoming White House performance. Horowitz was to give a recital for President Reagan and the First Lady in four days.

When Horowitz returned from his tour, the President had honored him with the Medal of Freedom. Before receiving it, he had said to me, "America doesn't care for good music. It's a junk culture. I don't like playing for Americans."

But upon the presentation of the medal, the great pianist became a superpatriot for a week or two. "I give a lot to my adopted country. I'm a very good American, you know. They all know my face. I can't take a walk for a block. Everybody stops me. I used to say, 'No, I'm not Horowitz.' But now, that doesn't work. I can't sit on my bench at the park anymore."

Horowitz had always been both annoyed and flattered by auto-graph hunters. But lately, he was constantly approached. While he was in Russia, he had been featured on the cover of *Time* magazine, which is death to privacy.

I told him, "Maestro, I was on an elevator in a building on Sixth Avenue, and two young women had a copy of *Time*. One said to the other, 'Isn't he cute!'"

Horowitz was absolutely delighted. "I'm cute. You see, Wanda, the girls still think I'm cute." The word *cute*, coming from Horowitz, sounded ridiculous.

I continued, "But Maestro, what was even better is the other woman said, 'One Sunday morning, I was changing the TV channels and I heard him play from Moscow. I didn't think I liked classical music, but he was beautiful.'"

"People think they don't like good music," Horowitz said. "But as soon as they *really* hear it, they love it."

Wanda—always glad when anyone came upon classical music—repeated the same sentiment. "If only they'd listen," she said.

Horowitz continued. "On Sunday, do you think Mr. President will sleep while I play?"

Wanda exclaimed, "Maybe he will, but Nancy will look like she is listening."

"You will be there in Washington for me, Mr. Dubal?" Horowitz asked.

"Of course I'm coming. It's going to be a great day."

"When I played in the White House for the President Carter, he was very nice to me," Horowitz said. "He was a real music lover. You know, I think Carter was a good man. He was for the people."

"Oh, yes, Maestro, a very pacific being."

"What is *pacific*?" he asked.

Mrs. Horowitz entered. "Volodya, he is like the Pacific Ocean, very peaceful. He talked in a terrible monotone, very soothing. But you could fall asleep."

"Yes," I said. "But the public wants the glamorous Reagan. Carter was too boring for Americans."

Horowitz then said, "I played for Carter in the seventies. Not so good, though. I wasn't feeling so good."

"You know," Wanda added, "Sunday at the White House will be full of celebrities to hear Volodya."

"Oh, sure," Horowitz concurred. "They all come."

Wanda asked, "Did you know he played at the White House for Hoover, too? Volodya was also asked by other Presidents, but he declined."

Horowitz reminded her, "But Wanda, you remember I did a birthday tribute for Roosevelt on the radio."

"Of course, I remember," Wanda answered. "Mr. Dubal, do you know the story of when he played for Hoover?"

"No, I don't. Tell me, please."

"My English was almost nothing in 1930," Horowitz began, "and I just returned from Europe where I am stopped at the Ellis Island because of some problems. I tell those people, 'I'm going to Washington to play for Mr. President.' They laugh at me.

"On the train to the White House, I was told there would be a reception after, and I must stand in line to shake everyone's hand. But all I needed to say was 'I am delighted.' So I memorized it. I said it over and over. After the concert, I had to meet the President and many others who came, mostly diplomats and their wives."

Wanda then blurted out, "Do you know what he said to the President and to each and everyone there?"

"What?"

"Volodya said, 'I am delightful'! Can you imagine? 'I am delightful'!"

I roared.

Horowitz said, "Hoover didn't give a damn about good music."

"But at least Truman and Nixon played the piano," I replied.

"Better for the world if they practiced twelve hours a day," Horowitz said, pleased with his statement. "I trust musicians more than anybody. They practice too much to do harm."

"You know," Wanda said, "we go, I think, on Friday."

Horowitz got up and shook my hand. "I see you in the White House after the concert."

"Good luck, Maestro."

Wanda took me down to the door, where I kissed both of her cheeks. She said, "Now I have to get him through this ordeal."

"You will, Mrs. Horowitz, as you always do."

23

A RECITAL IN THE
WHITE HOUSE

On October 5, 1986, the day of Horowitz's recital at the White House, the weather was cool and sparkling, the sky a brilliant blue.

Early in the week, the President's social secretary and security people called my office, providing a few rules for the occasion, including proper White House attire.

On Sunday morning, the Frosts and I flew the shuttle to Washington and appeared at the appointed hour at the White House. We had all been checked for security, and there was no red tape; all those who were invited had arrived.

Besides many friends of the Horowitzes, there were about one hundred guests, including Zubin Mehta, Itzhak Perlman, and Beverly Sills.

After the audience was seated in the large and beautiful music room, Secretary of State Shultz entered. He was not wearing the protocol black or gray suit, but was dressed in an ugly rust-colored suede jacket.

Soon afterward, Wanda sat down in the front row, followed by Giuliana, who took a seat next to the secretary of state.

After some minutes of quiet anticipation, a deep voice announced, "Ladies and gentlemen, Vladimir Horowitz." The great doors swung open and the pianist walked down the aisle, looking shockingly pale and nervous in his gray formal attire. He greeted the applause with only a nod and sat quietly at his own piano, which had been brought to the White House, where Franz Mohr had voiced and regulated the instrument to the Maestro's demanding specifications.

A few minutes later, the same voice announced, "Ladies and gentlemen, the First Lady and the President of the United States."

I had never seen the President close up and was surprised at his presence, which was much more imposing than I had imagined. His black suit was beautifully tailored, his shoes shined to a high gloss. Mr. Reagan looked taller, at least six feet two, trimmer and younger than on TV.

Nancy Reagan, in a lovely pink gown, also looked taller. She sat in the aisle seat, with the President between her and Wanda.

Horowitz played without mishap, but he wasn't in top form. That intangible extra quality was somehow missing. Still, this was Horowitz, and his Mozart and Chopin shone brightly. The President seemed to listen intently, but with no expression on his face.

For his encore, Horowitz played *Etincelles* deliciously. Nancy smiled sweetly through the elegant display of fireworks. During the applause, she whispered something into her husband's ear as the President nodded in agreement.

The proceedings continued with President Reagan, the First Lady, and Mr. and Mrs. Horowitz on the small stage, which was about two and a half feet high and surrounded by flowers. Nancy was seated on the platform near the edge.

Ronald Reagan spoke of Horowitz's early years, mentioning his piano teacher Felix Blumenfeld, a pupil of Anton Rubinstein. He talked of Horowitz's contribution to American culture and his recent return from his first trip to Russia after more than sixty years.

Then, just as the President began his next sentence, the First Lady fell off the stage with a loud squeal.

The fall sounded like a shot. Horowitz was terrified. He looked convinced that somebody had killed the First Lady and then would assassinate him. Richard Probst, from Steinway, gallantly helped Nancy return to the platform. The President rose to the occasion, saying, "Honey, I told you to do that only if I didn't get any applause."

After the President's speech came a reception. The White House looked beautiful and spotless. The Reagans were charming hosts, very much at ease and comfortable in their home.

Certainly Itzhak Perlman felt at home. In the large foyer, a military string quartet played background music. Soon, the first violinist of the group relinquished his instrument to the celebrated violinist, who then played happily with the other three.

As I wandered around, I realized I had not yet seen Horowitz. I returned to the East Room, but he wasn't there yet. I continued to walk about, looking at the many objects of Americana.

In a large side room, I found the pianist sitting alone on a sofa, looking forlorn.

He waved to me, saying hoarsely, "You and I are the only people here that really know that I was not at my best today. It wasn't so good."

"But, Maestro," I countered, "there were marvelous things."

"It was okay, but we know it was only that. I didn't feel relaxed."

I said, "Mr. Horowitz, you must come and see all the guests waiting for you. Believe me, Maestro, they all felt that what they heard was special because it *was* special."

"How did you like the mazurkas?" he asked.

"They were excellent."

Mrs. Horowitz suddenly found us, and I left them to talk.

Mrs. Reagan was in the receiving line welcoming guests. I felt the day would not be complete unless I, too, shook hands with the First Lady. My turn soon came, and I said, "Thank you for inviting me to your home to hear the great Horowitz."

Her handshake was exceptionally warm and tight, and her smile appeared to be real. She looked me straight in the eye, "It was a pleasure having you," she said.

I walked to a corner of the room and watched the President, who, for a moment, was somehow left unoccupied. Our eyes met, and I was amazed to see him walking toward me. As he shook my hand, I thought, My goodness, what do I say?

Ronald Reagan said, "Wasn't Maestro Horowitz wonderful?"

"Yes, he was, Mr. President." I said, "I was surprised to hear the names of Felix Blumenfeld and Anton Rubinstein being spoken in the White House."

At that comment, Reagan's face went blank. He didn't know what I was talking about. He had apparently forgotten that he had spoken those names. The speech he had made, I realized, had not been written by him.

That evening, a large contingent of New York's musical community returned to the Big Apple. Upon arriving home, I turned on the TV. I was sure that Mrs. Reagan's fall into the flowers at a Vladimir Horowitz recital would have news coverage. Just as I switched on CNN, I saw the First Lady topple over, and once again saw Horowitz looking shocked and frightened, as though convinced his time had come.

24

"I'M A GOOD AMERICAN"

A few days after the White House recital, I spent the evening with the Horowitzes.

The Maestro looked at me. "It was a good write-up in *Times*."

Mrs. Horowitz muttered, "I'm glad it's over. Every TV in America showed Nancy falling off the platform." She continued, "The klutz. Who cared about Horowitz!?"

"But," I said, "at least it showed that classical music can be heard at the White House."

Mrs. Horowitz said, "Who cares, the *nudniks!*"

Horowitz now said what I was waiting for. "You know, I thought Mrs. Reagan was shot, and then it would be me."

"Yes," I said, "I thought you felt that."

"At least I played the mazurkas good," he went on.

"Yes, you did, Maestro."

"But I'll not play in the White House again. My duty is done. I'm a good American."

"You are the best, Mr. Horowitz. *I'm* proud of you." Horowitz was still in his patriotic state of mind.

"I play better for Reagan than Carter. Few people know what is good and bad. That is the big pity."

"Yes, that's so true," I agreed. "But there is a segment of the public who may not know consciously, but intuitively they know what's good or what has depth. There is something that touches them." I continued, "Your career could not have been built on just a few people who know."

Horowitz said, "Only a few in an audience receive the spiritual message of great music. There are more who get the emotional excitement. But most come to a concert merely as a social event, to be seen."

Mrs. Horowitz agreed emphatically.

"From childhood every pianist experiences a real sadness," I said. "They are thrown in front of people who like to see a little manual skill or hear a pretty tune, but they don't know what is good. Liberace is enough for them."

"Exactly!" Horowitz said. "That's why I would prefer to play for a house full of good pianists. They at least know what is good.

"You know," he continued, "there is almost always a gap, sometimes a big gap between the intention and the realization of what you are trying to achieve. It is that gap which is so painful. The critic criticizing the concert doesn't know that you had worked forever in building up a crescendo, and that you didn't succeed in making it come out."

"I understand, Maestro," I said. "These are very important concepts."

"I think so," Horowitz went on. "You see, the world is full of prejudice and hatred. In a way, I work to fill that gap a little. I feel that if I can create beauty and emotion and sometimes a little perfection, then I am helping to close up the terrible gap where ignorance lives."

"You know," I said, "the poet Auden wrote that every high C accurately struck demolishes the myth that we are merely puppets of fate and charm."

"That's beautiful," Mrs. Horowitz interjected.

Horowitz went on. "When you hear the Chopin *Funeral March* Sonata, you don't have prejudice against it. You don't say at that moment the Chopin sonata is inferior to the Mozart sonata. It may have flaws. But my duty is to make the audience feel it's a great sonata, even with its flaws. I must help it along; that is a big job of the interpreter. This is no trick, believe me. This is work. And some days, you can't do it."

Horowitz was deep in thought. He leaned his hand on his chin. "Oh no, a good interpreter is always looking to make the music even better than it is, even the greatest pieces. But you see, I look at the music from a composer's mind. I think, Oh, Mozart was a little boring here. Chopin was not so good in this transition; how can I convince the listener that it is all perfect? That there is no boring moment in the Chopin nocturne?"

"I understand," I said. "Perhaps that's why we have so many dull performances. Playing the notes well is only the beginning. That is not nearly enough!"

Horowitz said, "Sure! But you know, when it's dull, I don't blame the composer. I blame me. I didn't accomplish my purpose."

At that moment, Horowitz, with considerable effort, pushed himself off the couch and wobbled toward the piano. "Look, Chopin wrote his F minor Concerto at eighteen or nineteen. He was in love with a beautiful singer. But Chopin had not yet become Chopin all the way. Listen—this part is dull, it is awkward. Chopin didn't yet know what to do. Everybody plays it the same, but I make the phrase this way so my ear is now ready to hear the next section."

Horowitz continued to play from each of the movements of the concerto, all the while talking and explaining as he demonstrated.

The old master played with fire, poetry, and originality. I sat spellbound; Wanda was enthralled. We looked at each other and smiled.

I had no idea that Horowitz played this concerto. He had never played it in public or recorded it.

Horowitz left his piano, satisfied with himself. "You see, a pianist can be a good American when he plays Barber, a good Pole when he plays Chopin, a good Russian with Tchaikovsky, a good Frenchman with Debussy, or a good German in Beethoven. A pianist is a citizen of the world. And that is the most important thing to be."

25

MOZART IN MY LIFE

Only six weeks after his White House performance, on December 14, 1986, Horowitz played a brilliant recital at the Metropolitan Opera House. He had long given up any thought of recording the Liszt Piano Concerto No. 1.

Lately, he had been consumed by Mozart's piano concertos. He had decided he would definitely record one. Week after week, he played for me the concerto he was momentarily in love with. Horowitz was a fickle lover, pouring his heart into one beautiful concerto after another.

Finally, after much deliberation, the Maestro decided to concentrate on Mozart's Concerto No. 23 in A Major, K. 488. This was the work he would record in Milan.

Artistically, Horowitz's increasing love for Mozart brought him great satisfaction. At this time of his life, he needed to escape the turbulent passions of Romantic music. His own musical temperament was Romantic to an extreme, but he also possessed a streak of Classicism, which periodically needed release.

Mozart is the Hellenic ideal, the supreme Classicist. However freely Horowitz played him, Mozart remained rational. As Aldous Huxley pointed out, "Mozart's melodies may be brilliant, memorable, infectious, but they don't *palpitate*, don't catch you between wind and water, don't send the listener off into erotic ecstasies."

For Horowitz, playing Mozart became a liberation. In Mozart, he found the crystallization of innocence and faith. Henry Miller wrote,

137

"The thing is to become a master and in your old age to acquire the courage to do what children did when they knew nothing."

Many pianists in their later years have gravitated to Mozart. Some, like Sir Clifford Curzon, played only Mozart. Perhaps Mozart's purity becomes for them the personification of a perpetual youth.

On this evening, Horowitz was sitting alone waiting for me, looking deep in thought as he motioned me to sit down. Wanda was in Italy visiting her sister.

"Madame has been gone a week," he grumbled.

I replied, "Do you miss her?"

"No! I don't miss her. But I get nervous if she is away for more than I expect."

"Look, Maestro, to cheer you up, I brought you a new edition of Mozart's letters."

"Really?" Horowitz perked up. "I love his letters. I love them."

He had been reading Mozart's delectable letters in French, German, and English, and would show me nuances that differed in the various translations. Anything about Mozart interested him. His eyes grew moist when I had told him that, at age eleven, Mozart had been blind for nine terrible days from smallpox.

"My God, what that boy went through.

"When I was young," Horowitz continued, "I didn't know how difficult Mozart was. Not so many notes. But now, I know. Yesterday, I was reading when Mozart made the first performance of the D minor Concerto in 1786. Papa Mozart came down to Vienna from Salzburg to hear it. Mozart was drinking punch, playing billiards, and still copying out the finale of the concerto. The household was in chaos, and Haydn dropped over. The piano movers came to take his piano to the theater. He was always busy, always behind. And after the performance, Papa wrote to the sister saying that the public didn't like the concerto so much, but Wolfgang was happy with the performance."

I said, "But most of the concertos were big successes, and once in a while, the audience demanded that Mozart repeat a movement."

Naturally, music lovers of the eighteenth century could buy neither radios nor records. Music was not yet mass produced. Nor was it composed in an ivory tower as art for art's sake. Music was bought, listened to, and then usually forgotten. Publication was rare. Mozart resurrected would be astounded by a Mostly Mozart Festival or monthly batches of new recordings of his music.

Horowitz asked, "How is it that Mozart composed twenty-five piano concertos?"

"Simply to pay his rent," I said. "Each season, he composed new ones for his own concerts. That's why he composed no less than fifteen piano concertos in five years.

"It was a time when composer and performer were one. The artist was not yet an outcast from society. Mozart was part of his world. But by the nineteenth century, bourgeois society was uncomfortable with the crazy Schumann, the mad Berlioz, or the megalomaniac Wagner shouting, 'The world owes me what I need.' Art was no longer a necessity for society, as it had been with Palestrina, Monteverdi, Bach, Handel, and Haydn. It was in the nineteenth century that great art was considered man's highest spiritual expression, and the great artist a prophet. Yet ironically, since the nineteenth century, the artist has been alienated from society."

Horowitz looked dejected as I talked. "Maybe music was better in Mozart's day," he mumbled. "Everything now is commercial. Everything is marketed. You know, most of the time, I think of myself as a commodity to be purchased for a ticket or for others to exploit."

I peered at Horowitz, who sat silently staring at me. Throughout his career, Horowitz had been a highly marketed artist. He was forever being duped into thinking about money. Was he getting the best terms, the best royalties? How much would he earn from his films? He was deeply concerned with money, caught up in the commercial aspects of his career. One part of him was repelled by commerce, but he always had too many people surrounding him who saw him as a dollar sign.

However, Horowitz the artist did not see art as a business. I think he was still rather amazed that he was paid so well to do what he loved.

Horowitz said, "Let me play for you from the A Major Concerto. Listen to the slow movement. Is it not tragic? So poignant. But it's eighteenth-century tragic. Mozart shows a tear coming through a gentle smile. It is glorious music.

"This movement is played too slowly by everyone. It's marked adagio; some editions have andante. The form is a siciliano, which is a dance. This movement is not a dirge. It has a slight lilt. I want to bring back this lilt. Ah, there is great emotion in these few notes."

When he concluded playing and talking through the slow movement, I said, "Maestro, how beautiful it is. Do you know that this is the only movement in all of Mozart's vast output that he composed in the key of F-sharp minor?"

Horowitz's eyes opened wide. *"No!"* he exclaimed. "No, not possible."

"Oh, yes, it's true. There are no other movements. You may look if you like, but no others exist."

Horowitz said, "It is sure a mystery why one composer loves a certain key and another does not."

"Yes, that has always interested me. For instance, Bach wrote some of his most sublime music in B minor, while Beethoven never touches the key except in one work, a tiny bagatelle for piano from his Op. 126."

"Mr. Dubal, I must tell you something important." Horowitz covered his mouth and almost whispered the words. "It's a big problem."

"Tell me, Maestro," I asked earnestly.

"I cannot play Mozart's own cadenza for the first movement of the A Major Concerto. It's not good. I'm sorry, it's far below the rest. It's foolish. It's too thin. What should I do?"

In a Classical concerto, a cadenza usually comes near the end of the first movement, and sometimes also in the last movement, when the soloist plays alone, using the themes from the movement. Eighteenth-century composers often left this moment for the performer to improvise. In some of his concertos Mozart wrote out the cadenzas, and in others he wrote nothing. In the Concerto in A Major, K. 488, however, Mozart had composed a cadenza for the first movement.

"Maestro," I exclaimed enthusiastically, "why not write your own cadenza? As you know, it was the tradition to do so. It would be a terrific outlet for you. I would love hearing your cadenza. Many pianists have disregarded Mozart's cadenza and have written their own."

Horowitz listened carefully. "I can't," he said. "No. The critics would kill me. And it's not my style to compose in the Mozart manner. It will sound artificial. I will look through some other ones. Maybe I find one that is interesting."

"Maestro, I'll look for some, too. I know that Busoni composed one."

Horowitz's face lit up. "Ah, I'd like to see that one. Busoni was a genius. I want to see it."

In the Horowitz household, the name Busoni was ennobled. Ferruccio Busoni was one of the fabled pianists in history. Born in 1866, he lived only to age fifty-eight. Horowitz had told me he wanted to study with Busoni in Berlin, but the Italian-born pianist-composer had died in 1924, the year before Horowitz escaped from Russia.

Busoni exemplified the highest moral and intellectual quality. His playing was titanic, even shockingly original. For many, its breadth and vision seemed boundless. In his memoirs, Arthur Rubinstein wrote, "With his handsome, pale, Christ-like face and his diabolical technical prowess, Busoni was by far the most interesting pianist alive."

Horowitz said, "You must get me the Busoni cadenza. It's late. I take you to the door. Wanda calls me tomorrow and she tell me when she comes home." He slowly went down the stairway and I followed. "Where is the maid? She has to put on the protection." The *protection* was what he called his security system.

There was no answer when he called for the maid. Suddenly, Horowitz became terribly frightened. "I'm here all alone but for the maid. I can't make the protection work." He became frantic. "Where is she?"

I tried to calm him down. Fortunately, the maid, who must have fallen asleep, heard the commotion and came down several flights of stairs. "Don't worry, Mr. Horowitz," she said. "I'll fix the protection."

I had never seen Horowitz so nervous. Without Wanda, his whole equilibrium was disturbed.

I bade him good night and promised, "I'll find the Busoni cadenza for you."

26

THE SEARCH FOR THE
PERFECT CADENZA

It was January 10, 1987. It had snowed heavily the night before, and Manhattan looked like a fairyland.

For several weeks, I had wanted to see the van Gogh exhibit at the Metropolitan Museum, an exhibition of his paintings from the last year and a half of his tragic life, before he shot himself at age thirty-six. With this great snowfall, I thought, nobody will be at the museum. I was wrong. It seemed nobody went to work that day, and the museum was more crowded than ever.

I stared in awe at the magnitude of van Gogh's last works. He must have been living in the very heat of creation.

By late afternoon, I decided to go to my WNCN office and work on the monthly programming. There I found two messages from Wanda, one saying, "Don't come tonight. The weather is too bad to go out to dinner," the second saying, "Do come." I called my machine at home to find two more messages from her. I phoned and reached her in person; her final verdict was "Don't come." Looking out my window and seeing it was again snowing heavily, I was relieved not to go.

Suddenly, Horowitz himself grabbed the phone. "Mr. Dubal, did you find the Busoni cadenza yet?" he cried impatiently.

"Yes, Maestro. A teacher I know gave me a photocopy. It's here on my desk. I'll bring it next week when I see you."

"No, no, forget what Madame just said. You must come over later. Even if you have to ski through the Central Park. I've been looking through many other cadenzas. They're all no good. I must see if the Busoni cadenza will do the job. I can't wait till next week."

I smiled to myself: How well I understand him. When I want a piece of music, I, too, *must* have it. Horowitz was to record the concerto in Milan in March, and I knew he couldn't stand not having a cadenza.

"Mr. Horowitz, you shall see the thing for yourself. It's six p.m. now; I'll be there by nine. But I must warn you, the copy I have is not perfectly clear; it's not a good photocopy."

"I don't care. Just come," Horowitz cried and hung up.

★ ★ ★

The maid let me in, and I zoomed up the semicircular stairway two steps at a time. Horowitz was waiting in anticipation.

"Ah, you got here. You're a good man, nothing stops you. Is that the cadenza?" Horowitz looked hungrily at the manila envelope, which he tore from my hand and quickly ripped it open. "Sit next to me," he ordered.

The only time I had sat next to him on "his" sofa was when I had written a short speech for his acceptance of the Grammy Award and worked with him on memorizing it. On the night of the awards, he totally forgot it and badly improvised his acceptance.

However, now I was to see another example of his great musical ability. His eyes devoured the music. He poked my arm here and there. "Ah, that is good. This is difficult. Look here, this is marvelous. Very good, very clever." I indeed knew how difficult it was, as I had played through it as slowly as a tortoise.

I was excited. So far, so good—he seemed to like it. But now, for the crucial test. He used both arms to lift himself from the couch, waved to me to join him, and put the music on the rack. At that, the legendary virtuoso played the arduous cadenza note-perfectly, as if he'd practiced it for weeks.

I was dumbfounded. What I had plodded through with difficulty, he breezed through as naturally as a bird in flight.

After he completed the cadenza, there was silence. He repeated it again. Already, his conception of it had ripened.

He looked up. Both Wanda and I waited for his judgment. "This cadenza is mine," he said happily. "I shall do this. I will learn it. But it is difficult, you know, very difficult. I'll have to work."

I laughed, "Maybe it's difficult for others, Maestro, but not for you." I was so pleased. He had found his cadenza.

"I think the cadenza is wonderful," Wanda exclaimed. "Volodya is happy. He can go to Milan now with his cadenza. You know, my father admired Busoni. He conducted one or two of Busoni's orchestral works. Busoni, I believe, dedicated his opera *Turandot* to Papa. After Busoni's premature death, Papa knew that his wife was in a bad way with money, so he made a personal contribution to her and appealed to other musicians." (Busoni's two-act opera, based on Carlo Gozzi's play, was composed in 1917 and preceded Puccini's popular treatment.)

Horowitz began walking out of the room. "I have to go peepee," he reported. "Tell Mr. Dubal about when Papa heard Busoni in the Beethoven *Waldstein*."

Wanda continued, "Oh, yes. Father was at a Busoni recital and thought the Beethoven was dreadful and walked out. Naturally, everyone noticed; it caused quite a stir. Busoni was told about it, but was not upset at all. In fact, he wrote a note to Father asking him to come to his next recital the following week, and he promised to play 'well.' Papa went, Busoni played marvelously, and Toscanini applauded with all his might."

Horowitz had now returned. "You see, even Busoni not all the time played well. You know, of course, that he transcribed many Bach works for the piano. At one party, he was introduced as Mr. Bach-Busoni. It's a true story." Horowitz laughed.

"Mr. Dubal, the weather is awful. You must get home. You did a good deed for me today, and now I hope you find a taxi. Many thanks for the Busoni. I will work at it tomorrow."

27

THE ARM-WRESTLING CHAMP

It was early February. Tonight, Horowitz was in a jocular mood.

"Do you think you are a strong man?" he said.

"Maestro, I'm not Mr. Universe, but I'm not a weakling. Feel my biceps."

Horowitz gasped. "It's like iron. How did you get that? You don't look so strong."

I told the old master that at thirteen years old, I was so thin I was embarrassed; I weighed only eighty pounds, and I thought I'd never grow or put on weight. One day, out of desperation, I bought a set of barbells and learned bodybuilding.

Horowitz looked amazed. "How long did you do this?"

"Till the age of fifteen. I took it seriously and it helped. By then, I started growing and putting on weight. And soon I grew bored with the weights."

He continued, "I would never think you were a sportsman."

"Oh, absolutely," I said. "When I was a teenager, my life was sports. I dearly loved playing baseball, and I was a darn good hitter."

Horowitz now flexed his biceps. "What do you think of mine?" he said.

I got up from my chair to grip his arm. "Not bad," I said. "Very solid, Maestro."

"Maybe I'm even stronger than you," Horowitz teased. His little pitch-black eyes gleamed. "Do you think you can beat an eighty-three-year-old man in arm wrestling?"

"Well, I don't know. Let's have a match and see. What will it be?"

"The winner must win two out of three matches," Horowitz said.

"Shall we do it straight, or do we put a flame on the table and the loser gets burned?"

"We do it without the fire," Horowitz laughed. "Let's do it with right hand."

We began, and I was quite surprised at Horowitz's strength. As I tested him out, I knew I could beat him, but I felt it would be more fun and better for his ego if I let him win the first match.

"You see"—he looked me straight in the eye—"I am the Hercules of old pianists."

It seems awfully important that old men feel they are still powerful. I remembered my grandfather, who was physically a wreck, always bragging that he was strong as an ox.

I proceeded to win the second round. This time, Horowitz showed even more strength.

By now, the Maestro was huffing and puffing.

Horowitz, who was very competitive, exclaimed, "Now we see who will be champ." He carefully placed his elbow on the table for round three.

This time, I really faked it because he was tired. There was no way he could beat me. After several seconds of give-and-take, my arm went down in defeat.

I cried, "The great Horowitz has downed the No. 1 challenger! You are still the world champion. The strongest octogenarian of all time."

Horowitz smacked his lips and looked pleased with himself.

I wondered if he thought he had really won.

His face was flushed a deep scarlet as he put both arms high into the air to proclaim his victory. "I'm the champion. But you're not too bad."

After a few minutes of silence and rest, Horowitz scrutinized me and said, "You want to bring young people to me. But here is a good reason not to see them. Read this." Horowitz shoved a magazine into my hands.

The article was an interview with the young hero of the keyboard, Ivo Pogorelich, who was playing his annual Carnegie Hall recital later in the week.

Pogorelich was born in Belgrade in 1958 and studied at the Moscow Conservatory. He won several competitions, but when he lost the 1980 Chopin Competition in Warsaw, some of the leading judges, including the Argentine pianist Martha Argerich, walked out of the jury. The uproar caused a stir that brought Pogorelich international attention. The exotically handsome young man has been receiving adulation ever since.

I had already read the article and was hoping that Horowitz would not see it. But somehow he saw everything that concerned himself.

In the interview, Pogorelich granted Horowitz the ability to play a few Scarlatti sonatas well, but not much else. Most alarming, he said that Horowitz was not a serious pianist. Horowitz was not his only target: he panned others, and called Arthur Rubinstein a "dilettante."

Horowitz was livid.

"Maestro," I said, "this article only shows his ignorance. He is a master at self-promotion; that's why the press loves him. I know very well not to take what he says seriously. He is very irresponsible. I know he grew up listening to your records, and he only heard you once, and that was in Japan when you were below par."

"I ask you this question, Mr. Dubal. Do you think I am serious?"

"Please, Mr Horowitz, it is all so absurd Such silliness should not bother you. Cf course I know how serious you are. You live for your art.

"Believe me," I went on, "I'm not making any excuses for Pogorelich. He is obviously immature. He has a case of unabashed self-love, and an unshakable belief in his own playing. Once we sat in my office in 1983. I played him various performances I thought he would admire, such as Kapell's Liszt *Mephisto* Waltz and Lipatti's *Alborada del gracioso* of Ravel. He smirked at both of them. He looked at me with a straight face and told me Kapell was a dilettante and Lipatti lacked technical control. Please, Maestro, why do you take him seriously?"

"Mr. Dubal," Horowitz said, "you know, I, too, was good in making a career. But I never attacked any colleague in the press. *NEVER!* Mr. Dubal, you are with many young pianists all the time. Tell me this, are all the young people today cruel like Pogorelich?"

"Maestro, the young are not cruel. They love you. I know that even Pogorelich admires you. His wife, Alicia, with whom I was a judge at a piano competition, said to me, 'There are only three great pianists of the century.' I said, 'And who may those be?' She answered, 'Rachmaninoff, Horowitz, and Pogorelich.' I flinched.

'And what about Busoni, Schnabel, Friedman, Michelangeli?' On
and on I continued. Maestro, they both talk nonsense, but it gets
them attention."

I turned the topic away from Pogorelich to Horowitz's Mozart
concerto.

He said, "I am having trouble memorizing the last movement.
Maybe I use music at the recording session in Milan."

"Why not? You are not playing it in public," I said.

"But you know, they are filming this, too. People will think I
cannot memorize anymore."

"Who cares what people think?"

It never ceased to amaze me that Horowitz was continually
concerned about what others thought of him. A sense of insecurity
plagued him. He could never be loved enough. Even a pinch of
criticism was escalated into complete rejection.

Mrs. Horowitz had just returned from a party.

As she entered the room, Horowitz said, "Mr. Dubal tells me that
all young people today are not cruel like the Yugoslavian boy."

Mrs. Horowitz pretended to spit at the floor. She said, "I wish
these things wouldn't bother Volodya so much."

Horowitz got up, shook my hand, and walked me to the staircase.
"What you do this week?"

"Oh, nothing much," I answered, neglecting to say that I would
be hearing Pogorelich at Carnegie Hall.

28

THE BOW-TIE AWARD

It was a cold, windy mid-February night. I arrived at the Horowitz house exactly at nine-thirty p.m. I was always slightly late for everything—except to my Horowitz appointments.

Mr. Horowitz bounced into the living room with particular verve. "What do you think of this one?" he cried, pointing to a brilliantly colored bow tie.

"I think it's a beauty," I said.

"Feel it. It's a beautiful silk."

"It sure is. And it looks great on you," I said with brio. The bow tie was a Horowitz trademark, and his collection included over eight hundred.

I added, "When Liszt was on tour, he had three hundred sixty cravats, one for each day of the year."

Horowitz smiled. "But I can beat Liszt. I can wear a different bow tie every day for over two years. But I don't do that, because then I miss my favorites. But come here. I will show you something that just arrived yesterday."

He proudly lifted a framed document. It was the annual award of the Bow-Tie Association, given only to prominent bow tie wearers.

Horowitz laughed and laughed. "I like this award better than others," pointing to a glassed area with his collection of medals, ribbons, and medallions from dozens of places. "Those are all serious. But this award is fun. The world is sinking. Schumann, you know, wrote a piece called 'Almost Too Serious.' The Germans are always serious. That's a bad trait. And the Russians, oh my God. They are now so poor. I go back to my country to see where I was born and raised, and I find that nobody eats, and the faces are sad. The Russians keep building bombs. This country will be poor, too, if it keeps making bombs. In Russia, they are frightened. That you can see on the street."

Horowitz sat silently for a bit. "They still love the music, but I get to play in Moscow only once. I'm glad it was on TV. But television is not real. Even when live. No, you must hear music only when it's real. When it is transmitted, it is the wrong sound." Horowitz looked pensive.

I asked, "What are you remembering this moment, Mr. Horowitz?"

"I was thinking of my mother and father and sister, and how after dinner the samovar would be heated, and the neighbors would come for tea and cookies. My father was a brilliant man, and they would have conversation."

"Was your mother a good pianist?" I asked.

"She was good, but my sister was better. You know, my sister died just before my visit to Russia. All those years," he gasped. "More than sixty years. And I see my sister's daughter, my niece, and she is old woman. My God, where does the time go? I married to Wanda fifty-three years already. Wanda is out tonight.

"You know, Mr. Dubal, I never talk about it, but my own daughter is dead."

"I know that, Maestro. It must have been very hard on you."

"Oh, it was. But it broke Madame up very badly. Don't ever have children," he said.

"Maestro, I don't think I will. The responsibility is too great. And in these times, you have to be wealthy to raise a child well."

"Believe me," Horowitz said, "take my advice, and you know, I don't give advice much."

"That's true, Maestro."

"But I must admit," Horowitz continued, "I wanted to have a son. But maybe it was better not, after all. You know, a pianist has to practice. I couldn't go play baseball with him."

I started laughing at the thought.

"What are you laughing at?" Horowitz asked.

"I just don't see you, Maestro, as the coach of your son's Little

League team. Or in the stands at Yankee Stadium, eating popcorn and a hot dog."

Horowitz, too, gave one of his little snort laughs. "But you know," he said, "I like to watch the baseball sometimes. You know, I am a good American. I pay plenty of taxes. But where that money goes, I wouldn't want to know."

"Well, Maestro," I responded, "someone said, you can bet every dollar will be used against you."

"That may be truer than true. I told Wanda that we should live in London. It's better there, maybe. We looked at a house recently. I think it cost a million pounds. More pianists live in London now than in New York. And at least there, I can play duets with Shura Cherkassky."

Horowitz and Cherkassky—a phenomenal child prodigy who studied with Hofmann—had been friends for years. Although Horowitz was only eight years his senior, he treated Cherkassky like a child, while Shura adored Horowitz unconditionally. Cherkassky once said to me, "Horowitz is like nothing on this planet. He is not even of this planet."

Horowitz continued, "I miss four-hand playing. I used to play four hands, the Schubert F minor Fantasy, with Rachmaninoff. Oh, yes, we do it a good many times."

"I sure wish that had been recorded," I said. "That is the greatest of all piano duets, in my opinion."

"That's for sure." Horowitz nodded his head vigorously.

Once more I felt Horowitz's isolation from other musicians. I was fully aware that in London, or anywhere else, his life-style would remain the same.

"Maestro, if you leave New York, I will miss you very much."

"Thank you, but you will come to see me."

I knew very well that Horowitz was not going to move to another city.

He went on, "Who knows, maybe I go. Wanda has even more friends in London than in New York. Oh yes, she does. I still have a sense of adventure. I'm a prisoner in this big house. I haven't even seen the top floors for years."

Horowitz continued, "I play duets in London. Shura will love it with me. You know, Wanda can't play the piano good enough to play with me. If a pianist marries, he should get someone who plays good enough to play duets. It is much better than playing cards. I used to play two pianos a lot."

He continued, "Rachmaninoff, a few years before he died, wanted to record his two suites for two pianos with me, but RCA didn't want them."

I looked at him in disbelief. "Imagine! Because of some foolish executive, the world has been deprived of those recordings."

"Oh, yes. And Rachmaninoff and I played on two pianos his *Symphonic Dances.* I used to have two pianos in here, but no more. I don't need two mastodons any more.

"I bought this house in 1940 for only forty thousand dollars, I think. Imagine! It's now worth millions. Yes, this room has seen lots of practicing in forty-five years."

"By the way, Mr. Horowitz, I've been meaning to ask you how it felt to play in Paris again last May."

"Oh, very good. I always play well in Paris. The audience is attentive. I lived there. I speak French good, you know. I remember when I first played in Paris, I made such a hit that I cannot tell you how they love me. I also met all the important people there. I come there in '26, I think. I met Poulenc, a marvelous, very debonair man. Great savoir faire. You know, he loved my playing. His Toccata, a wonderful piece, is dedicated to me."

"Yes, I know," I responded. "I love your recording of it."

In Poulenc's little book, *My Friends and Myself,* the composer said, "My Toccata is very well known, thanks to Horowitz's fantastic playing." Of his famous *Pastourelle,* Poulenc wrote, "I can no longer listen to it except when it's played by Horowitz, who gives it a new freshness each time."

I asked the Maestro, "Did you play the Liszt Sonata in Paris when you were first there?"

"Oh, absolutely. The Liszt Sonata traveled everywhere with me. I remember after a concert in Paris—and I must tell you, the French are not musical: they listen well with the head, but they don't feel music. One society lady comes to me, and says, 'M. Horowitz, the Liszt Sonata is a charming work.' I look at her like she is crazy. 'The Liszt *Valse Oubliée* is maybe a charming work, but the Liszt Sonata *charming?*' I laugh out loud. But I had good times in Paris. I knew everybody.

"I played the *Emperor* Concerto with Cortot conducting. He called me the Prince of Pianists. He was very nice to me. We had dinner together often. Cortot was very intellectual. He liked me and I admired him very much. He played Schumann like nobody, absolutely divine. Oh, yes, it was. He told me he loves Schumann. His playing could be very messy. Rachmaninoff heard his recording of the Chopin etudes and complained they were too 'musical,' which for Sergei meant they lacked technical refinement. But Cortot had a bad disease. He had bad anti-Semitism."

Alfred Cortot was one of the great pianists of the century, and an inspiring teacher. His recordings are treasures. During the war, he became the High Commissioner of Fine Arts for the Vichy government, an inexplicable act. After the war, he was tried and found guilty of collaboration with the enemy, and his musical activities were banned for one year.

I continued, "It seemed everyone was in Paris during the twenties and thirties."

"Oh, yes. It was the center of the world, and not so expensive."

"Did you know many Americans during that time?"

"Not too many. I saw a lot of Alec Steinert [an American composer who lived in Paris]. He was a good friend."

"Did you know Virgil Thomson, who had been in Paris from the early twenties?"

As I spoke Virgil's name, I remembered that Thomson had given Horowitz and Toscanini many bad reviews.

Thomson was a composer and, at one time, America's most powerful music critic. His prose style, in his words, was "sassy and classy." Thomson resented that "Horowitz was out to wow the public and wow it he does." The critic was notorious for dozing during concerts. Wanda once hit him with her program booklet when she saw him sleep through one of her father's performances.

Horowitz looked at me in disgust. "No, I didn't know Thomson in Paris. But when he came here to review for the *Herald Tribune,* he hated me. He was a bad character, believe me. I wait for him to die. I look every day in the obituary page. He didn't like Toscanini, either."

I said, "I've read all of his criticism, and it's true he didn't really like your playing. However, he did write some flattering and interesting things about your Liszt, which he thought had 'a diabolic incandescence.' He didn't love Jascha Heifetz too much, either. He called his violin playing 'silk-underwear music.'"

Horowitz asked, "Do you know that hooligan?"

"Oh, yes. He's a very interesting person. When he went off to

Paris in the twenties, he said to friends, 'I would rather starve where the food is good.' I brought him to WNCN years ago and he did a weekly show for a year. I once asked him where he placed himself in the history of English criticism. He replied, 'Next to Shaw, naturally.' He's really a fantastic character, and an intriguing composer.

"You know," I added, "he has written many *Portraits* for piano. One sits for him, like having a picture painted. He did my portrait in 1982—*David Dubal in Flight*—and he liked it so much he orchestrated it. Unfortunately, I'm not fond of the piece, and I've never learned it."

"I don't know." Horowitz gave an ugly grimace. "I never hear a note of his music. I don't give a damn for him or his music." He then muttered, "He must be even older than me."

"Yes. He's ninety-one now. I gave a speech at the Harvard Club last year for his ninetieth birthday. I worked hard on it, and afterward, I said, 'Virgil, how did you like what I said?' He responded, 'You *know* I'm deaf. I didn't hear a word.'"

Horowitz, I could tell, wanted to drop the subject of Thomson. I felt he was in the mood to play for me.

As he began to play, he said, "I bet you won't be able to guess what I'm going to play for you tonight." After twenty seconds, he looked at me. "Now, what is it?"

"Maestro," I said confidently, "it's the Medtner First Concerto in C minor."

Horowitz played for at least twenty minutes, playing sections from Medtner's three concertos as well as parts of sonatas and shorter pieces. Then he returned to his couch.

Mrs. Horowitz had returned home just in time to hear her husband play. She said, "You know, Medtner is like Rachmaninoff, but more intellectual. I'm afraid he will never catch on."

I said, "What a pity you never recorded any Medtner."

Horowitz replied, "I did. One piece for Columbia around '69, I think. A Medtner *Fairy Tale*."

"Oh, yes," Mrs. Horowitz said. "I think it was one of those tiny records, a Christmas promotion for the record company."

She went into the side room and began searching for the disc. In five minutes, she returned. "Here, I've found it." We listened avidly to the three-minute work.

Wanda commented, "A very good piece, I think."

Horowitz listened carefully, bending over with his arms on his legs and his hands on his cheeks. Afterward, he said, "The playing is not too bad, but the public will never like Medtner. I knew him. He was a good pianist. He was crazy for my playing."

Horowitz pointed at the table. "Why you not having the cookies and coffee there?"

I first poured a cup for Wanda.

The rest of the evening, Horowitz and I spoke about Hummel, Czerny, and Moscheles, three pianists born in the late eighteenth century.

Horowitz said, "I think maybe I will restore the Hummel E-flat Rondo. I never recorded it, but it's a good program opener."

I agreed. "It's an elegant little work. Very graceful."

As I left, Horowitz said, "Okay. I look now at the TV news and see what's new in violence. Maybe the weather will be better tomorrow."

Then he waved and added, "Remember, look around for the Moscheles *Memoirs*. I want to read them again." Horowitz had twice asked me to try to find this book. His copy had disappeared.

"I will. I have some people looking also. Thank you tonight for your gift."

"What gift? I give you no gift!"

"Oh, yes, you did, Maestro. The gift of Medtner."

29

THE RUBINSTEIN
RIVALRY

A week had passed since I last saw the Horowitzes.

As I plopped down in my usual chair, Horowitz began, "Did you find me a copy of the autobiography of Ignaz Moscheles?"

"No, Maestro, not yet. But I've asked around. As I told you, I lost my copy, too."

Moscheles, the teacher of Mendelssohn, was a remarkable pianist-composer who knew Beethoven, Weber, Chopin, and Liszt. His memoirs offer a valuable fund of information concerning the nineteenth century.

"I miss that book!" Horowitz exclaimed. "The last time I saw it, Arthur Rubinstein was reading it—in the same chair you are sitting in. He wouldn't put it down. I'm sure he stole it. I never saw it again. Yes, I bet you, Rubinstein stole it."

"Maestro," I replied, "maybe Rubinstein borrowed it and forgot to return it."

"No, he took it. That I'm *sure*! I never loan books. Nobody returns anything."

Horowitz was a bundle of contradictions. I said, "But, Maestro, you loaned me two books on Medtner, and just tonight, I've brought them back."

Horowitz replied, "With you, I make exceptions. I would loan you anything. But you know, I tell you, Rubinstein lied about everything." I thought, Poor Rubinstein, now he's a thief and a liar. "Oh, yes, he lied about everything."

Just then, Wanda marched in, and I got up to kiss her hand.

"Isn't that so, Wanda? Didn't Rubinstein lie about everything?"

"Oh, he could exaggerate a bit, I think," Wanda replied.

Here I was sitting in the same chair as the great Rubinstein, and the poor pianist could not defend himself.

To the world, Horowitz and Rubinstein were the masters of the grand manner, the Romantics par excellence. For decades, the two great pianists were rivals. Although they maintained a tenuous friendship, each artist envied the other, for good reason, and each of them was clearly fascinated with the other.

Horowitz—finicky as a cat, enigmatic, and neurotic—was always waiting for the exact moment to do anything, especially to play in public. He told me, "The tragedy of the performer is to have to be at your best at a certain day and time. What a horrible fate! Your best might have been two days before or after." And so Horowitz could be inert for years. Finding even the right hour of the day to practice the piano could be a monumental problem.

Horowitz would stick his foot gingerly into the river of life and scream it was too cold, while Rubinstein swam like a fish, living a lusty, triumphant existence. Rubinstein was fearless and lived "unconditionally," as he put it. He said, "I can be happy in prison." Horowitz's life was sterile in comparison.

Rubinstein was extroverted and healthy, as was his playing. He was comfortable in the world. Horowitz saw the world as dangerous and hostile. Rubinstein, with unnerving vitality, swept through life, giving abundantly and in turn, being showered with adulation and applause. Horowitz sat at home, plagued by mood swings of every nuance.

Rubinstein, who lived "in the moment," was baffled by Horowitz, who lived almost totally for the piano—his very being and identity were linked to his instrument. If the humidity outdoors affected the piano badly, Horowitz might despair. Rubinstein, the pianist, painted alfresco and never quite understood Horowitz's endless obsession with a pianistic detail. It irritated Rubinstein when Horowitz would run to the piano saying, "Listen, I did something different to the *Carmen* Variations."

Horowitz was thrilled by his tactile contact with the keyboard. Of course, the importance of craft varies in degree with all accomplished pianists. But in Horowitz's case, technical wizardry was the attainment of a transcendent glory.

Rubinstein was deeply jealous of Horowitz's mighty technical powers. Although he was himself a superb technician, he could not bear the fact that Horowitz could do things at the piano that no other pianist, perhaps in all history, was capable of accomplishing.

For a pianist to know that he can work till eternity and never play scales, arpeggios, and octaves with such accuracy, glitter, and reckless abandon as Horowitz is serious stuff indeed. All the good reviews in the world calling a performance musical and beautiful mean little when a player is confronted with technical feats beyond his own abilities.

Horowitz was capable of giving his audiences an electric shock which was never to be forgotten. Rubinstein, too, could arouse his audience to a high pitch of excitement, but he had too long relied on his "fatal facility" to camouflage flaws in his craft. He had such joie de vivre that not until he heard Horowitz, seventeen years his junior, did Rubinstein truly submit to disciplined practicing. And by then, he was in his mid-forties.

During Rubinstein's career, a new reverence for note-perfect accuracy had arisen because of recording. Pianists at the turn of the century, the so-called Golden Age, just preceding Horowitz, were miraculous technicians, but often careless. Indeed, many despised and feared the recording apparatus, and their playing for it could be stilted and repressed.

Before the advent of the phonograph, many music lovers were unfamiliar with a great deal of the piano literature, except for smaller salon pieces which had popular appeal and were the domain of the amateur pianist.

As recording matured and the recorded repertoire expanded, the critics and public became more educated. They frowned upon such things as changing the composer's text or sloppy rhythms. Paderewski, for example, was criticized for his excessive mannerism of not playing with his hands together. Audiences began to sneer at inaccurate playing.

Horowitz emerged just as electrically recorded discs had come on the market in 1925, and his steely, very "modern" sounding precision made many pianists further aware of note-perfectness. After hearing him, Ignaz Friedman, one of the great pianists of the Golden Age, pronounced, "Our careers will never be the same again," and he was right.

After Horowitz's Paris debut in 1926, Rubinstein began hearing about Horowitz-mania from his own Parisian friends Coco Chanel, the dancer Serge Lifar, and Misia Sert, the great hostess and herself a student of Fauré. Rubinstein's engagements prevented him from hearing Horowitz at the time. He wrote in his memoirs, *My Many Years*: "I must frankly admit that the great ado and excitement about Horowitz gave me a little pang of jealousy. My staunchest friends and supporters, my most loyal admirers, were now talking of nothing else but young Horowitz."

However, when Rubinstein heard Horowitz soon after in Paris, he was astonished. Half a century later, he wrote:

> I shall never forget the two Paganini-Liszt Etudes, the E-flat and E Major ones. There was much more than sheer brilliance and technique; there was an easy elegance—the magic something which defies description. He also played two major works by Chopin, the Polonaise-Fantaisie and the Barcarolle, both masterly performances even if they went against my conception of Chopin. The greatest success of the evening was his encore, his own arrangement of the dance in the Second Act of *Carmen*. He brought the three repetitions to a shattering climax which made us jump up. When he had played his final encore, in a high state of excitement I rushed with the others to see him backstage. While he was dressing, his admirers, among them most of my friends, were shouting enthusiastic comments at each other and I was the loudest.
>
> Horowitz came out of his dressing room sweating and pale and received the great homage with regal indifference. When I came up to him he said, "Ach! I played a wrong note in the Polonaise-Fantaisie." I would gladly give ten years of my life to be able to claim only one wrong note after a concert. On the way out, one lovely and very musical lady, a great friend of mine, said, "Arthur, pour la Barcarolle, il n'y a que vous." (The Barcarolle will always be yours.) This little sentence stuck in my mind for a long time. It caused me to feel a deep artistic depression. Deep within myself, I felt I was the better musician—my conception of the sense of music was more mature,

but at the same time, I was conscious of my terrible defects—of my negligence for detail, my treatment of some concerts as a pleasant pastime, all due to that devilish facility for grasping and learning the pieces and then playing them, light-heartedly in public; with all the conviction of my own musical superiority, I had to concede that Volodya was by far the better pianist... My self-esteem was at its lowest. The pianistic exuberance and the technical ease of Vladimir Horowitz made me feel deeply ashamed of my persistent negligence and laziness in bringing to life all the possibilities of my natural musical gifts. I knew that I had it in me to give a better account of the many works which I played in concerts with so much love and yet with so much tolerance of my own lack of respect and care....

After discussing with Horowitz what Rubinstein had written in his memoirs, I asked, "Do you have anything good to say about Rubinstein?"

"Oh, we knew each other for years. But you know, he had a good technique. I hear lots of his records on radio lately, on your station, too. Very good playing, that's for sure!"

Wanda agreed, "Oh, yes, Rubinstein could play the piano."

Horowitz continued, "They once said of Paderewski that he did everything well except play the piano. But Arthur was a real pianist."

"Yes, he had a large mechanism," I joined in. "His records are perhaps a shade careful because he was so damn scared of wrong notes."

"You know," Horowitz said, "he played Spanish music very well. Albéniz *Navarra,* and things like that. But nobody plays Spanish music better than Alicia de Larrocha."

Horowitz always praised de Larrocha, Spain's greatest pianist and a brilliant interpreter of Spanish piano music of all periods.

Wanda exclaimed, "Yes, she is unrivaled in Spanish music. I heard her just the other evening at Fisher Hall playing the entire cycle of the Granados *Goyescas.* Nobody can touch her in this music."

"Maestro, do you think such playing as de Larrocha in Spanish music can be taught? Or is it pure instinct?"

"It can never be taught, *never!*" Horowitz said vehemently. "But you know, I'm Spanish, too, when I play Scarlatti." Scarlatti is

Spanish, *not* Italian. The Maestro sang from a Scarlatti Sonata in D Major. "That's the changing of the guards at the Madrid court."

Horowitz continued. "Rubinstein made a big splash in Spain and South America. He was the most popular pianist there. Brailowsky also had lots of success in South America."

Alexander Brailowsky had a major career during the thirties and forties, and along with Rubinstein was one of Horowitz's rivals at RCA.

"I could have made piles of money in South America, but the timing never worked right. In the late twenties, I performed in Madrid once. I hated it. The food didn't agree with me."

I continued our discussion of Rubinstein. "So you see, Maestro, you were very important in Rubinstein's life. You made him aware that he was superficial in his work methods. He envied you."

"Maybe that is true," Horowitz replied. "How you work is the most important thing of all. Envy can be good, jealousy is stupid. Envy can stimulate someone to work harder. If you admire a quality, you can work for it. But jealousy is senseless. My hand is born to me. Why compare? You cannot be jealous of my hands. That's a waste of time."

I said, "Then Mr. Rubinstein did a good job of envying you because he got down to hard work, and became one of the important pianists in history."

Horowitz interjected, "I saw a lot of Rubinstein in Paris. We played together often at Alexander Steinert's home. We play Wagner on two pianos. Rubinstein knew Wagner's music well. And me, too. When I was a boy, I play Wagner with Henrich Neuhaus. Then, everyone couldn't get enough of Wagner. He was like a narcotic."

"You mentioned Alec Steinert, I knew him quite well in the 1970s."

"Really?" Horowitz brightened. "He was a good friend of mine."

Wanda interjected, "Alec was a composer—a sort of socialite. He knew everybody. He was good-looking and charming, and rich."

"Oh, yes, I knew him in the late twenties," Horowitz said." He had all of Paris at his home. He came from Boston and was a member of the family of the Steinert piano firm."

"Maestro, he was very fond of you. He spoke a great deal about you to me. But I think he was deeply hurt that you let the friendship lapse."

Horowitz didn't respond.

I went on, "He composed a piano sonata for you, and dedicated it to you. Do you remember it?'

"I don't remember," Horowitz said glumly.

"Oh, yes. I have the score. It's a fine work. Neo-Romantic, quite French. Steinert told me you sight-read it magnificently, and taunted him by promising to play it in a concert, but you never did."

Wanda said, "I don't remember the piece."

"Perhaps you never heard it. It was composed in 1930, before you two met."

"I liked him," Wanda said. "But over the years, somehow, we didn't see him."

I continued, "Alec loved your playing and I'd see him at your concerts. But he never tried to see you. I think he died in 1982. He was a true gentleman, a fascinating man and a prodigious musician. I went to a memorial service at a church on Madison Avenue and Seventy-third. Only a few people were there. However, John Steinway came to pay his respects."

Horowitz looked sad. Perhaps he was thinking of those far-off days in Paris. "Rubinstein liked Steinert a lot."

"David, you never met Rubinstein, did you?" Mrs. Horowitz asked.

"Oh, yes I did," I responded. "On two occasions. In 1972 and in March of '76, right after he played the last Carnegie Hall recital of his career. He was eighty-nine years old, already blind, but his playing was rapturous. I was amazed not only by the ardor of his playing but by his technical audacity that night. At the conclusion of the recital, he spoke briefly to the audience, as if he knew this would be his last recital in the concert hall he loved most of all.

"The next morning, I did my daily eleven a.m. radio show, and I raved about the Rubinstein recital and played his recordings of the works he performed the night before. I was euphoric and told my audience that Rubinstein had never played more wonderfully."

"So how did you meet him?" Horowitz asked.

"After the show, I went back to my office. I was tired in the empty way one is after doing a live performance. Well, the receptionist rang me saying that Mr. Rubinstein is on the phone.

"I said, 'Betty, don't put me on.'

"'No, seriously, Mr. Rubinstein is on the phone.'

"Indeed he was, and he began by graciously complimenting me on my program. He said he was especially exhausted after last night's recital, but his daughter told him to listen to my program and, much to his delight, it was about last night's concert.

"He said, 'You touched me deeply. I receive lots of applause, but seldom such a verbal tribute.' Rubinstein then said he was having guests at lunch the next day and asked if I would join him.

"At lunch, we talked alone for quite a while. His blindness prevented him from seeing me at all, nor did I remind him that we had spent an afternoon together five years earlier. He told me he was pleased with his playing the previous evening. He shuddered at the thought that the critics and public might think him a tottering old man of ninety who should be retired. I told him I was thrilled by his performance of *Carnaval*. The fiendishly difficult section titled 'Paganini,' Schumann's portrait of the violinist, was played with a rousing virtuosity that went far beyond his recording.

"When I mentioned this to Rubinstein, he was overjoyed. He said, 'Do you know why it was so good? Since my blindness, I can't read my favorite authors like Proust and Joyce, and I don't like being read to. And worse, now I can't take walks to look at the beautiful women. So I am bored, and do you know what I do? Yes, I practice, and on all those tricky little places that I've neglected all my life. That's why 'Paganini' was so good last night.'

"He was pleased telling me this, and his good-natured laughter boomed through the room.

"Several hours later, without help, he walked me to the hotel elevator. He took my hand, looked me straight in the eye, and said in his raspy voice, 'We shall be friends forever.'

"I never saw him again, but one year later, out of the blue, I received in the mail, with no note, a photo of Rubinstein and myself talking intensely, sitting at a table in the midst of flowers."

Wanda smiled. "Oh, yes, he could be a charming man. What about your first meeting with him?"

Horowitz was listening with rapt attention.

"Oh, that was five years earlier and quite different. RCA gave him a lunch at La Côte Basque. I was introduced to him, and miraculously, we talked for almost two hours after lunch. I told him that a mutual friend, the pianist Allen Tanner, had once sent me a snapshot of him with his friends, the violinist Paul Kochanski and the composer Szymanowski, on a ship leaving New York for Paris in 1921. During our conversation, he made no mention of the photo.

"It was getting late. In those days, I still smoked. As I was helping Mrs. Rubinstein with her coat, I had a lit cigarette in my hand, and somehow I burned her hand. I was mortified, and in my horror I actually said, 'Thank God I didn't burn Mr. Rubinstein.' She said that she deserved the little burn since she herself smoked."

Wanda cried, "Thank goodness you stopped smoking. You are dangerous."

"Yes, but the euphoria of the day disappeared. What a stupid ending. I wrote him a note at the Drake Hotel, saying how wonderful it was meeting him, but that I was anguished at having burned his wife. I also asked him about an interview on WNCN. Many weeks later, I received a letter. Much to my chagrin, he misunderstood me and wrote, 'My hands have other troubles with piano technique than with a slight burn of a finger.'"

Horowitz roared. "So now, he thought you burned him."

"Yes. I was flabbergasted. He also told me that he would be happy to be interviewed by me."

Horowitz interrupted. "But in your book, there is no Rubinstein interview."

"I know," I said. "Can you believe it? What a fool I was! At that time, I hadn't thought of doing an interview book of pianists. Somehow, I let it pass, and then it was too late.

"However, I was amazed at Rubinstein's superb memory. I thought it curious that when we spoke, he passed over the subject of the Szymanowski and Kochanski photograph. At the end of his letter, he told me he lost all his photos of these two 'beloved friends' during the war, and asked me to send a copy of the photo. This I did. But I never knew if he had ever received it, and when I met him again in 1976, I forgot to ask him. In 1980, eight years after my first meeting with him, I read the just-published second volume of his memoirs and was excited to find the photo I sent him included in the book."

Horowitz said, "It's a shame that you never interviewed him. But at least, you got to know him a little. I think he was ninety-six when he died. That is a long life. I'll never live that long."

Wanda arose from her chair. This was to be our last evening together for a while. In a few days, the Horowitzes were to leave for Milan, where the Maestro would record Mozart's A Major Concerto.

He had no idea what an arduous month he was to have making his recording.

For Horowitz, life was never simple. Perhaps that was the major difference between Horowitz and Rubinstein. Everything was difficult for Horowitz. Everything was easy for Rubinstein. One saw life as a tragedy, the other as a comedy. Horowitz thought with his feelings, which makes life murky. Rubinstein thought with his head, which makes life clearer and happier.

30

LISTENING WITH
TREPIDATION

It was early April 1987—over a month since Horowitz had gone to Milan to make his Mozart recording. Soon after their return, I received a dinner invitation.

Mrs. Horowitz said, "Tonight, we shall go to Piccolo Mondo on First Avenue."

When Horowitz entered a restaurant, all eyes were on him. Sometimes an admirer could not contain himself and came to our table asking for an autograph. Wanda usually scowled.

Horowitz liked the attention, but occasionally he declined to provide his signature. Tonight, he signed his name, but made no comment nor looked at the autograph hunter who plied him with compliments.

New Yorkers are accustomed to celebrities, and they usually respect their privacy. In the case of Horowitz, however, I noticed they often could not suppress their interest in him, and his autograph, that of a great artist, had the extra attraction of having permanent value.

After dinner, we returned to the Horowitzes' lovely drawing room. It felt good to be there once again.

Mrs. Horowitz began the conversation. "Tom and Lynne were here last night. Tom brought Mozart's G minor String Quintet for us to hear because we didn't know it."

169

"What a magnificent work," I said. "That's one of the great chamber works."

"The slow movement is the most beautiful imaginable," Horowitz chimed in. "Today, I'm reading a letter by Tchaikovsky. He was a great soul. He tells his friend how much he loves Mozart. He talks of this very G minor Quintet. When he hears it, he weeps. You know, I own two Tchaikovsky letters. I give them to Yale when I die. Here I am, almost eighty-four, and I never hear this quintet before. I still don't know so much music. We live with treasures everywhere, and we don't have the time to know them. Mozart died at thirty-five. He composed enough for twenty composers, and I don't even know all that he did."

Mozart was Horowitz's favorite topic. "Mozart remained a child," I said. "I think that near the end of his life, his angelic nature was awakened to the cruelty of the world. Speaking of the quintet, someone said it was Mozart's late discovery of the world's pain. Mr. Horowitz, I think Mozart was duped. As a child, he was deceived."

"How do you mean?" Wanda wanted to know.

"Well, because his genius bloomed so early, he grew up as a spoiled prodigy. And I mean spoiled. No other child in history was so feted and observed. At a dinner party in Paris, the tiny Mozart gave Madame de Pompadour his cheek, which she refused. He glared at her. 'Who are you,' he said, 'to refuse to kiss me when my own Empress Maria Theresa showers me with hugs and kisses?'"

Horowitz was enthralled. Any bit of information about Mozart enchanted him.

"Little Mozart was a true snob," I went on. "The anecdote shows that he expected equality from the highest society. He forgot his middle-class origins. The great trick played on Mozart was that, as soon as he was no longer the *wunderkind,* his amusement and amazement value was over, and he was simply dropped. To the aristocrats, he became just another musician, and that amounted to servant status. Soon, Mozart was forced back to provincial Salzburg, a small town he hated, and had to work for the even more hated archbishop."

"A *nudnick,*" Mrs. Horowitz exclaimed.

"Yes, and Mozart could not suffer fools. He was never a good diplomat. That's why he never got the good posts in Vienna. After his father died in 1787, Mozart started a slow decline. He had many illnesses and drank heavily, and he spent way beyond his means."

"What about his wife?" Mrs. Horowitz asked.

"Constanza probably was not the woman Mozart loved," I continued. "It was her sister. His wife was of little help to Mozart. She was just as childish, impractical, and frivolous, but they stuck together."

Mrs. Horowitz said, "Volodya, today everyone loves Mozart. But after he died, he wasn't that much played. Isn't that right?"

Horowitz replied, "*Oh, sure.* When I grow up, Mozart was still not very big. The concertos were not played. Only a few sonatas. Even Bach's preludes and fugues were considered good *exercises* for the mind and fingers. I remember playing to Rachmaninoff some Scarlatti. He didn't like them at all. He didn't even know there were Schubert sonatas. Why do you think we change now so much?"

I explained that the nineteenth century saw everything in terms of evolution and progress. Mozart was merely a gallant rococo predecessor of the mighty Beethoven. Music before Bach was virtually unknown. Also, the nineteenth century was a great age for music. Chopin, Liszt, Schumann, Berlioz, Verdi, Wagner, Grieg, Brahms, and others stole the show from the past. While, in the late twentieth century, very few are interested in new music, so the past has been rejuvenated.

Horowitz and Wanda nodded vigorously. "I think you are right. Now, people can't get enough of Mozart."

I continued, "I saw a French film recently. I think the title was *Get Out Your Handkerchiefs,* and the hero was in love with Mozart's music. His friend got irritated and said, 'Can't you listen to anyone else? There's Schubert and Brahms and Chopin and Mahler.' But he said calmly and firmly, 'Mozart is enough for me'"

Horowitz shook his head. *Me, too!"* he responded. "Mozart is enough for me, that's for sure. Mozart is my number one man!"

Mrs. Horowitz said, "No, I'm like the other person. Sometimes I beg Volodya, 'Can't you play anything else? Mozart is coming out of my ears.'"

Horowitz looked at me. "Mr. Dubal, do you want to hear *my* Mozart concerto? I have a copy of it already."

"You do, Maestro? Of course I want to hear it."

"It's not the finished product. That won't be out for months yet. I never thought I would go through such hell in Milan, day in and day out. I don't know why we even go there. Maybe because it's Wanda's town. I should have recorded with the Berlin Philharmonic. The orchestra of La Scala—who are they? And I'm not used to doing concertos. Giulini and me are different for Mozart. He likes slow tempos. But he is a gentleman, a noble-looking person."

Carlo Maria Giulini—a most experienced conductor—was Horowitz's own choice for this concerto, and he did his best to please the pianist in every way.

Horowitz continued, "The orchestra was not so good. I myself had to train the bassoonist. Oh, yes, I help improve them all. Maybe nobody likes my Mozart, but I don't care. I do my best."

In his first recording of a Mozart concerto, Horowitz was more susceptible to criticism than ever. He desperately wanted the world to see him now as a major Mozart interpreter.

"Are you ready to hear it?"

"Of course, I am, Mr. Horowitz. I can't wait."

Horowitz said, "Wanda, put the cassette in the machine. Mr. Dubal doesn't know how to make machines work."

She teased, "He's as bad as you, Volodya."

During the long orchestral tutti, I mumbled, "That's a good tempo."

Horowitz's eyes were glued to the floor.

Wanda sat silently, as she usually did when her husband played.

As I listened to Horowitz's Mozart, I was fascinated by the Maestro's indelible stamp of individuality. Liszt once said it was his goal to merge his own individuality into the ideas of the composer. If this was the ideal for an interpreter, then Horowitz was utterly successful. His Mozart was luminous, the technical flexibility astounding. But Horowitz's lavishly expressive Mozart, especially in the slow movement, I felt, would be disparaged by conservative critics.

With the concerto's last chord, the three of us stood up. Better, perhaps, to hear my verdict.

"What do you think?" Wanda seemed a bit impatient.

I thought quickly. To say "I love it" was simply not enough. Horowitz had been living intensely with this concerto for months. I decided to tell a story. While the three of us remained standing, I began.

"Sometime in 1840, the pianist Ignaz Moscheles played Weber's *Konzertstück* for piano and orchestra. An audience member who heard the Moscheles performance happened to hear Liszt perform the same work several weeks later. He was dumbfounded: the composition seemed transformed under Liszt's hands. After the concert, this man met Liszt. He told him that he had heard Moscheles play the *Konzertstück* recently and it was excellent, 'But your playing brought the score to another sphere.' Liszt listened carefully and responded, 'Oh, yes, my friend Moscheles is a very fine artist indeed. But sir, what I do with the Weber *Konzertstück* is quite another thing.'"

I paused a second. "Maestro, I have only to say that *your* Mozart is 'quite another thing.'"

At that, Horowitz was beaming. He grabbed my hand, "So my Mozart is 'quite another thing.' Good! Then I've done the job. Now I won't have to read the reviews."

Alas, after the recording appeared, he did read the reviews, which poured in from everywhere. He was always ambivalent about critics, seldom trusting them and knowing from experience how pedantic they could be. As I suspected, many of these reviews were critical, condemning him for his more unconventional style in Mozart.

"All pianists have one thing in common," he once said. "They are all insecure."

Here was the most famous pianist in the world, with a best-selling recording, but it still hurt him when a critic from London or Berlin found his slow movement too fast or too Romantic. For me to say Horowitz's Mozart was "quite another thing" was fine, but the whole world had to agree, too.

As he read me a batch of reviews, he would say, "What do they know?" always ignoring the many good reviews.

"Maestro," I said, "you know that your Mozart was bound to bother some people. You knew also that a few would take exception to the Busoni cadenza instead of Mozart's own. We live in conventional times."

"I know," he replied. "What do they understand? What can you do with a concerto anyway? The only thing one can do is play in time. But the Mozart sonata on the other side of the record, ah, there I really do interesting things. But they don't notice."

"Maestro, I knew they would pick on your Mozart because the time has come for you to receive a critical backlash. All your reviews since Russia have been raves. It's time to 'get Horowitz.'"

"You are right. I don't give a damn anyway."

I said, "It will take a little time, but I think that your playing of Mozart will change the way many pianists view him."

"Do you think so?"

"I sure do, Maestro."

"Maybe I record next No. 20 in D minor. I love it, too. I think I do a good job with it."

However, I knew then that Horowitz would never again record a concerto. Basically, it repelled him not to have total control. He had gladly sacrificed the glamour of playing concertos to preserve his individuality and artistic freedom. His mentality was definitely not collaborative.

31

RACHMANINOFF: THE
HOROWITZ ICON

The major musical influence in Horowitz's life was Rachmaninoff. As a child, the moment he heard Rachmaninoff's music, he attempted to learn it. His early ambition to be a composer was inspired by Rachmaninoff as well.

Around the time Horowitz played for Scriabin, in 1914, he was also to be evaluated by Rachmaninoff. However, this meeting never took place. The eleven-year-old Volodya went with his mother to meet Rachmaninoff in a Kiev hotel, where the boy was to play for him. The appointment was scheduled for four p.m., but Rachmaninoff left town at three that afternoon.

Years later, when Horowitz confronted him about it, Rachmaninoff said, "I hated prodigies. And I began worrying that if you were no good, I would have to tell your mother, and so I left. I cannot lie."

Rachmaninoff's musical idealism became, for Horowitz, a standard of measurement. Once, in an unguarded moment, I asked Horowitz where he placed Rachmaninoff in relation to himself.

He said, looking up, "Rachmaninoff is a giant redwood. I'm only a tree, a big one or little one, I don't know. Ah, there was only one Rachmaninoff in this century." Horowitz put his arm straight up.

"Rachmaninoff is there," he said. And lowering his hand, "Maybe, I am down here somewhere."

I was curious to see if we were of the same opinion as to Liszt, who I felt must be a musical entity ranked even higher than Rachmaninoff. "Where then, Maestro, do you place Franz Liszt in relation to Rachmaninoff?"

Without hesitation, Horowitz stood up and pointed straight up. "Liszt," he proclaimed, " is so high that we can't even see the top. It will still take years for us to fully understand his importance in music."

Horowitz's musical respect for Toscanini bordered on veneration, whereas Toscanini said that his son-in-law was possessed by demons. He said, "Nobody but Liszt could play like Horowitz." Although Toscanini was not fond of Liszt's music, he called Horowitz's Liszt playing "superhuman."

Much to Horowitz's regret, the intractable Toscanini detested the gushing voluptuousness of Rachmaninoff's music. Horowitz was irked that Toscanini would not perform Rachmaninoff's Third Concerto with him, the work he loved more than any other concerto.

The Third Piano Concerto in D minor, the most resplendent of Rachmaninoff's concertos, loomed large in Horowitz's life. Mrs. Horowitz told me that during November 1989, only days before her husband died, he had thought once again of playing it with Claudio Abbado conducting the Berlin Philharmonic. His desire to do so was extraordinary, because the Third Concerto demands the strength of a lion; only a few years before, Horowitz had told me that he could no longer hope to play such a gigantic work. Yet at eighty-six, his strength, general health, and mental outlook had so improved that, in his mind, at least, such an undertaking seemed possible.

I once asked Horowitz if he thought the Rachmaninoff Third Concerto was the most difficult of all Romantic concertos.

He thought for a moment, putting his hand to his chin. "I think so. Yes, definitely it is. There are maybe more notes and chords than *all* the Mozart concertos. Somebody will count the notes and they will see. But even as a teenager, I knew that I could play that piece in a way that the people would know that Rachmaninoff in No. 3 went beyond what he did in No. 2."

"When did you first play it?" I asked.

"Oh, I remember it was a big event. Glazunov himself conducted, and Milstein played the Glazunov Violin Concerto in the same evening. The audience heard something that night. Glazunov was one of the big composers in Russia at the time. I was around eighteen, maybe seventeen, when this happened."

Horowitz continued, "Maybe Rachmaninoff composed No. 3 when I was a teenager, because it was unknown in Russia."

"No," I said, "he composed it when you were around five or six years old. And he premiered it in New York when he had an American tour in 1909."

Horowitz pursed his lips and nodded. "I see. I never read a biography of Rachmaninoff. I didn't know he was here that early."

"Yes," I said. "He played it in New York first with Walter Damrosch, and a few days later with no less than Mahler himself."

"Imagine!" Horowitz howled. "I didn't know that."

"Oh, yes. What a collaboration. The last great Russian Romantic and the last great German Romantic. Two such different artists."

"My God!" Horowitz shrieked again. "I would love to have been there."

"I don't know of a greater combination of musical genius on stage," I said. "The earth must have trembled. The only other combination of two such titans that comes to mind was in Weimar, when Liszt premiered his First Concerto with Berlioz on the podium."

"What do we have today?!" Horowitz roared. "I don't play concertos because I can't even find a good conductor. Did Rachmaninoff like Mahler's conducting?"

"Very much, Maestro. Both Busoni and Rachmaninoff were greatly impressed with Mahler the conductor. Otto Klemperer called Mahler the greatest conductor who ever lived."

"Rachmaninoff was a first-class conductor, so he knew. Did they like the concerto in New York when it was new?"

"No, the critics said it was too loosely made. They liked the Second Concerto better."

Horowitz intoned, "Rachmaninoff was upset that he never had the kind of success that he had wished for it. Rachmaninoff, I think, was glad to give the piece to me. He said he composed it for elephants. Maybe I'm an elephant.

"But I must tell you, Rachmaninoff dedicated the concerto to Hofmann, and I know for a fact that he was disappointed that

Hofmann never played it. Rachmaninoff loved Hofmann's playing, especially in the years before the alcohol. He was always telling of Hofmann's playing."

"I wonder why Hofmann didn't play it."

"That I never found out," Horowitz replied. "But it was good for me that he didn't, because then, *I own the concerto*," he yelled. "Maybe Hofmann was a little bit lazy. He had hard time reading music. He used his ear too much and maybe all the notes scared him. Maybe Hofmann's hand was not good for the piece. He had very small hands, but powerful. He had Steinway build him a piano which made the octave into seven keys. Or perhaps he felt it wasn't as good as No. 2."

"Did you know, Mr. Horowitz, that in 1907, Rachmaninoff asked Hofmann for a lesson on the Tchaikovsky Concerto because he was asked to play it somewhere? Hofmann could not understand why Rachmaninoff asked for a lesson, and he refused."

Horowitz said, "I must tell you that Rachmaninoff was *very* insecure about everything. There is an old Russian proverb, You can't hunt three hares. And Rachmaninoff was composer, pianist, and conductor, and he was most insecure about the pianist. That's why he never played much of any music but his own until after the Russian Revolution. Then he decided he would rather make his living as a concert pianist than conductor. You know, he was offered the posts of Cincinnati and Boston Symphony. When he declined, Koussevitzky took the Boston.

"Oh, yes, Rachmaninoff could have had an easy life as conductor, but he was obsessed with piano playing. He practiced constantly, scales and arpeggios every day. Although he learned faster than anyone, he worked harder. He could only give the best in himself. Oh, sure, he knew he was great pianist, but he wanted to be better and better. He was never lazy, not a minute was wasted."

Horowitz continued, "After the revolution, he kept composing, but *much less*. He said he could not compose on trains. And he told me that he could not conduct and then play, because whenever he conducted, he couldn't play well for a long time after because the muscles he used when conducting ruined his playing.

"But Rachmaninoff was always unhappy and complaining. Nothing was right, and nothing was perfect. You know his transcription of the Scherzo from [Mendelssohn's] *Midsummer Night's Dream?*"

"Of course I do," I replied. "It's horribly difficult."

"Terrible. Terrible!" Horowitz screeched. "He told me that when he recorded it in 1930, I think, he did it forty-eight times. Even though it was perfect on many of those takes, he could never get it good enough. Those were the days of 78s, before editing. One time he comes back and says, 'I played seventy concerts and only three of them did I play well.' Oh, yes, Rachmaninoff was after perfection, and he had the biggest integrity to art. He was very unhappy if he did not reach his goal.

"He lived to seventy, and nobody worked harder. Believe me, he was a big influence on me in lots of good ways. His picture is always behind me when I work. It's good to know that he is there on the wall. It keeps me from being too lazy. But he was never satisfied and he didn't like anyone's playing all the way. He found fault with everything. He was crazy about Ignaz Friedman's playing and his singing tone. He thought him a tremendous virtuoso, and very elegant, too. But he complained that he sometimes played too much to the gallery. With Rachmaninoff, bad taste was a sin."

Horowitz went on. "Rachmaninoff was hard to get to know. He laughed very little, but with me he could laugh. I would imitate Russian singers for him. I knew all the Russian operas. Rachmaninoff adored the basso Feodor Chaliapin. I try to imitate him and Rachmaninoff burst out with laughter. Rachmaninoff was convinced that Chaliapin was the greatest singer of all time.

"Rachmaninoff trusted me, but very few ever got to know him well. He helped me a lot and encouraged me always. He was a very strong-minded person. Not mentally off-balanced at all. He had his job to do, and he did it.

"He missed Russia terribly," Horowitz said. "Before the revolution, he had a good life on his estate. He was not bitter, though, and America treated him like a king. He respected America and how they opened everything up to him. But at times, he said, 'America only cares for the money.' Rachmaninoff himself was very fond of money, and was very careful that nobody cheated him in any way. He could complain about a fee, or not play because it was not enough. Believe me, he knew he was Rachmaninoff.

"He laughed or even cried at things you wouldn't expect. For instance, the finale of Liszt's *Faust* Symphony, with the chorus, the worst part of the piece, he would weep.

"I remember once, at a party, Gershwin was there and he could not be dragged from the piano. Rachmaninoff was there, too, and suddenly, I heard like a bomb Rachmaninoff's voice booming out, '*Horowitz,* play your *Danse Excentrique!*' This piece, which I composed when I'm eighteen for my brother's birthday party, Rachmaninoff was mad about. I remember, I was very embarrassed. But Rachmaninoff's word was like law. So I obediently go to the piano. The piece is only two minutes, so Gershwin didn't have to wait long to get back to the piano.

"Rachmaninoff didn't like when others would say, 'Horowitz is a good pianist.' *He* was allowed to say I played well, but not others. He was a secretive man, and he kept things to himself. I once asked him why he never gave interviews. I said, 'A whole generation would be interested in your views on music and life in general. Nobody knows what you think about composers.'

"Rachmaninoff looked at me with a very hard face and said, 'Mr. Horowitz, I must tell you something. I was brought up never to lie, and I *cannot* tell the truth.'" Horowitz laughed loudly as he recounted this enigmatic statement.

"You see, Mr. Dubal, it was not so easy to figure him out. He was a puzzle, and you never knew what he would say. He was very unpredictable, too. Once I was stunned when I play the Third Concerto and he actually came out of the audience to the stage to hug me. You never knew what he would do."

"That's fascinating," I said, "that he felt incapable of telling the truth. One biography of Rachmaninoff says that when he arrived in New York in 1909 to play the Third Concerto, there was a great deal of publicity, and he told the press that he only learned the piece while on ship, practicing on a dumb keyboard."

"He had never learned it before!" Horowitz exclaimed. "My God! That's how he learned his Third Concerto? But to learn that concerto on a dumb piano on a ship, that is pretty good. But it is not the way Rachmaninoff worked."

I said, "Exactly. I once read a diary that was published some years ago called the *Amazing Marriage of Marie Eustis and Josef Hofmann,* and in it, Hofmann's wife reports that in Moscow, Rachmaninoff, just before his American debut, 'magnificently' played the concerto for Hofmann."

At that moment, Mrs. Horowitz came in from a party. Horowitz called to Wanda. "We have been talking of your favorite."

Mrs. Horowitz said, "Oh, Rachmaninoff. He was the best person.

The most aristocratic man, a man in the grand style, the kind of man they no longer make, a gentleman! Of course, he had his strangeness. I never understood why he lived so austerely. His apartment in New York was very bare and simple. Yet his estate in Switzerland was very lavish."

Horowitz continued, "I remember when we were in Switzerland, during one summer when he was composing the *Rhapsody on a Theme of Paganini,* a terrific piece. A little more modern-sounding, difficult, too, but not so many notes as the Third Concerto. Rachmaninoff played it the best.

"Each day, Rachmaninoff would call me over, and he play for me his newest variation. At the No. 18 Variation, I say to him, 'Oh, this sounds like the older Rachmaninoff,' and he tells me, 'Yes, I compose this variation for my manager. Maybe it will save the piece.' You know that Rachmaninoff suffered that the critics didn't like his music? He tried to change his style a little. They always said he composed like Tchaikovsky, he's not of our century. This hurt Rachmaninoff very much."

Wanda said, "Critics or not, Rachmaninoff's music is played more than ever because it tells of human feelings. As long as people *feel,* Rachmaninoff will live. I went to his funeral. Volodya didn't go."

"How come?" I asked. "You loved and respected him more than anyone."

"I was friends with him until his eyes closed. But I could not bring myself to go to the funeral."

Wanda said, "Where is it in Westchester that he is buried?"

I said, "It's a cemetery in Valhalla, New York. I went there several years ago to see where he was buried and put a lilac on the grave in commemoration of his song."

Horowitz said, "Better he should have been buried in the famous cemetery in Leningrad with Anton Rubinstein, Pushkin, and Tchaikovsky, where they are all resting. Then each day, they would put flowers on his grave. That is how it should be. He missed the soil of Russia. He should be there. That I am sure."

"Did you know, Maestro, that supposedly, one of the last things he ever said in the hospital while looking at his giant hands was 'Farewell, my dear hands. Farewell.'?"

Horowitz said, "They were tremendous hands. Hofmann asked him to loan him his hands for one year. The last thing Rachmaninoff ever said to me was 'Please play my First Concerto, my favorite, and nobody plays it.' As you know, I never played it. I worked on it, I thought about it, but I never could bring myself to do it. It's a good work. You know Rachmaninoff's own record? It's the best job he did on his recordings of his concertos."

"Do you feel guilty about not playing it?"

"Oh, yes. I do a little. I should have done his last wishes for him."

"But in a sense, you did it through Byron Janis, your very own pupil, who played it, and his recording is superb."

"Maybe you are right, I should not have the guilt. I have done much for Rachmaninoff's music, and I would like to restore the Second Sonata again. I can still do it."

Horowitz was in good spirits. He lifted himself from the couch and asked if I would like to hear him play Rachmaninoff. "But not the gloomy Rachmaninoff," he said, and he proceeded to toss off his dazzling Polka. With that witty composition, the evening ended.

32

ON OLD AGE

On this particular Wednesday evening in early May 1987, I had worked late and had no dinner. I gobbled down three slices of pizza on Ninety-second and Madison and rushed over to the Horowitzes' home.

When I walked in, I found him alone.

"Wanda went to some fancy party," he said. The pianist was in a thoughtful mood.

"Did you work today, Maestro?"

"Yeah, a little on Liszt. But I still don't know if I will do this piece on the record. Nobody knows this Liszt piece. Probably not even you."

"Play it for me and I'll see if I know it."

Horowitz was intrigued to find out if I knew his latest Lisztian discovery. He went to the piano and began playing the *Csardas obstiné*, a work of Liszt's old age. I gave him no indication that I knew the piece. When he finished, my face looked blank.

Horowitz said, "Hah, you don't know it!"

"Maestro, of course I know it. I know all of Liszt's late music."

"What then is the name of this?"

"*Csardas obstiné*," I said. "Composed in 1884."

"You know your stuff," Horowitz said.

"I like the work, Maestro. I studied it myself."

He returned to the couch. "You know," he began, "I am an old man, but life is a little too short. There is not enough time."

183

Horowitz said this with an unforgettable sadness. Here was a man who had accomplished so much, who should have felt great fulfillment. And yet, there was still so much to learn and so little time.

Horowitz continued, "How much I wanted to be a composer. But then, all of a sudden, I had to earn money. I found myself on trains, trains, trains. Once, when Rachmaninoff was leaving on a tour, someone said to him, 'When will you be home?' and he looked at the train, saying, 'Home, home, this train is my home.' I know how he felt. But what can you do? I had to support myself. When I come out of Russia, the little money I had I put in my shoes so they wouldn't take it at borders. I have nothing, and believe me, I didn't want to go back there. So I play, and the success came. And you buy clothes, you have good dinners, and there is no time to compose."

"Mr. Horowitz, did you resent your prowess as a virtuoso?"

"Oh, sure. I thought if I was not a good pianist, then I would be composing. But when that godforsaken revolution comes, you do what you can. So I play the Tchaikovsky Concerto."

"Did you ever expect the world to love your playing immediately?"

"Never, never. I was glad. I was happy. But I didn't expect much. You know, Russian Jews don't expect good things."

"How well I understand. There should be a lot of bad first, and then maybe a little good can come."

"You damn right," Horowitz muttered.

"Mr. Horowitz, were you afraid of getting old?"

"Yes, because a virtuoso needs strength. Not just a dancer, you know. But now, I'm ugly and I'm old. I still play okay, and new things are happening. I'm still playing concerts, and I know there are many Mozart concertos to learn. So many. How did Mozart do all of it? It makes me sick that he dies at thirty-five."

"Maestro, do you know what Schubert wrote in his diary about Mozart when he was nineteen? It's so pure and innocent. He wrote, 'O Mozart, immortal Mozart, what countless images of a brighter and better world you have stamped upon our souls.'"

Horowitz said, "How beautiful. Can you write it down for me? How did Schubert do it all? He was even younger than Mozart when he died."

"Mr. Horowitz, for me, Schubert is one of the divine ones. Can you imagine composing such an amount, nearly six hundred songs alone? He is thirty-one years old, dying of syphilis, weakened by a deadly typhus fever, and the musical storms in his soul wouldn't let him alone. He is composing the last three great piano sonatas on his deathbed. Mr. Horowitz, why did he bother to compose them? He was burning alive with the fever."

Horowitz's eyes squinted; he was thinking deeply. "I think he had to. I think he must have felt that it was his responsibility to the human race to compose until his last breath."

"Yes, I think you are right. A composer of the magnitude of Schubert is a creator first and foremost. A lover of life, a giver. He had no idea that he was the last representative of the Viennese classical school. He didn't wake up in the morning saying, 'Ho, ho, I'm Franz Schubert, the harbinger of Romanticism and the creator of the German art song.' No, he had a responsibility to his gift and to humanity."

Horowitz said, "This Schubert was a brave and courageous man. And Beethoven, too, was a brave man." Horowitz continued, "Look what he go through with the deafness. I read that Schubert was a pallbearer at Beethoven's funeral."

I explained that Schubert and Beethoven probably never met. Although he was practically unknown, somehow Schubert managed to be one of the thirty-six torchbearers at Beethoven's funeral. Vienna was proud of him, and when he died, schools were closed and a day of mourning was declared. The cortege to the cemetery consisted of perhaps twenty-five thousand people.

Horowitz interrupted, "But how come Mozart was buried in pauper's grave?"

I replied, "Mozart lived in a great age of patronage, but he was not very adept at getting the good positions, like Haydn or Salieri. Beethoven, in fact, never really worked at an official post. He was a master at extracting money from wealthy Viennese aristocrats. The Archduke Rudolf received no fewer than twenty-five dedications from Beethoven."

"How come Schubert was not famous?" Horowitz went on.

"Schubert was born twenty-seven years after Beethoven. By the time of the Congress of Vienna, 1814–15, the world had changed. The middle-class emerged. There was no patronage for Schubert. Nor was he a performer, so he couldn't make his living that way. He literally lived the life of a starving bohemian artist, which was popularized in the 1830s in Paris by Murger's novel *Scènes de la vie Bohème*. But it was already being lived in Vienna by Schubert and his circle. They were destitute, and it was during those early stages of Romanticism that the phrase 'art for art's sake' was coined."

Horowitz said, "Yes, art for art's sake. It's okay if those rock-and-roll hooligans make hundreds of millions a year, but God forbid I ask good money for my concerts. People don't like that. I am artist, I can't ask to be paid well. They don't care when I play for one hundred or five hundred dollars a concert. Now, I'm rich, so I am money-grabber. They forget the years I didn't play. I had to sell the paintings in my collection to live. Hollywood wanted to give me big dollars, I don't remember, if I play on film Gershwin *Rhapsody in Blue*. But I can't play the piece, I could learn notes, but that piece is not me. I can't play it and I can't take money for it either. So I lose out on big deal. But poor Schubert, I think he would really starve today."

"I think you are right," I said. "Schubert tried to be a respectable bourgeois when he was a schoolteacher for a while, but he couldn't stand it. He had to compose. He wore his glasses while sleeping so he could begin composing the minute he awoke, because he already had a new song surging in his head. He didn't waste a minute. But today, he would have to get up and take the subway to work. So no song would be composed."

"You see," Horowitz said, "time is everything. If you have to make a living, you are beaten to a pulp."

"Absolutely!" I exclaimed. "But fortunately, Schubert had no blocks, no conflicts about composing. Actually, I think Schubert seemed to be freed in some way when Beethoven died. Suddenly after Beethoven's death, in the last year and a half of Schubert's life, his genius flowered. The Ninth Symphony, the Octet, the *Winterreise,* the String Quintet, the last piano sonatas. It was a miracle, a magic fountain; Benjamin Britten called the eighteen months between the deaths of Beethoven and Schubert the greatest eighteen months in music history."

"I had no idea," Horowitz responded. "All that!"

"All that and more. He never stopped."

"What else during that time?" Horowitz asked.

"Oh, it was staggering. Quite a bit for piano duet including a great favorite of yours, the Fantasy in F minor. Also for duet the Lebensstürme, the C Major Fantasy for Violin, the second set of Four Impromptus, and just after the *Winterreise* cycle, he composed the song collection *Schwanengesang.* Also the two great piano trios in B-flat and E-flat, the E-flat Mass, and other church music."

"It's unbelievable!" Horowitz gasped.

"And during much of this time, he was physically wretched, dizzy with headaches. He finished the great B-flat Sonata on September 26, 1828. Then the String Quintet. He died November 19. The last eleven days, he ate or drank nothing. His last words were to his brother: 'Here is my end.' At his death, Schubert's possessions were worth less than fifty dollars. His funeral and the final illness, combined with his debts, amounted to nearly a thousand dollars. His friends were shattered. The poet Grillparzer wrote an epitaph which is on his grave, but I must say I think it's a selfish thought."

"What does it say?" Horowitz's attention was riveted.

"It says, 'The art of music here entombed a rich possession, but even far fairer hopes. Franz Schubert lies here.' I think it's selfish because people are seldom grateful. Schubert is one of the immortals of the immortals, and Grillparzer wants even more."

"I'm satisfied," Horowitz said. "I don't even know a fraction of his music."

Horowitz shook his head. "Schubert dies at thirty-one. I'm eighty-four. Maybe I can keep going a little more."

Maestro, you *are* doing marvelously. I'd like to write an article on the development of artists in old age to crush this myth that the creative powers have to die in old age. It's only this damn body that makes things difficult. I'm going to quote to you from a letter that I memorized from the Japanese painter Hokusai. Just as Beethoven said when going deaf, 'I shall seize fate by the throat,' Hokusai said, 'I will break the barrier of old age.'"

"Tell me what he said," Horowitz asked avidly.

From the age of six, I had a mania for drawing the form of things. By the time I was fifty, I had published an infinity of designs; but all I have produced before the age of seventy is not worth taking into account. At seventy-three, I have learned a little about the real structure of nature, of animals, plants, birds, fish, and insects. In consequence, when I am eighty, I shall have made more progress; at ninety, I shall penetrate the mystery of things; at a hundred, I shall certainly have reached a marvelous stage; and when I am a hundred and ten, everything I do, be it but a dot or a line, will be alive.—Written at the age of seventy-five by me, Hokusai, an old man mad about drawing.

Horowitz was moved by the Hokusai letter and asked me to repeat it again.

"Ah, he was an optimistic man, he wrote this at seventy-five. Did he live to a hundred and ten?"

"Maestro, who has ever lived that long? No, he never made it, but he did go to eighty-nine, not bad. He died in 1849, the same year as Chopin."

"Chopin wasn't so lucky," Horowitz exclaimed. "But a lot of old people should know that Hokusai letter. It gives hope. Anyway, I'm alive. My doctor told me if I get up in the morning and I have no aches and pains, then I am dead. Wanda likes this saying, too. I'm not depressed anymore. I was, you know, a little, before you came. You tell me lots of things."

"Well, Maestro, I have served my purpose."

"How will you go home?"

"I'll get a cab. And tomorrow, practice your Liszt, okay?"

"I will. I'll look at the news now and see what's up."

33

HOROWITZ AND ROCK-AND-ROLL

The summer of 1987 was rapidly disappearing. I had been visiting the Horowitzes frequently, usually twice every ten days. Lately, he had not wanted to go out for dinner. I was coming mostly to talk, and occasionally we ate in their lovely dining room, with Rouault prints covering the walls.

On this late August evening, when I arrived the couple were watching a documentary about jaguars on public television.

Mr. Horowitz was intrigued by the gorgeous jungle beasts. "Can you imagine?" he said. "They are supposed to be extinct in a few years."

Mrs. Horowitz exclaimed, "Just think, such beauty and elegance will forever disappear from the earth. All my money will be given to the protection of animals when I die. This house will be a shelter for them."

"That's good," I said. "Let's hope it's not a losing battle. The whole planet is endangered."

"What do people have children for?" Horowitz snorted. "They will have nothing to see, no elephants, no lions, no trees, no water. All destroyed for greed. I see all these documentaries, and they all tell me the same thing: everything is dying. Birds don't know their way in the sky anymore because the pollution has confused them. They are not good pilots anymore. The elephants used to give the piano ivory keys. At least they feel good to touch. Plastic feels terrible."

Mrs. Horowitz was fully absorbed in the conversation. She had a profound sorrow for the plight of animals. And if she showed little respect for humankind, she was in awe of the animal world.

At that time, she had no animals in her household, and she felt lonely for the lack of a cat wandering the large brownstone.

She continued, "The poachers, no matter what the laws, won't be stopped. They kill the elephants mercilessly for the tusks. But that ivory is never used for keyboards. Today, they are ripped off before they even die."

"Yes, Mrs. Horowitz, elephants are wonderful creatures. They are intelligent; they have funeral rites, they are kind to each other. Do you know how long it takes for an elephant to give birth?" She shook her head. "I believe two years is the gestation period."

Mrs. Horowitz remarked, "That's like the whales."

"Yes, the whales are musical and sensitive. They, too, will be wiped away from earth by man."

Mrs. Horowitz said, "It is inexcusable that humans think they can murder other animals because they murder themselves. I must tell you, I hate humans. They terrify me."

"They should," I continued. "I interviewed Yehudi Menuhin the other day."

Horowitz interrupted, "He is a very intelligent person. I know him since he was a boy."

Mrs. Horowitz continued, "Oh, yes. My father was very fond of him. What did he say?"

"Well, we were speaking of the animal question, and I told him whales are good musicians. As you know, Menuhin is greatly concerned with world problems. He asked a most intriguing question. I have the transcript with me. I'll read it to you."

What is more worthwhile to save: the last twelve whales or a hundred thousand people somewhere? That is a very difficult problem. The answer isn't automatic by any means, because we are wasting people by the millions anyway. We are wasting them in famine, in cholera, in cancer, in routine, in mental madness. Are those human beings that are being wasted anyway and destroyed, are they worth twelve healthy whales? I don't know who is the Solomon to give us the answer.

Mrs. Horowitz replied, "Menuhin's question is good. I don't think I would hesitate but to save the whales. They are innocent. But I am not a Solomon."

Horowitz continued, "Do you think Solomon was a Solomon?"

"I doubt it, Mr. Horowitz. But only the old can be wise. That doesn't mean the old are always wise; in fact they are usually as stupid as they were when young."

Horowitz added, "And more foolish-looking and uglier than when young."

"Not always, Maestro. Toscanini, Casals, Miró, Picasso, Braque, Cocteau, and many other artists looked wonderful when old."

"Yes, that's because they still work well," Horowitz replied.

"Yes," I said, "that is the reason. Erik Erikson said you have to be old to be wise, and all societies have instinctively known this except our Western society. Today, there is no chance to find wisdom because the young have been lobotomized forever with the most horrid propaganda of all time, rock-and-roll. It soaks the brain and sucks out the life of a child. They may grow old, but they don't achieve wisdom. Their brains are burnt out, and their ears are deaf. And believe me, I'm not being too harsh.

"I've been reading a most provocative book by Alan Bloom, called *The Closing of the American Mind*. He has a chapter on rock music that is devastating. Bloom believes no classical music has any impact on the young, and that rock has risen from the ashes of classical music. He sees rock as a constant sexual stimulant, the beat of sexual intercourse. The only piece of classical music they seem to relate to is the incessant, orgiastic beat of Ravel's *Bolero*. And rock is one of the world's largest industries. Bloom says that if parents took rock away from their children, the children would leave them rather than give up rock."

Mr. Horowitz looked interested. "Did you see the ad for my new record in the *Times*? It's mixed in with all the rock-and-roll albums. I tell you, the piano recital is almost dead now. In fifty years, good music will only be a memory. Nobody will want it but a few old-fashioned collectors."

"Maestro, it is very disheartening."

Wanda said, "Speaking about *Bolero,* my father played it in Paris, and Ravel went backstage very angry to tell him that he conducted it much too fast. I don't think they ever talked again."

"Maybe your father made it too sexual," I said.

Horowitz replied, "That may be true. I knew Ravel, and he was not very interested in sex, I think."

"Do you know who Bloom considered the great heroic figure of the last fifteen years, the man who played the role that Napoleon did in the lives of ordinary young people in the nineteenth century?"

"Who?" Horowitz boomed out. "Not me, the young don't know who I am."

"No, Maestro, not you. It is Mick Jagger."

"Oh, God," Horowitz gulped. "Then it's worse than I thought. Even I know who he is."

"Bloom says he discovered that students who boasted of having no heroes secretly had a passion to be like Mick Jagger, to live his life, have his fame. He calls him a 'gutter phenomenon' and asks, 'Is this all we have left in our exhausted Western heritage?'"

Horowitz continued. "I tell you, when I was young, the popular music wasn't so dreadful." Horowitz went to the piano and began playing his dated repertoire of operetta and popular tunes, which, on occasion, he pulled out to show he was one of the good guys. Horowitz, the arch-elitist, like all monarchs, liked to show his democratic goodwill. His playing of these tunes, at least when I heard them, sounded tepid and trite. Wanda smiled graciously during her husband's little excursions outside the lofty regions of art. Horowitz smiled up at me, as if to say "See how well-rounded I am." Tonight, however, he was not really in the mood and soon went back to the sofa. "I am an anachronism, I tell you," he said.

"I hope not, Maestro. Can you imagine a world without Chopin and Liszt?"

For the rest of the evening, we spoke of the plight of the homeless and the tragedy of our cities.

I said, "The homeless will grow to half a million soon. If cities are civilization, then we are crumbling. It's all cold, furious, and without a shred of compassion on the streets. Maybe New York will die before classical music does."

"I will die before New York does," Horowitz said. "Tonight, we have been very pessimistic. I'm glad I never go out."

Wanda said sternly, "Before you go, I want you to sign a petition."

"About what?" I asked.

Mrs. Horowitz handed me a brochure and a petition. "Look at this picture. It's terrible. Look at those dogs, hanging up!"

"What is that?" I said.

"Don't you know?" she said. "Those crazy people in Korea eat dogs. They torture and kill them. They are served in restaurants. It's very common. They eat the dogs for health reasons, they say, and for men to be virile. Such superstition, such primitive things go on. There is a worldwide committee to stop these atrocities which take place all over Korea. These people will have the Olympics soon. They want to be part of the world community but they kill dogs by the millions."

"What a world!" Horowitz said. He sounded gloomy. "And the lion, jaguar, cheetah, and leopard will be extinct because of us. We are a bad species. Next time we will talk of music. That is never depressing."

34

PADEREWSKI: THE NOBLEST SPIRIT OF THEM ALL

In late autumn 1987, I had been seeing Horowitz for two years. Although this year had not been as eventful for the pianist as the preceding, he had been to Europe, giving recitals in Berlin, Hamburg, Amsterdam, and Vienna.

As I entered, the Maestro shook my hand from the sofa. "I can't get up," he said. "It's too comfortable. What is the book you bring?"

"Oh, just a few snippets that I read. It's a 1932 biography of Paderewski. And in it, there is a conversation with the author, Rom Landau."

"What's it called?"

"Ignace Paderewski: Musician and Statesman."

"No, I don't think I know it," Horowitz replied.

"Mr. Horowitz, you were born forty-three years after Paderewski. He was the most famous pianist in the world then, as you are now."

"Oh, yes, Paderewski was a golden name. I must tell you that not everybody thought he was a good pianist, though. But you know, he was also past his prime when I heard him. He had not the technique like a Rosenthal and others of his day. But he did things with little pieces that were beautiful.

"You know, he meant something to me. I had much pride in him. He was like a knight-errant on white horse. He was a hero figure. You see the inscribed photo on the wall? That is always with me. Paderewski gave me that photo. Look at him, an old lion there. I was only about sixteen when he became the first President of Poland. Imagine how all pianists felt. He had signed the Versailles Treaty in Poland's name."

"Maestro, he had the most glamorous career imaginable. He *was* the epitome of the Artist as Hero."

Horowitz continued, "He was a good statesman, too, I heard."

"Definitely. Woodrow Wilson, Clemenceau, and Lloyd George were deeply impressed with him. They thought he had high diplomatic abilities."

"He was the symbol of Poland," Horowitz said. "You know, I have Polish blood, too."

"Yes, you've told me that." I continued, "Paderewski was also a good composer."

"Very good. By the way, I think I told you, when I play for Scriabin when I was about eleven, I play, besides a few other things, the Paderewski *Melody*. But he did ambitious things, too."

"Oh, yes, he composed an opera, *Manru,* and a huge eighty-minute B minor Symphony. I've heard the recording. Not so wonderful, I'm afraid."

Horowitz asked, "When was it composed?"

"Around the turn of the century."

"Those big, long, dreary symphonies," Horowitz went on, "they are horrible. There is more music in one mazurka of Chopin than, I think, in all the Mahler symphonies."

"That's interesting you said that about the Chopin mazurka. George Sand said that there is more music in one Chopin prelude than in all of Meyerbeer's operas."

Horowitz cried, "She is right. I am right. Chopin choose her for good reasons."

"When did you first hear Paderewski?"

"I don't know. But I remember when I heard him in some Chopin mazurkas. Wonderful. Really! I must tell you, I spent, I think in '38, one whole day with him at his beautiful villa in Switzerland. I knew he liked me. Brailowsky had just been to see him, too."

"What was he like, Mr. Horowitz?"

"Very kind, very beautiful, wonderful-looking. Oh, I tell you the word, *noble*. I have a long lunch with him, then tea, then dinner. I spend all day. We talked of many things. Not politics, but music. He wasn't so sure about Debussy, who was still modern to him. I told him Rachmaninoff wasn't too sure of him, too."

"What else do you remember?" I asked.

"Not much. He was sad, you know. Europe was dying, and Poland would go down first."

I told Horowitz that the French tenor, Doda Conrad, once visited me at WNCN. He told me that he had been for a time Paderewski's secretary. In 1940 the former president of Poland was eighty, exhausted and ill. He was to make some records, with the proceeds going to the war effort, but Conrad, who was with him, said he could hardly move his body. He looked like a corpse. It was a hot summer day, and there was no air-conditioning then. By the conclusion of the session, news spread through the neighborhood that Paderewski had been recording, and a crowd gathered outside of his limousine. When Paderewski saw them, with great difficulty, he stood to his full height, brought his head high, and walked majestically, suddenly flushed with the color of life. The crowd was almost silent except for people in tears, crying, 'Long live Poland! Long live Paderewski!'"

Horowitz said, "Oh, yes. He had nobility of soul, that is what I felt from him, and you don't get that feeling often. But read to me. What did Paderewski say about me in the book you bring?"

"Here, Maestro, on page 283, in a chapter called, 'Conversations at Riond Bosson,' Landau says—"

"Yes. That was the name of his château," Horowitz interjected.

The author began:

"Mr. President, nobody seems to know your opinion about the younger generation of pianists. Have you ever heard Vladimir Horowitz?"

Without a second's hesitation, Paderewski replied: "I heard him a few years ago in Chicago. I must admit that I liked him very much; I like both his playing and his appearance and his general bearing." (I remembered how important Paderewski considered the latter point in a pianist.)

"What did you like best about him?"

"He was self-disciplined, and above all, he has rhythm and

tone. I only heard him play the D minor Concerto by Rachmaninoff, but it was very fine indeed. Of course, I cannot téll you how he tackles the great classical composers, what he does with Bach, Beethoven, Chopin or Schumann. If he does not get spoiled, and if he can keep up his present power, he ought to go very far."

Horowitz seemed very pleased. "I didn't know of this. I had heard he came to a concert of mine. He heard me probably in Chicago around 1930. It was Frederick Stock who conducted me there in Third Concerto. I was playing it everywhere. Mr. Dubal, what do you think?"

"About what, Maestro?"

"Do you think I get spoiled over the years?"

"Mr. Horowitz, I think you were born spoiled. But you somehow got through that defect."

"Go on with that book. What else did he say?"

The author asked Paderewski,

"Did his technique impress you?"

"I think it was good enough to carry him over any difficulties, and it was not obvious. Without any doubt, he is the most convincing among the younger pianists..."

Horowitz interrupted, "I wonder if I am now the most convincing of the very old pianists. Maybe Serkin and Arrau still convince the public, too."

I said, "Maestro, you are only a child compared to your old friend Horszowski, who is ninety-five."

Horowitz giggled. "I think he lies. I think he is really a hundred years old. I'll never make it so long. But go on about what Paderewski says."

"Well, he says he has also heard José Iturbi, 'who was very effective and whom I like, though much less than Horowitz.'"

"My God," Horowitz interrupted. "Iturbi had big career, too. He's dead also. Everyone is dead. Go on, what more does he say about pianists? I must write my memoirs, you will help me."

"Of course I will, Mr. Horowitz. Paderewski says here, 'I also very much appreciated the playing of the German, Gieseking, in whom there is taste, musical refinement, and a subtlety which is quite un-German...'"

Ferruccio Busoni around 1910. Horowitz used Busoni's cadenza in a 1987 recording of Mozart's Concerto No, 23, K.488.

Horowitz recorded more of Chopin's music than that of any other composer. This daguerreotype shows the dying Chopin in London in 1848 after he left Paris.

Horowitz gave the American premiere of Prokofiev's Sonatas 6, 7, and 8. An ink portrait of the composer by David Dubal.

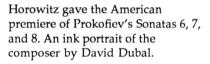

Publicity photographs of the debonair Horowitz from the 1940s. (Photos courtesy RCA Records)

Wanda and Vladimir in their living room. On the wall is Picasso's 1923 *Acrobate au Repos*. (Photo courtesy RCA Records)

Horowitz with the composer Samuel Barber around 1950. (Photo by Bender)

The program for Horowitz's historic comeback recital.

The twenty-fifth anniversary program of Horowitz's debut.

JANUARY 12, 1953

THE
PHILHARMONIC-SYMPHONY SOCIETY
OF NEW YORK

Gala Pension Fund Concert
at Carnegie Hall

VLADIMIR HOROWITZ

Celebrating the Silver Jubilee
of his American Debut with the
New York Philharmonic
in the
Tchaikovsky Piano Concerto in B-flat minor

JANUARY 12, 1928

Sunday Afternoon, May 9, 1965, at 3:30 o'clock

THE CARNEGIE HALL CORPORATION

presents

Vladimir Horowitz

Pianist

Bach-Busoni Organ Toccata in C major
Prelude
Intermezzo: Adagio
Fugue

Schumann Fantasy in C major, Op. 17
Fantastic and with passion
Moderato, energetic throughout
Lento sostenuto sempre dolce

"Through all the tones that vibrate about Earth's mingled dream, one whispered tone is sounding for ears attent to hear."
FRIEDRICH SCHLEGEL

INTERMISSION

Scriabin Sonata No. 9 in One Movement, Op. 68
Poem in F sharp major, Op. 32

Chopin Mazurka in C sharp minor, Op. 30, No. 4
Etude in F major, Op. 10
Ballade in G minor, Op. 23, No. 1

*In memory of the composer on the 50th anniversary of his death, April 27th, 1915.

COLUMBIA RECORDS   STEINWAY PIANO   RCA VICTOR RECORDS

Net Proceeds for the Program Fund of The Carnegie Hall Corporation

The line for tickets for Horowitz's famous return to the concert stage after a twelve-year retirement, on May 9, 1965. (Photo courtesy Steinway and Sons)

The author with Arthur Rubinstein in 1976, two days after Rubinstein's last Carnegie Hall recital. (Photo courtesy RCA Records)

Horowitz at the White House with President Jimmy Carter. (Photo courtesy Steinway and Sons)

In 1986 with Mrs. Horowitz and Richard Probst, then Steinway's Director of Concerts and Artists. Horowitz receives an award for his six decades as a Steinway artist. (Photo courtesy Steinway and Sons)

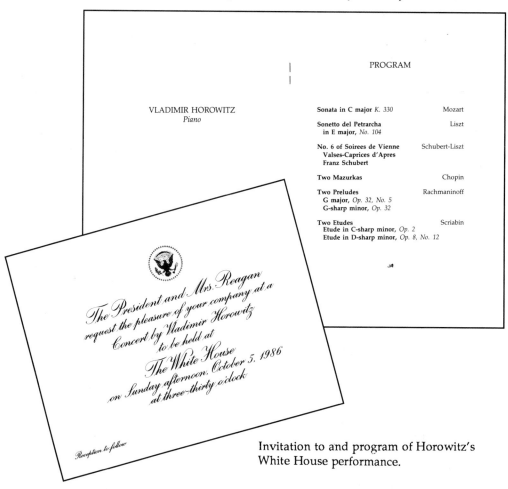

PROGRAM

VLADIMIR HOROWITZ
Piano

Sonata in C major *K. 330*	Mozart
Sonetto del Petrarcha in E major, *No. 104*	Liszt
No. 6 of Soirees de Vienne Valses-Caprices d'Apres Franz Schubert	Schubert-Liszt
Two Mazurkas	Chopin
Two Preludes G major, *Op. 32, No. 5* G-sharp minor, *Op. 32*	Rachmaninoff
Two Etudes Etude in C-sharp minor, *Op. 2* Etude in D-sharp minor, *Op. 8, No. 12*	Scriabin

The President and Mrs. Reagan request the pleasure of your company at a Concert by Vladimir Horowitz to be held at The White House on Sunday afternoon, October 5, 1986 at three-thirty o'clock

Reception to follow

Invitation to and program of Horowitz's White House performance.

Horowitz with the author at a Deutsche Grammophon press conference on September 30, 1985. It was the first time the two had seen each other in five years. (Photo courtesy Shawn Randall)

Horowitz with his recording producer, Thomas Frost. (Photo courtesy Shawn Randall)

METROPOLITAN OPERA

Sunday Afternoon, December 14, 1986, at 4:00

The Metropolitan Opera
presents

Vladimir Horowitz
Piano

SCARLATTI	Two Sonatas Sonata in E major, Longo 23 Sonata in E major, Longo 224
MOZART	Adagio in B minor, K.540
MOZART	Rondo in D major, K.485
MOZART	Piano Sonata in C major, K.330 Allegro moderato Andante cantabile Allegretto
RACHMANINOFF	Two Preludes Prelude in G major, Op. 32 Prelude in G-sharp minor, Op. 32
SCRIABIN	Etude in D-sharp minor, Op. 8, No. 12
	Intermission
SCHUMANN	Arabesque Op. 18
LISZT	Consolation in D-flat major, No. 3 Valse Oubliée No. 1
SCHUBERT-LISZT	No. 6 of Soirées de Vienne, Valses-Caprices d'Après Franz Schubert
CHOPIN	Mazurka in B minor, Op. 33, No. 4
CHOPIN	Scherzo in B minor, Op. 20, No. 1

The last recital Horowitz gave at the Metropolitan Opera House in Lincoln Center.

Wanda Toscanini Horowitz
Vladimir Horowitz

A 1987 photo of Mr. and Mrs. Horowitz at home. Mrs. Horowitz wrote: "To David, 'molto simpatico,' Wanda Toscanini Horowitz," to which Mr. Horowitz added: "I am of the same opinion. Vl. Horowitz." (Photo courtesy Christian Steiner)

1933   1988

Mr and Mrs. Vladimir Horowitz

request the pleasure of your company

at a dinner buffet

to celebrate the occasion of their

Fifty-fifth Wedding Anniversary

on Wednesday, the twenty-first of December

at half after eight o'clock

Fourteen East 94th Street

R.S.V.P.   Black tie

The invitation to the pianist's fifty-fifth wedding anniversary party.

Photos courtesy Shawn Randall

Among the last photographs taken of Horowitz by the pianist Mordecai Shehori. (Photos courtesy Mordecai Shehori)

The author standing in front of the Toscanini crypt at the famous Cimitero Monumentale in Milan. Since the photo was taken in 1990, there was no mention of Horowitz being interred there.

Horowitz said, "He is right. I must tell you when I was a young man, Gieseking's playing bowled me over. I had never heard such pianissimos, like a dream. But later, I got bored because he treated all music the same. He was big artist, sure. But as a person, I wanted nothing to do with him."

"Didn't you protest his coming back to the United States to play after the war?"

"Absolutely, and I'm not sorry I do that. Rubinstein and me and others didn't want him on the stages. He stayed in Germany. He was supporter of the Nazi."

"Did you know, Maestro, that when Paderewski died, he was given the funeral of a hero? In 1941, at Saint Patrick's Cathedral. And did you know that, by order of Franklin Roosevelt, Paderewski is buried at Arlington National Cemetery?"

He said, "I didn't know such a thing."

"Yes, Paderewski was more than a pianist."

"Thank you for reading those pages."

"I loved doing it."

"How do you get home?"

"A taxi, Maestro." Horowitz often asked how I was to get home, as if this in itself was a monumental burden.

35

BRAHMS: THE LITTLE B

It had been blustery cold, and damp. The usual New York February. Tonight Horowitz looked dejected. "What's wrong?"

"The weather is getting me down. Too much rain. Only two good days all month." The eighty-five-year-old pianist was ever-watchful of the weather. His body reacted to every climatic change, and he could predict what the weather would be.

"I am a weatherman. The best one, better than on TV," he stated proudly. He could hear the merest hint of thunder in the distance and was seldom wrong if it was about to rain. Most importantly, his daily and therapeutic walks depended upon the weather.

Wanda said, "My father felt nature is man's worst enemy. But I'm not concerned with the weather, whatever it is. What can you do?"

"But Wanda," Horowitz replied, "that's because you were raised in Italy. If you grow up in Russia, the weather is of big concern, always. Read Tchaikovsky letters. That's what he talks about most. The Russian yearns for spring. He begs for spring. He dreams of it. By April, in Russia, you are mentally ill from the hardship of winter. It is a long nightmare, and then there is the mud. Russia is not easy. New York is good."

Horowitz continued, "I hear on the Philharmonic broadcasts, Vladimir Feltsman playing the Brahms B-flat Concerto with Mehta conducting."

Feltsman, a Soviet Jewish pianist in his thirties, was virtually stopped from pursuing his career in Russia. He had recently come to

201

the United States in a wave of publicity, and made his Carnegie Hall debut in November 1987.

Mrs. Horowitz was upset by his instant celebrity. "Only in America," she said. "Who is he? All they have to do is walk off the plane and they are given a career, a house, a teaching position, a Carnegie Hall debut, a White House appearance. And you know, Mrs. Reagan was coming to the Carnegie Hall debut, but the rain stopped her."

"Nobody even knew if he plays well," Horowitz joined in.

Mrs. Horowitz said, "What is worse is nobody cares if he's good, but he's already on Mike Wallace. It's incredible."

"Well, the American publicity machine eats up any Russian defector," I said. "To the average American, if they are Russian, they have to be good."

"They wanted us to help this Feltsman when we were in Russia," Mrs. Horowitz said.

"He even wants to come to visit me. I don't want to see him."

"When did this Russian mystique start?" I asked Horowitz.

"Well, believe me, I had some of this mystique, but in the twenties, the world was full of pianists who were great. But Russians were big from Diaghilev's time. Russians have always been something a little exotic to the Americans."

"Oh, yes," I said. "I think it started as early as Anton Rubinstein's coming to America in 1872. Steinway brought him here, and he was the great Russian pianist, as Hans von Bülow was the great German. Rubinstein looked like Beethoven, and he looked mystical. He took America by storm. He played 215 concerts in 239 days."

"God help me," Horowitz shook his head. "He must have been iron. I would never give more than two concerts a week, and that was when I was young. My manager would say, 'I booked you in Columbus, Dayton, and Cincinnati in one week.' I tell him, 'Take Dayton out or I won't play well in Cincinnati.' How can you do well under such strain?"

"You know," I said, "Anton Rubinstein played the entire existing repertoire of his time, but he did not play Brahms. He didn't like him."

Horowitz's dim eyes looked brighter. "Do you know, Mr. Dubal, that I don't like Brahms anymore either? I cannot warm up to him. I have not played him for forty years. He is long-winded."

"Well, Maestro, that's almost a sacrilege. Brahms is one of the three Bs."

"He may be one of the three Bs, but, Mr. Dubal, he is a very little B compared to Bach or Beethoven."

"Yes, I think Brahms is a great master, but you are right. He is not of the magnitude of Bach or Beethoven."

Wanda also agreed with Horowitz. "But Father admired Brahms. He conducted the symphonies like a demon."

"That's for sure. His recordings are wonderful. And Maestro, you played both Brahms concertos."

"I know. But I don't like them," Horowitz said. "I recorded the No. 2 with father-in-law."

"Brahms is many things," I continued. "But felicitous for the pianist, he is not. You know, Brahms was embarrassed by being called the third B. It was Hans von Bülow who invented that epithet, 'the three Bs.' When he conducted the Brahms First Symphony, he called it Beethoven's Tenth."

Horowitz smirked. "But we had enough with nine symphonies of Beethoven."

I said, "You didn't mention how you liked Feltsman's playing of the Brahms B-flat Concerto."

"Not so good," Horowitz declared. "Did you hear it?"

"Yes, I was at the actual performance, and I must say, I was more impressed with Feltsman in the concerto than at his Carnegie Hall recital. I thought the first two movements especially were marvelous. Do you know what Brahms said of his gigantic Second Concerto?"

"What?" Horowitz replied gruffly. He wasn't pleased that I disagreed with him on Feltsman's performance.

"Well, Maestro, Brahms called it 'a tiny tiny pianoforte concerto with a tiny tiny wisp of a scherzo.' Wouldn't you say the Brahms Second Concerto was one of the most difficult of all concertos?"

Horowitz answered, "The Brahms Second is not difficult at all."

Horowitz, when in a contrary mood, was not going to give Brahms or his Second Concerto their due, let alone Feltsman. I decided it was wise to stop discussing Brahms.

Suddenly, Horowitz went to the piano, alighting on it with a tremendous crashing and exaggerated sonority, playing the opening of the Brahms F minor Sonata, screaming, "Terrible music! *uh—uh*—terrible. I heard the other day on television the Brahms B Major

Trio played with a terrible pianist. It's terrible music, terrible playing, horrible. And violinist was bad, and cellist, too. And the music and the tempi, everything terrible."

"I see, Mr. Horowitz, that the Hamburg master is not your cup of tea. Next week when I come over, I'll read to you a wonderful essay on Mozart that the critic Paul Rosenfeld wrote in the 1930s."

"Good! It's better to talk Mozart. He was an angel come to earth."

36

HOROWITZ AND I DINE ALONE

Wanda was visiting her sister in Italy, and the Maestro was not down yet from his bedroom. As I waited for him, I fixed myself a drink.

"How do you like this jacket?" the Maestro exclaimed as he entered the living room. "I never wore it before. I got it in London." He reported this information as if something bought in London was automatically better.

I replied, "Mr. Horowitz, it's a marvelous piece of cloth and it looks perfect on you. And I like your bow tie, too."

"You look chic tonight, also."

"And I see you are losing some more weight," I said.

Horowitz was always aware of his weight and his appearance in general. It was a matter of pride to him as well as a form of personal dignity.

"I know. I've lost three pounds. I feel pretty good lately. Giuliana and I took a ten-block walk today."

The maid came to the large double doors to say that the chauffeur was outside. "Okay," Horowitz said. "We will be soon. I hope you are hungry tonight."

"I certainly am, Mr. Horowitz." I proceeded down the curved stairway ahead of him and went to the closet, which always smelled of cloth and furs. Horowitz wore his favorite hat, a fine black one which made him look ten years younger.

He walked cautiously but securely from the house. At times when he walked, he looked wobbly, and it seemed he might topple over. However, he was steadier on his feet than he looked.

We made our way downtown via Park Avenue and then toward Piccolo Mondo, the restaurant on Sixty-third and First, where the Horowitzes were regulars.

During the ride, Horowitz told me he had heard his recording of the Schumann F minor Sonata on the radio at three in the morning.

"How did you like your Schumann?" I asked.

"It is awful!" Horowitz burst forth. "It is so affected. Why didn't somebody stop me?"

Horowitz often disliked his own records after not hearing them for a period of time. An accent or rubato from a year ago could be intolerable in the present.

Horowitz said, "My playing is so neurotic. Schumann was crazy, but I ruined him."

"Ah, Mr. Horowitz, you are going too far. I like your recording. But you are the creator of that record, and you have every right to dislike it. You may think it's too neurotic, but I don't. It is music of great yearning and emotional stress. And I'm glad you recorded it because it is unduly neglected. But you said an interesting thing a minute ago."

"What did I say?"

"You said, 'Why didn't somebody tell you it was too affected?' This reminds me of an idea that Whistler once had."

"Who was Whistler?" Horowitz asked.

"James Whistler is a late nineteenth-century American painter whose most famous work is a portrait of his mother. It's so well known that the world refers to it as *Whistler's Mother*, instead of its actual title, which is *Arrangement in Black and Gray.*"

"Oh, I know him. I almost bought a Whistler once on Madison Avenue. What did he say?"

"That it takes *two* to paint a picture: the artist and another person, who stands next to the painter with a revolver, ready to blow out his brains if the painter begins to *overwork* the painting."

"Ah," Horowitz replied. "That is very good. And that is what I mean. Somebody should stop a pianist from the excess. That's a good lesson."

After considerable traffic, we arrived. As we walked toward the restaurant door, two ladies passed us and turned around with "Isn't he famous?" Whereupon the great pianist looked at them, eyes wide open, and stuck out his tongue.

"Stupid people," he exclaimed as he reached for his comb before entering the restaurant. He gave me his hat to hold and ran the comb through his hair several times.

As always, Horowitz was greeted with quiet flourishes, then Carlos took us to a waiting table. Since it was Saturday evening, the restaurant was more crowded than usual, and the clientele less elegant-looking.

Horowitz glanced around. "Who are these people? The place is full. Why don't the men wear ties?"

Just then, Carlos trotted up to our table. "Maestro," he said brightly, "tonight, we have your favorite carrot soup."

"Carlos," I interrupted, winking at him, "will you throw all these men out? They are not wearing ties. What disrespect to your establishment!"

With a wicked gleam in his eye, Carlos asked, "Maestro, should I throw them out, as Mr. Dubal suggests?"

"I think Mr. Dubal is right. But let them stay. You need the business."

"I'll bring you the soup, Maestro. Mr. Dubal, should I bring you a salad?"

Horowitz asked, "Who are these people, where are they from?"

"Well, let me speculate. This being Saturday night, Manhattan is jammed with people coming in from New Jersey, Westchester, everywhere. Everyone wants to be in the Big Apple on Saturday night. Now this group, judging from the women's hairstyles, the bleached hair, and clothes, comes from Queens. They're in from over the bridge, Italian middle-class, about thirty-five to fifty. The men are very proud not to wear ties. Notice the gold chains around their necks."

"But this is a fairly expensive restaurant," Horowitz said.

"Yes, this is their big night out and they want to eat good Italian food. Italians love Italian food all the time. Just like Mrs. Horowitz. And this is northern Italian, a step up from their southern heritage. You see, this restaurant has a certain status for them, like their gold chains."

"How do you know this?"

"Naturally," I replied, "I'm guessing and generalizing. But living in Manhattan long enough, one can tell a lot from the look of different people or groups. You learn by looking, listening, being in buses, subways, and taxis. Remember, you stay in one place in Manhattan, but I'm all over the city. And each area is different."

Horowitz interrupted, "You ask Carlos if you are right about these people."

I signaled Carlos to our table and described his clients to him. Carlos said, "Mr. Dubal is absolutely right. These people are regulars, almost every Saturday night. The same crowd of Italians from Queens."

With Carlos's seal of approval, Horowitz gave me a look of amazed respect.

"By the way, Maestro, tonight, you are not the only famous person here."

"Who else?" he asked.

"Do you see the man at that table?"

At that very moment, the man came toward us. "Maestro, I am honored to be in the same restaurant as you."

Horowitz didn't have a clue who this person was, and looked totally uninterested as Howard Cosell, who was somewhat high, started talking to me.

It was all rather awkward, and when Howard returned to his table, Horowitz asked, "Who is that man? You seem to know him."

"No, I never met him, Mr. Horowitz. But he is the most famous sportscaster in America."

With a wave of the arm, Horowitz dismissed him. "Who cares?"

Horowitz ate his soup with his napkin tucked in at his neck, as he did wherever he went. In this habit, I imitated him whenever I dined with him. Horowitz was an impeccable eater, and his manners were perfect.

Because of his delicate stomach, he was meticulous about what he ate. For instance, he had not eaten a salad for decades; he said it would kill him. He was usually careful not to overeat, because he wanted to leave room enough for a little dessert. Dessert was like a reward to him. If a restaurant didn't have good desserts, he would occasionally bring a couple of cookies, carefully wrapped, to eat with his chamomile tea. These he himself picked out at a bakery during his afternoon walk.

Just as Horowitz contemplated his first bite of gray sole, Howard Cosell got up to leave. Once again, he walked to our table, and with overbearing flair, began genuflecting in front of him.

"Maestro, you are the legend of legends," he bellowed. "I heard you in Carnegie Hall last year. It was a revelation."

Horowitz just stared at him, a little dazed and not quite understanding what the sportscaster was saying. I was embarrassed when Horowitz failed to respond, so I said, "Howard, you are one of the most famous persons in America."

"Yes, I know," he sputtered. "But I am nothing compared to Horowitz."

The opening was too wide to resist, and I said, "Howard, that is true."

At that, the sports commentator disappeared, and we continued our meal.

After the last bite of dessert, Carlos came to the table and presented Mr. Horowitz with a Sunday *New York Times*, which he had gone out to buy for him.

When the check came, Mr. Horowitz took his green American Express card from his wallet to pay the bill. The great pianist obviously had no need for the extra status of the gold or platinum card. He carefully wrote in the amount.

"Tonight, it's less without Wanda," he noted, and showing me the slip, he asked, "Is this a correct tip?"

"Exactly enough."

It was nearly eleven when we left. In the car, Horowitz said, "I'm a little tired. The driver will take me home and then he will take you home. I will read the *Times* and listen to *Eugene Onegin* on the radio later. I love that opera."

Horowitz had the ability to look forward to events, big or small, whether it was hearing an opera on the radio or giving his next Carnegie Hall recital.

As I took him to the door, he said, "We had good time. Wanda will be home soon, and we all go together next week. Giuliana will call you Monday to see when we meet again."

37

SCALING THE IVORY TOWER

Horowitz was all too isolated from the pianistic world. Living in an ivory tower over the years, "the Emperor of Pianists" seemed more and more alone.

He would say, "Pianists in this city don't even know I live here." And I would assure him that every serious pianist not only appeared at his concerts, but also knew that he lived in isolated splendor on East Ninety-fourth Street. But he seemed unapproachable.

It had been years since the Maestro had taught a few pianists on a regular basis. I was convinced that he would greatly benefit from contact with younger pianists as well as from hearing a few of my Juilliard students.

Such a project seemed simple enough. I knew dozens of important pianists, and in my Juilliard classes I was blessed with some of the world's finest pianistic talents. I had even told Horowitz that several students reported to me how they waited outside on Ninety-fourth Street for the slim chance of hearing him practice.

Such an observation would automatically frighten Mrs. Horowitz. The slightest scent of exploitation made her Toscanini nostrils flare. The chance that the Horowitz name would be "used" was a real fear of hers. On occasion, both her father and husband had indeed been exploited for the glamour of their names. In the past, for example,

Horowitz had discovered that several pianists who had played for him just once advertised themselves as Horowitz pupils.

Horowitz said to me, "Liszt always told everyone, 'I am not a professor of the piano.' But he loved to give master classes, and the pupils followed him everywhere he went. When he packed up for Rome, they follow him. When he went to Budapest, they follow him. And every summer they come from all over the world to Weimar to study with him.

"He was too generous. He heard anybody who came and they wasted his time. Liszt had a heart, better than anyone else's. But as soon as someone plays for Liszt, they go home and they print up the card. And it says, 'So-and-so, a pupil of Liszt,' and they make the money teaching on his name. Everybody was pupil of Liszt.

"One day, his real pupil, Hans von Bülow, who you know, married Liszt's daughter before she married Wagner. He saw what was happening and tried to put a stop to all the good-for-nothings. He made sure only the worthy ones could play for the master."

I said, "Liszt had a motto, 'Génie oblige.' And I think this was one of his ways of giving to the world."

Wanda said, "My father did not like Liszt, you know."

"Why?" I asked.

Horowitz explained, "He couldn't believe that a man was so good, so helpful, and asked so little in return. Toscanini called it a pose. 'Well,' I said to Toscanini, 'if it was a pose, it was a good one.'" And here, Horowitz burst out laughing hysterically.

I said, "If I may be so bold, I don't think it was a pose. Your father may have been a little suspicious about good deeds."

Wanda agreed. "He was a lot suspicious. And if we let some people come play for Volodya, we also would have to have a von Bülow to clean them out."

"Well," I said, "I think that everyone could be screened. Wouldn't it be fun for the Maestro to talk to some of his young colleagues? They would be so honored and thrilled."

"Honored? Thrilled? What do they know?" Wanda said.

Horowitz did not respond. He was thinking it over, and as was usual with him, the process was slow. The thought was churning in his mind, and, perhaps, he would open his home once again to some pianists in the future.

He said, "I'm no teacher, but maybe I can give a few tips, some hints. We will see."

Horowitz never failed to read the Sunday *Times,* paying particular attention to the Arts and Leisure section. "How can such a word *leisure* be used in connection with the arts?" he wanted to know.

Once, as he was reading aloud with his ever-present magnifying glass, he said, "I don't see my name in the *Times,* but I see *your* name. You are giving some classes called 'The World of the Piano.' Maybe I show up. What do you think?"

"Maestro, that would be fantastic," I replied.

"Did you see the article about Alexander Toradze? Do you know him?"

Toradze had defected from Russia and was enjoying a big career in the United States. I had interviewed him at WNCN, and we struck up a friendship.

"Oh, yes. His nickname is Lexo. His friends call him that."

"Do you think he plays chess?" Horowitz inquired.

"I don't know. But if he does, would you like him to play with you?"

"Maybe," Horowitz replied.

Several weeks later, I happened to see Lexo and casually dropped into our conversation, "Do you play chess?" His answer was yes, but I managed not to tell him why I asked.

The next time I saw Horowitz, I said, "Oh, by the way, Maestro, I asked Toradze if he played chess, and *he does!*"

Horowitz looked at me quizzically, saying, "Who is that?"

"*You know,* Maestro, the pianist you read about in the *Times.*"

"I don't know," he said abruptly.

He knew perfectly well whom I meant. "Would you like me to bring him over to play a game or two?"

"*No,* I don't play chess much anymore."

Toradze, who admired Horowitz, would have been good company for the Maestro. They could have spoken Russian together.

It was nearly spring. My goal was to have some students play for him by the summer, which was a dangerous time for Horowitz because he had little stimulation during those months.

But before I accomplished my purpose, I wanted Horowitz himself to choose someone to see, a pianist who was still young but who had an established career.

The pianist had to be male, as Horowitz had no interest whatever in woman pianists. He had many prejudices. More than once he said, "Women are not interested in careers. I think like Leschetizky. He said he wanted no more female pupils. 'They aren't serious. I kill myself teaching them. They get married and have children, and they give up music.' I agree with him." Horowitz continued, "What do they give to art? More babies!"

Horowitz also had an aversion to physically unattractive people, especially those who were fat. However, he took pains to explain that he didn't mean that people should only be handsome, but that they should be clean and "normal" looking. He was appalled by how slovenly people looked and dressed.

Earlier in the week, Wanda had gone to Tiffany's, where she examined a clock that Mr. Horowitz had liked. She returned exhausted and depressed because of the way people looked and acted. "How things have changed!" she exclaimed. "I can't believe the clothes people slap on themselves!"

"This is not the age of elegance," I replied.

"No, the age of brutality," she concluded.

Horowitz chimed in, "I am looking for some character in faces. Liszt's face had character, not only handsomeness. Paderewski had not only beauty, but nobility."

"Look at Rachmaninoff," Wanda continued. "Maybe he was no beauty, but there was much in his face, suffering, too."

Horowitz said, "Busoni was beautiful. Where are the faces today that have something spiritual in them? I think Arthur Rubinstein was rather ugly, but there was something in his face. Yes, there was," Horowitz agreed with himself.

"Absolutely, there was. And your father," I remarked, looking at Wanda, "had a face of passionate intensity."

"Maestro, you really think that a person who does not possess a spiritual look can't play the piano artistically?"

"Maybe they can play," he said. "But there is something missing. That I am sure of. I even know when I hear a record."

"What about violinists?" I asked.

Wanda replied, "Well, I must tell you, Heifetz was not much in the head, but he wasn't ugly. And Menuhin is not and Kreisler was not."

"What about yourself, Maestro?"

"I'm ugly now, but I hope something good still shows in my face. But you know, when I was younger, I was fairly good-looking. Oh, yes. Maybe the nose a little big, but *not bad*. Some people say I looked like Chopin. I was very slender."

"Maestro, you look wonderful now. You know, Chopin said, 'I have only two faults, a big nose and a weak fourth finger.'"

Horowitz roared. "Yes, but Chopin looked spiritual."

"Oh, yes. And in the Delacroix painting, he looks absolutely Byronic."

"These days," Horowitz continued, "I am content if the person looks *normal*."

38

MURRAY PERAHIA
PLAYS FOR HOROWITZ

At the Horowitzes' I was now hearing about a budding new friendship. None other than Murray Perahia was pursuing Horowitz and playing for the Maestro when he was in New York.

I was delighted. Perahia had a major career as a pianist and did not need Horowitz's name to promote himself. In his case, the exploitation issue was closed.

Perahia, who lives in London, called Horowitz every Sunday. A bond quickly developed between the two musicians.

"What did Perahia play for you, Maestro?"

"Beethoven's *Les Adieux* Sonata. Not bad! You know, he came to play for me twenty years ago, but he didn't want to listen to a thing I said. He was frightened to change anything."

Mrs. Horowitz gave a nod. There was no doubt she approved of Perahia. "He's a nice man, a good person. And so is his wife. He wants to learn from Volodya."

"That's quite a tribute to Perahia," I said.

"I know it is," Horowitz replied. "He's not a young boy. I think he is almost forty." Horowitz checked in my book *Reflections From the Keyboard* for the exact year. "Born 1947. Yes, so he is over forty now."

217

"What did you think of his playing, Mrs. Horowitz?"

"He plays wonderfully, of course, but he is somehow inhibited. And I think he knows it."

"Well, I will fix that," Horowitz said.

I added, "Yes, I'm impressed with him. After all these years, he wants to listen to what you have to offer him. That surely says a lot about him and his desire to grow. I think he finds the 'big' element missing from his playing. He probably wants to break out of his rather intimate style and project the grand manner as well. He plays in big halls and he needs more punch and drama."

"And he needs more color," Horowitz said. "I have to extend his repertoire. I think he should study more Liszt. I'll tell him to do Twelfth Rhapsody and the *Spanish Rhapsody*. That's a good piece. Yes, he must do the *Spanish Rhapsody*."

"Maestro, that's a fine idea. And what a splendid and neglected work the *Spanish Rhapsody* is."

"It's a big piece. It needs much projection," Horowitz continued. "Yes, Perahia could do worse than playing *Spanish Rhapsody*. Barère played it very good. You know, Busoni made good arrangement of it for piano and orchestra. Oh, he knew the piano. Busoni made it easier, a good job!"

"Oh, yes," I replied. "Do you know what pianist gave the first performance of Busoni's version of the *Spanish Rhapsody?*"

"Who? Not Busoni?"

"No, it was Béla Bartók, who was a marvelous pianist. Did you know that Bartók came in second to Wilhelm Backhaus at the Anton Rubinstein Competition in the early 1900s?"

It is little known that Bartók, the greatest twentieth-century Hungarian composer, was a virtuoso pianist of the first order.

Horowitz loved historic tidbits. "I heard that Bartók was supposed to be good pianist," he said.

"Oh, absolutely, very original conceptions. I've heard all of his recordings. You wouldn't believe some of it. He played with an amazing freedom, and his tone was beautiful. So different from the ugly percussive style that so many others use to play Bartók. His Brahms Capricccio in B minor is especially arresting. There has never been such a Brahms capriccio. Believe me, Maestro."

Horowitz asked, "Did he have a big technique? Who did he study with?"

"Oh, yes, a dazzling technique. His Scarlatti is very fleet and virtuosic. He had a large repertoire. In fact, he gave a series of historical recitals of the piano literature in Budapest in the late thirties. His teacher was István Thomán, an important Liszt student. One of Bartók's specialties was Liszt's *Totentanz.*"

Mrs. Horowitz said, "He died here around 1945."

"Yes, that's the exact year. He was very poor and ill. There is a plaque on the building on Fifty-seventh Street where he lived."

I continued, "It's very interesting. Bartók never gave composition lessons. He concentrated all of his teaching on *the piano.* And, by the way, he made some interesting editions of the Mozart sonatas and the Bach *Well-Tempered Clavier.*"

Horowitz said, "You know everything. That's why I need you here. Who studied with Bartók?"

"Oh, many pianists. Lili Kraus was one, and György Sándor, whom you know, studied with him for several years. Sándor worked on all Bartók's major works with him."

Mrs. Horowitz said, "Oh, yes. Wasn't Sándor at Michigan University?"

"Yes, but now he's teaching at Juilliard. He gave the world premiere of the Bartók Third Concerto with Ormandy in 1946. You know, Sándor is a great admirer of yours."

Horowitz said, "Is he in your book?"

"Yes, and he talks about Bartók in the interview."

At this point, Horowitz picked up my *Reflections From the Keyboard*, which was always near him on the table, as well as Ernest Hutcheson's *The Literature of the Piano* and books on Mozart. He took his big magnifying glass, and, after I pointed out the place to him, he began reading. "Oh, yes, you say:

DUBAL: Was Bartók a great technician?

SÁNDOR: He was technically a virtuoso on the level of Prokofiev, Dohnányi, Rachmaninoff, and Busoni. And as an interpreter, there are no words to describe the fusion of his world with that of the composers he played. Sequences of notes were turned into richly expressive melodies, harmonies and chords were bursting with tension or brought soothing relief. His rhythms danced with grace or angularity. His Scarlatti, Bach, Mozart, Beethoven, and Debussy were highly personalized and filled with the spirit and pulsating life of the creative instinct. . . .

"That's a good description. Maybe you bring sometime his recordings and I listen. I'm sorry, but I never much liked Bartók's piano music. But the third Concerto has good things."

"Oh, definitely," I replied. "A fine concerto and, sadly, the last piano concerto to enter the international repertoire. I recently heard Andras Schiff play it very well."

"Schiff is a good pianist." Horowitz responded. "And I like the way he looks. He looks *normal*. I heard him play the Mozart F Major Concerto in London. Very good, a little slow maybe. He didn't know I was there. Nobody knew. I was concealed."

"What a shame," I said. "He would be proud to know you were there."

Hungarian-born Andras Schiff has a major international career. His playing reveals an exceptional lyric talent with a technique of unusual flexibility.

"Maybe this Schiff doesn't like my playing. I don't think he would like my Mozart. Maybe you bring him to see me sometime."

Mrs. Horowitz scowled. "I don't know why Volodya wants to see him."

"Well," I said, "it would be a thrill for Andras, I'm sure."

Horowitz responded, "Who knows!"

Now that Perahia had entered Horowitz's life, perhaps the event had created a desire to see other younger colleagues as well. But Horowitz could not be rushed. Everything that happened in his life had a long gestation.

39

THE COMPOSER COMES
FIRST

Tonight a March wind was howling but the Maestro was in a particularly fine mood. The pains he had recently experienced in his legs had subsided, and he practiced his new Mozart sonata for a good two hours. "Do you want to hear it?" he asked.

"Of course I do, Mr. Horowitz. I think recording the B-flat Sonata, K. 281, is a great idea, since nobody knows it."

The improvement since the last time I heard him play it was astonishing. The gallantry, the agreeable smoothness, the rococo fluff of this Viennese cream puff sounded delectable in Horowitz's hands.

Horowitz said, "I heard a record of this by Gilels. Awful, just awful. Too slow. Listen, this is the tempo he plays at. Mr. Dubal, you see this marking in the slow movement? It is andante amoroso, the only marking like this in all of Mozart. *This is Mozart in love*," he shouted. "How old was Mozart when he composed this sonata?"

"Around nineteen."

"Nineteen? And he was in love, believe me! Listen to this. It's like an opera scene." As he played, Horowitz looked up at me with a disarming smile of tender sweetness. After he concluded the sonata, he said softly, "Not bad. It's going to be good."

As he dropped onto the couch, he reported, "Today, I heard Schiff on the radio. Maybe it was your station. It was the Mozart Sonata in A minor. The slow movement was too slow, but nice sound. If he comes to New York, maybe I will see him."

Horowitz picked up my book and scrutinized Schiff's photograph. "A nice face. Maybe a little pretty, like his playing. But tell me, is he neurotic? You and me, we are neurotic. In fact, I am *normal* compared to you. Oh, yes I am."

Saying this to me amused Horowitz. He liked using this phrase. Whenever he did, I would glance incredulously at Wanda, who would shake her head, saying, "Sure!"

"Well, Mr. Horowitz, Schiff is not nearly as neurotic as we are. I think he is probably very settled. He seems quite balanced to me."

"Is he married?"

"I believe he just recently married a Japanese violinist."

"Oh, that's bad. Now he will be forced to accompany her."

"That I don't know, Maestro. But I do know Schiff is going to be in New York very soon. And I can call him or his publicity person and say that you would like to meet him."

"*No, no,*" Horowitz and Wanda cried abruptly in unison.

"You must ask him if he would like to meet *me*. Don't say I would like to meet him."

Mrs. Horowitz ardently agreed.

I replied, "Of course I would do it that way."

"But you know," Horowitz went on, "I don't know if he likes my playing. I don't think I'm his type."

I had a feeling I knew what he was getting at, but I waited.

Sure enough, the cagey old master turned to the Schiff interview in my book and said, "Do you know what he says? You were there when he said it. You interviewed him."

Naturally, I knew every word in my book. Horowitz shoved the volume in my hands and commanded me to read it.

DUBAL: Then tremendous virtuosi like Horowitz and Hofmann are not usually for you?

SCHIFF: I admire what they can do instrumentally. They have tremendous ideas, and they produce such pianistic color and effects as to make one's hair stand up like a punk-rocker's. But I believe that I am not in that line. They are great instrumentalists but they are not great musicians, because the composer is secondary. The public says it is going to hear Horowitz and the composer is in his shadow. When I go to a concert it is to hear a performance of a Mozart concerto, or a Chopin sonata. A pianist I adore is Mr. Arrau; I have the utmost respect for his art. He never loses sight of the composer.

As I read this portion, I thought, Oh, no, this is deadly. I had hoped Horowitz had not read this because he really seemed interested in meeting Schiff.

Horowitz said, "Mr. Dubal, do you think that, with *me*, the composer is secondary?"

Wanda joined in. "How ridiculous. Why do they keep saying such a thing? This Mr. Schiff is not different from others. And what he says is stupid because people don't just go to a concert to hear a Mozart concerto. They always go to hear who is doing it, as well. Why would they go to hear a second-rater play? The performer makes the music."

"I agree with you, Mrs. Horowitz. And I know, Maestro, that the composer is never secondary with you. Indeed, nobody knows better than I do. I think that many pianists who are less than virtuosi seldom produce extraordinary effects because they can't. So when a real virtuoso produces anything startling, especially in the classical masters, they are condemned for being show-offs."

Horowitz protested, "But Haydn, Mozart, Schubert, and Beethoven need effects and surprises just like Liszt does."

"Of course, Maestro. But the minute this happens, the scream goes up: 'Horowitz violates the score. He has no respect for the composer. He plays the classics with too much color and freedom.' and on and on."

"I know," Horowitz went on. "I'm always accused of such nonsense. As if Haydn has no blood and guts."

"I know, Maestro. And in the case of Schiff, I think he really is, as he says, in a different line. But he is a much quirkier musician than some think he is, nor is he truly at home with the Romantic composers. He is more interested in Bach, Mozart, and Schubert. I think Beethoven is too rough and tough for him."

Horowitz again surprised me. "Well, he looks good. When he comes to town, bring him here if you can find him. But not for dinner. At nine-thirty. And we will talk. But you must be here, too."

I said, "Of course, I will come with him. I'll try to arrange it."

Wanda said, "I will not meet him, though. Not yet."

"Well, when he deserves to meet you, Mrs. Horowitz, he shall."

For several months, I had wanted a photograph of Mr. and Mrs. Horowitz together. But every time I was with them, I would forget to ask. Tonight, as the evening was drawing to a close, I remembered.

"Is there a recent photo of both of you?"

Wanda said, "Let me look," and went to another room.

In a few minutes, she returned, annoyed. "I can't find the photo I wanted, but here is one that I like. I think it was used on a record."

Horowitz held out his hand. "Let me look."

As he gazed at the likenesses, the pianist sighed, "Ah, how ugly I've become."

Wanda retorted, "That's not true. It's a very nice picture."

I said, "Nonsense, Maestro. I think you look very good."

Wanda reached for the photo, found a pen, and wrote an inscription:

"To David, 'Molto simpatico.' Wanda Toscanini Horowitz."

Horowitz looked at me helplessly. "What should I write?"

"Whatever you want."

The Maestro bent over to write, but nothing happened. He looked at Wanda for help, but she was silent and winked at me.

Horowitz said, "I don't know what to write. You are too complicated to write one line." Suddenly he said, "I have it. You are molto simpatico to Wanda, and you are to me, too."

Under his wife's words, he wrote, "I am of the same opinion."

I looked at it and smiled with satisfaction. "Maestro, it is perfect. I shall treasure this picture."

40

ANDRAS SCHIFF VISITS EAST NINETY-FOURTH STREET

The next day I phoned Agnes Bruneau, a friend of mine who was Schiff's public relations manager. She was certain Schiff would be excited by the possibility of meeting Mr. Horowitz, and she intended to call Schiff in London immediately.

As Agnes predicted, Andras was delighted by the prospect.

Upon his arrival in New York, I called to say that Horowitz preferred Tuesday, March 8, 1988. Schiff readily agreed: "Whenever he wants."

En route to pick up Schiff, I wondered if Horowitz would like him. Perhaps bringing younger pianists into his life was a mistake. Would Andras show the proper respect?

It was not easy to enter the Horowitz kingdom. Everything concerning the Maestro was problematic and could easily backfire.

When I arrived at Schiff's West End Avenue apartment, he introduced me to his wife and fixed us a drink. I hadn't seen him for a few years, and we sat for a while chatting and catching up.

I warned Andras that Horowitz had read our interview saying he was more interested in effects than in the composer.

Schiff gulped. "We'll get past that, I hope." Andras was dressed casually but carefully. He had on a tie and looked his "normal" self.

At nine-thirty on the dot, I rang the buzzer at the Horowitzes'. The maid announced, "The Maestro will be down momentarily."

Wanda was not in the living room, which meant she would not appear.

I deposited Schiff in her chair, which would enable Horowitz to hear him better. The Maestro was a little hard of hearing in the left ear, although he would not admit it. Schiff appeared calm and comfortable and was looking forward to the encounter.

Horowitz soon appeared, looking particularly natty in a bright and dashing bow tie. It was, he said, a new item in his formidable collection.

Schiff quickly stood to greet Horowitz, who gave him a long, dazzling smile and welcoming handshake. Schiff seemed instantly at ease with Horowitz; I was certain Andras felt the unmistakable aura of Horowitz's presence.

The master plumped down on his flowered sofa and began the evening by complimenting Schiff on his playing. Schiff countered with a compliment about Horowitz's recording of the Mozart Concerto No. 23.

Horowitz said, "It is probably not really to your liking. The critics say I play the slow movement too romantically and too fast."

Schiff responded, "What does it matter what critics say? The recording is by Horowitz."

Horowitz, too, was feeling comfortable with Schiff and said, "I will interview you." He asked Schiff about his childhood, life in Hungary, whom he studied with, and so on. All was going well. Every so often, the Maestro would include me in the conversation.

"Where did you just play?" he asked Schiff.

"I just returned from Princeton, where I gave a recital."

"What did you play?"

"The *Hammerklavier*," Schiff said proudly.

"Oh, *no!*" Horowitz made a face. "Not that! What do you want to do, kill the audience? Why do you play such a thing? It's so long, so pretentious, and how do you give such a piece in a little town?"

The twenty-ninth and longest of the thirty-two Beethoven sonatas is one of the great monuments in the piano literature. The subtitle, *Hammerklavier*, means "piano" in German.

Schiff sweetly argued that Princeton's audience was sophisticated, capable of appreciating Beethoven's Op. 106, and that he was playing the *Hammerklavier* everywhere this season.

I interjected, as if to referee: "Mr. Horowitz has his problems with late Beethoven sonatas. But, Andras, believe me, he knows every note of the *Hammerklavier.*"

Horowitz appeared not to listen to my explanation of this Horowitzean blasphemy.

I looked at the Maestro, saying, "You know, Anton Rubinstein called the *Hammerklavier* the Ninth Symphony for the piano. When it was published, in 1818, Beethoven said to a student, 'This will keep pianists busy when it is finally played in fifty years.'"

"I know. But to subject the public to it is too hard."

Horowitz turned to other topics, one of them being Bach's *Well-Tempered Clavier*, a great specialty of Schiff's. "I know you record Bach preludes and fugues. I don't know if Bach is good for large halls."

Schiff agreed that too large a concert hall was not conducive to Bach's keyboard music.

Andras is one of the younger generation of pianists who play Bach on the piano without any apologies to the harpsichordists, who have propagandized for Bach on his original instrument.

Horowitz said, "I have good memory usually, but the fugues of Bach, I cannot memorize them."

We all agreed. No music is more difficult to memorize than Bach.

Horowitz asked Schiff if he cared to play for him.

"No, Mr. Horowitz, I'd rather not, at least not tonight."

"Okay," Horowitz said. "Maybe you play some other time if you want to come back."

"Mr. Horowitz, I would love to come back."

"Good."

Just then, the maid came to ask if I would go upstairs to visit with Mrs. Horowitz.

Horowitz quickly made excuses. "Madame is not feeling well tonight and can't be here. Mr. Dubal, will you go up and be with her for a while?"

I was a bit disappointed, since I was curious to see how things would progress between the two pianists. I had no choice, however, and dutifully went to Madame's boudoir. Wanda, always gracious to me, asked how the interview was proceeding.

"Fine," I said. "I think Mr. Horowitz likes him."

I stayed with Mrs. Horowitz for over half an hour, until she said, "Perhaps you should go back now."

Schiff and Horowitz were talking comfortably, testing out their Russian on one another. Schiff talked about many of the Maestro's recordings, displaying a fine knowledge of the Horowitz discography while showing deep and moving admiration for his art.

The evening ended around midnight. I had hoped that Horowitz would play, but because Schiff didn't, I felt he wouldn't, either. Horowitz stood up and, with great cordiality, said good night. The maid ushered us to the door.

Schiff was exhilarated. Instead of hailing a cab, we walked down Madison Avenue, talking about the evening.

"He was so real," Schiff said. "I was so comfortable with him."

"Oh, yes, if Horowitz likes someone, as he did you, he makes him feel comfortable."

"Wasn't Mrs. Horowitz well?" Schiff said.

"She was tired. She will meet you another time. It was actually easier that she wasn't there."

Schiff raved on about Horowitz, saying, "I was amazed at his Mozart A Major Concerto. There is nothing in it that I agreed with, but the magnetism of his playing is overwhelming."

We found a taxi and I took Schiff home. I asked if he would like to see Horowitz again. He assured me that he would love to, but that he would be on tour nonstop for nearly a year and wouldn't be back in New York until next February. However, my little goal was accomplished. I had brought to Horowitz one of the distinguished younger pianists of our time. I had helped a little to reduce the generation gap and the isolation of Horowitz's life.

41

THE FIVE HUNDRED
DOLLAR BET

A week later, on my next visit to the Horowitzes, we spoke of our evening with Schiff.

"He looks good, just like his photo. I think he talks in an exaggerated way." Horowitz launched into mimicry.

Horowitz could imitate someone with amazing accuracy. Not just the speech patterns, but the facial expressions as well. His imitations were slightly malicious but very funny. I thought, How would the Maestro react if he heard my imitation of him?

In Schiff's defense, I said, "I think that is his way of expressing himself in English, but it's not an affectation."

Horowitz said, "I know! But Mr. Dubal, why is it that I invite him to my home and he does not send me a thank-you note? Maybe he didn't have a good time."

"Oh, no, Maestro. That's not true. I know he had a smashing time. He raved about you on our way home, and also about your Mozart Concerto."

"Then why didn't he thank me for the hospitality?"

"Well, you are perfectly right," I said. "But people today are a little too informal, and they are always busy."

Wanda insisted, "He won't send a thank-you note. I guarantee you."

Horowitz adamantly agreed with his wife. "I will bet you that I never get a letter from him."

"What do you want to bet, Mr. Horowitz?"

"I bet you fifty dollars," he said.

"No, I'm so sure that he will send one. Let's make it for five hundred dollars, because I need the money."

Horowitz held out his hand, and we shook on our bet. Wanda laughed: "He will not send it."

Our evening continued uneventfully and I went home during the eleven o'clock news.

The next day I called Schiff, but he had already left town. I then phoned Agnes Bruneau because I didn't want their one meeting to end badly simply because of the lack of a thank-you note. I confided in her, mentioning that Andras had not written them.

"I don't know if he will be doing it or not, but the Horowitzes are formal, and it would be good form to write."

Agnes said, "Oh, Andras would no doubt be writing one, but just in case, I shall remind him."

I said nothing about my bet with the Maestro and hung up.

Less than a week later, I joined the Horowitzes for dinner. They were both in good spirits.

As the Maestro munched on bread sticks, he said to me, "I only love three things in life."

"And what might they be, Mr. Horowitz?"

"I love beautiful perfume," taking out his handkerchief and letting me smell the fabric. "This I got in London; it's delicious. It's Stephanotis, by Floris."

"Do you know Tchaikovsky loved scent, too?" I said. "So did Chopin. He always had eau de cologne near him. What else, Maestro, do you love?"

"I love *money*! Oh, yes, that I love."

"Well," I said, "that's not an unusual love. But I'll ask you one simple question, which for me will determine if you really love money."

Horowitz looked quizzically at me, awaiting the question. Mrs. Horowitz was quietly amused.

"Do you know how much money you have?"

Horowitz looked puzzled. "No, no. Of course not. I don't know. Why would I know? I don't count my money."

"Well, there is your answer. If you *really* loved money, you would know what you have. You would watch it and count it."

"Maybe you are right, Mr. Dubal. I'm glad I'm not poor, but I don't watch my money."

Horowitz, like many artists, never made money a priority. Money simply meant freedom to him.

"Now, Maestro," I said hesitantly, "what is your third love?" I glanced at Wanda, who was also waiting for the answer.

Horowitz looked surprised. "What do you think it is? You should be able to guess. My third love is *music*. I love music more than anything. That's for sure."

Since the mood was light, I was able to say, "But what about Mrs. Horowitz? Don't you love her?"

Wanda said smiling, "He doesn't love me. He *needs* me."

"I was not speaking of people."

Wanda said sweetly, "I forgive you, Volodya."

When the food was served, Horowitz smelled the risotto. "They make a good risotto here. I don't even talk about music when I eat. I love good food, too," he assured me. "But eating is more important than love."

After dinner, he ordered chamomile tea and a baked apple for dessert. Just before the tea arrived, Horowitz pulled out a letter from his pocket. "Do you know what this is?" he said teasingly.

"What is it, Maestro?" I asked.

"I must tell you, Mr. Dubal, that *you* won our bet. This is a letter from Schiff. You were right. He is a good man."

"What does it say?" I asked, appearing surprised.

Horowitz read it out loud. "Dear Mr. Horowitz, Because of our mutual friend, David Dubal, I was able to meet you. It was a wonderful evening, and I hope I am able to repeat the occasion. Next time, I hope I shall be able to meet Mrs. Horowitz. Again, thanks for inviting me to your beautiful home—with all admiration, Andras Schiff."

Horowitz was gleeful. As he put the letter carefully back in his jacket, he pulled out his wallet and took out a five-dollar bill. "Here is your winnings."

"But Mr. Horowitz," I protested, "our bet was not for five dollars, but for *five hundred* dollars."

Horowitz smiled widely. "You must hear wrong. I don't have such money. Take the five."

I took the money and said, "I told you he would write. You should know by now that I'm never wrong."

Horowitz's eyes twinkled; he knew very well that our bet was a joke. I said, "What a wager. From fifty dollars to five hundred dollars to five dollars."

In money matters he was careful, but in no way was Horowitz cheap. He never deprived himself or Mrs. Horowitz of anything, but there were actually very few things he wanted. He was even negligent about money. Once, when showing me an item in his drawer, he showed me a six-figure royalty check.

"Oh, I forget to have it put in the bank. It's been sitting here for two months."

It was an unwritten rule that the Maestro always paid for dinner. In the early stages of our friendship, I had offered to pay and he gave me a frozen look. "Never!" he said authoritatively.

On the few occasions when I dined with Mrs. Horowitz alone, I naturally paid.

In any case, I won the bet. I would never know if Andras would have sent the note if I had not intervened. Was it ethical to do what I did? No, but the world is not black and white.

I am sorry that Schiff never had a chance to see Horowitz again. However, this encounter led the way to my bringing several of my students to his home later in the year.

42

THE 500,000TH PIANO

Late in March 1988, Richard Probst called me to have lunch. He wanted me to help create and program a grand concert to celebrate Steinway's 135th anniversary and their 500,000th Piano.

I thought it would be an interesting challenge and accepted the offer. Although we did some work on the program in April, it was not until May that we realized the time was drawing close. The Carnegie Hall spectacular was to be held a month later, on June 2.

Richard Probst is a man of tremendous energy, with abilities to match.

He said, "Officially, you will be music director of this gala and choose the twenty-five pianists who will play. In my position, as you know, all Steinway artists must be regarded as equal. Otherwise, I will be lynched by those who were not asked. Naturally, I have certain people I want in this, such as Shura Cherkassky."

"So my friend, you are saying you want me to make the enemies."

"David, that's exactly correct."

"Well, Richard, I've done these things before, and I'm not too concerned about making enemies. Believe me, just getting them all here and ready to play without pianist X, Y, and Z cancelling at the last second will be a triumph of the first magnitude."

Richard nodded with understanding. "Now," he said, "let's talk turkey. Wouldn't it be something else if our Volodya would consent to be the first pianist to play the 500,000th Piano." This specially

233

designed space-age-looking instrument had the signatures of all the Steinway Artists laminated into the case.

"Oh, glory," I said. "But will he do it?"

Richard, like myself, had become a weekly guest at the Horo-witzes'. As the liaison to the Steinway Artists, Richard felt duty-bound to pay extra homage and attention to the supreme Steinway Artist. All eight hundred Steinway Artists throughout the world were, in theory, equal, but Horowitz was the grand exception.

A Steinway Artist is a pianist chosen by the firm. These pianists endorse their preferred instrument with no financial remuneration, and Steinway promises to provide them with a good Steinway piano wherever they perform.

However, we were by no means confident that, between us, we had the power to influence Horowitz to play at the gala.

"If we succeed," Richard said, "we will be heroes. Carnegie Hall will explode from the applause."

We decided our plan of attack would be through Mrs. Horowitz.

During our next visits, Richard and I did not mention the gala. We did not want to be refused early in the game.

At the strategic moment, we invited Wanda to a cozy Madison Avenue restaurant. Richard and I were excessively attentive to her; charm poured from us. But we were reluctant to ask her to persuade the Maestro to participate in the concert. One was not only respectful of Mrs. Horowitz, but careful, too. She could be more temperamental than ten thoroughbreds at the starting gate.

After half an hour of banter, Wanda said, with a sly smile, "It certainly is unusual for both of you to ask me to lunch."

In a serious tone Richard said, "Mrs. Horowitz, to put it bluntly, we'd like your husband to be the first to play the 500,000th Piano on June second. Can this happen? In fact, Steinway would love to give you an award for your years of service to music, because the house of Steinway has had a magnificent association with you as well as your husband."

Although Mrs. Horowitz replied, "I don't need to be given an award," we both felt she was flattered by the idea and would willingly accept the recognition. "I will try to convince Volodya," she added, "but you know him."

"Mrs. Horowitz, Richard can't say this, but I can. Steinway has always been marvelous to Mr. Horowitz, just as Mr. Horowitz has been loyal and faithful to them. I really think that Steinway deserves this from him. Tickets are being sent to each of the Steinway Artists and probably no concert will every have so many distinguished pianists in the audience. Can you imagine the thrill when your husband, the pianist of the century, comes on stage? It will cause pandemonium."

"What would he play?" she mused.

"Anything he wants," I said. "The other twenty-five artists have a limit of four minutes. I'm trying to program works that are unusual. I think it would be fabulous if Mr. Horowitz would play his own *Danse Excentrique*. I know it's in his fingers; he tossed it off for me recently. It's an insinuating little piece and only two minutes long. It would be great fun to hear."

Richard agreed with my idea. "But, naturally, Mr. Horowitz could play as long as he likes."

Wanda said, "I will do my best. I think he should do this for Steinway."

After lunch, Richard and I congratulated ourselves.

"So far so good," I said.

Richard went on, "Wouldn't it be great if we get Horowitz and Cliburn, too? What a coup. I talked to Van today. He said he was seriously thinking of coming. I told him his mother, Rildia Bee, would get an award. The problem is Van probably won't play."

"Be careful," I warned Richard. "These awards can get tricky."

"I know what you mean. John Steinway is also getting an award."

"Awards are time-consuming," I said. "I'm worrying about the length of the gala."

Later that week at my regular visit, Horowitz said, "Probst tells me you are helping him on the big Steinway concert at Carnegie Hall."

"Yes, I am. It's lots of work, but it's going to be an exciting event." I said nothing about the Maestro participating.

I continued, "Probst tells me that Cliburn may come. He's played a piece or two at the White House recently when Gorbachev was there. And who knows, maybe he'll play at the Steinway event."

Wanda said, "Did I tell you that we had dinner with Cliburn recently? His mother and Susan Tilley, the chairman of the Cliburn Competition, were with him. We had a nice evening. Cliburn was gracious and sweet."

"Yes," I said, "he really is just like his image. I was at his home in

Fort Worth last month after I played at the Dallas Women's Club. I got there nearly at midnight, but he and his mother were just starting their day."

Wanda said, "I hear the house is extraordinary!"

"It's incredible! Cliburn lives in the grand manner. In the back, there's a fleet of automobiles. The house is huge, the furnishings unusual, with many antiques. In room after room there are Steinway grands, I think seventeen or more of them. Sometimes Van gives them away to churches or the like."

Wanda asked, "Where did all the money come from? He hasn't played in ten years."

I replied, "I heard the money was made early in his career by very wise investments.

"Van and I had an extremely pleasant conversation. At four in the morning he took me for a walk around the magnificent grounds. The honeysuckle was blooming and the air smelled luscious. Van showed me how to 'pop' a honeysuckle blossom and sip the drop of nectar inside. While were were walking, he told me what a wonderful time he had being with both of you. He said he invited you down in the summer to stay as long as you'd like."

Mrs. Horowitz said, "Yes, that's right, he did."

"Perhaps you should go. Believe me, you would receive royal treatment. Cliburn told me that he would be so pleased if you visited him, he said he would hire a special chef for you."

"I'm sure he means it," Wanda replied. "Did you talk to him about the upcoming Steinway concert?"

"No, I didn't. I didn't discuss it at all." I noticed Horowitz was listening but said nothing.

"How are you coming on the program?" Wanda asked.

"Not bad. Lazar Berman is coming from Moscow, Alexis Weissenberg from Paris, Cherkassky from London. Things are shaping up. Unfortunately, I have to go to Seoul, Korea, on Saturday, the twenty-first, and won't be back until the twenty-eighth. But I'll be in touch with Probst from there."

Horowitz said, "You just went to Korea."

"I've been asked back. Can you believe it? It's been exactly two years." I told the Maestro I would call as soon as I returned.

Wanda walked me downstairs to the door.

"It's up to you to plead our case," I said. "I really think he should be there June second, even if he doesn't play. I'll see you right after I get back."

From the moment I returned from Korea, I was on the phone, working on the final arrangements for the gala. I was the host, script-writer, and programmer, as well as one of the performers. This was a complicated concert and many things could go wrong.

Horowitz still gave no indication that he would appear. Carnegie Hall was sold out, with the top ticket going for one hundred dollars. We still hoped that Horowitz would be the first to play the 500,000th Steinway.

Cliburn, true to form, was as elusive as Horowitz, and we still didn't know if he would attend. The chances were we would be in trouble, left without a superstar to unveil the super Steinway.

It was Tuesday, May 31. The concert was only two days away. That morning, Bruce Stevens, the president of Steinway, had invited me to come to their factory in Long Island City to play on the instrument for the employees who had worked on it.

Steinway's chief technician, Franz Mohr, gave No. 500,000 some finishing touches in the voicing and regulation of the instrument. He said, "David, Volodya himself might even like this piano."

I said, "Do you really think so, Franz?"

"Well, he replied with a gleam, "perhaps not."

Back in Manhattan, Richard and I had lunch at the Jockey Club, and afterwards, I went on to WNCN, where I was on deadline for the station's programming. I couldn't get rid of the jet lag from Korea and felt I would collapse from fatigue.

That evening, Probst and I went to see the Maestro after meeting beforehand to discuss a few last-minute diplomatic tactics.

As Horowitz experts, we immediately sensed that the great pianist was not in a good mood.

Richard was direct. "Maestro, I suppose you know why we are both here."

"Yea," he responded, looking at us with a sharp glare. "Why should I be in this damn concert?" Horowitz boomed as he gave off a loud belch.

Mrs. Horowitz seemed forlorn.

Hesitantly, I said, "Maestro, I really thought that you would enjoy being part of this. Your colleagues would love to see you walk out onto the stage. I can imagine the ovation the audience would give you. The piano is quite fine. I went over today to try it out. Franz Mohr told me that he thought you might like it."

Horowitz answered gruffly, "You know I hate the new acoustic at Carnegie Hall. I told you I will never play in that hall again."

I had forgotten he had said that. "But Maestro, we are only talking about playing a two-minute piece."

"Well, then," Richard continued softly, "if you don't want to play, what about appearing on stage just to be seen? It would be a great gesture to Steinway."

At that, Horowitz grew angry. "What am I, a *piano salesman!*"

I tried to calm him, and Wanda screamed, "But Volodya, it is a pledge of goodwill to Steinway. They have been loyal to you."

"I have been loyal to them. I play only their piano."

I had remembered at Horowitz's birthday party, Richard brought him a beautiful brass desk paperweight from Czarist Russia with the words *faith and loyalty* printed on them. It was one of the many Steinway gestures to Horowitz. But tonight, Maestro Horowitz was not going to reciprocate. Richard and I looked at each other with defeat in our eyes.

Richard reminded Horowitz that Wanda was supposed to receive a plaque. That seemed to make him even angrier.

I had never seen him so out of control. Suddenly, he took his trusty magnifying glass, brought it far back in the air, and slammed it down on the table with a shattering thud. The large magnifying glass nearly shaved my head; if I had been hit, I would have been seriously injured. So great was his strength that the sterling-silver-mounted glass dented the coffee table. Horowitz turned red. The vein on his forehead bulged. We were all frightened. Wanda began crying. We had lost. Horowitz would never change his mind.

Probst and I stayed on for twenty minutes of small talk. Nothing more was said of the gala.

I had erred in thinking that Wanda was the key to enticing him to the gala. I now realized that her domain was domestic, with some involvement in financial matters. But when it came to Horowitz's career, that was *his* territory, and ultimately he had the final word.

Richard and I said good night. We walked in the sultry May night, depressed and silent.

After a few blocks, Richard said, "I feel it in my bones."

"What do you feel?"

"I feel it in my bones that Van won't come either."

I said, "Forget Van. If he comes, he comes. And if he does, it will be a last-minute decision. I can't even think of him. Tomorrow, we must figure out who is to play the 500,000th."

Early Wednesday morning, Richard and I discussed who we could get on such short notice. Nobody came to mind. We were stuck. Richard now heard from Cliburn that he would attend but wouldn't play. We needed a star, but there was none to be had. Pollini, Perahia, Brendel, de Larrocha, Arrau, Argerich, and Pogorelich were all in Europe.

Suddenly, I thought, It doesn't have to be a pianist. Why not a duo? Navah Perlman, Itzhak's daughter, was the youngest Steinway Artist in the gala. It would be fantastic if she accompanied her father in a violin transcription of a Chopin nocturne.

I called her. She was all for the idea, but had to convince her father. The day was passing quickly, and Perlman couldn't make up his mind. In the meantime, I needed another plan.

I decided if I couldn't have a star, perhaps I would find an unknown, a child who would symbolize the future of the piano. I was told of a nine-year-old Korean boy who studied at the Manhattan School of Music who would fit the bill. I called his parents, who were excited by the prospect of their son's playing at such a grand celebration and in Carnegie Hall. I gave them no guarantee and told them that I was waiting to hear if Perlman would play, but to bring him to Steinway Hall to be auditioned by Richard and myself.

That evening, Perlman and I again talked on the telephone. He had been wavering all day. I used all my persuasive power, which was working better on the famous violinist than it had on Horowitz. However, Perlman felt he didn't want to be seen as the doting father, and he argued that this was a piano event.

"But," I said, "you are going to play Chopin."

During our talk, however, I felt that Perlman, always the consummate showman, in this case really didn't want to do it. He was torn between his daughter and my arguments.

Suddenly, I said, "Itzhak, you really don't want to do this, and I can't stand the fact that I'm manipulating you into this by using Navah as a pawn."

"David, you are right. You are convincing. Just let me be in the audience and enjoy myself."

I left the phone feeling better. Within minutes, the adorable pudgy-faced Albert Kim arrived. Richard and I listened to him and approved. He was perfect, the very picture of childish confidence. He didn't have a nerve in his body.

From Horowitz to Albert Kim was not exactly what Probst and I had dreamed of, but, after all, children have a way of stealing the show.

Early Thursday morning, the day of the concert, Richard called me. He was frantic. Vladimir Feltsman was ill and had just canceled. The concert was to have two intermissions. The third part was to be Schumann's half-hour *Carnaval*, with each of the evening's pianists playing one of the selections. Feltsman had been honored with the assignment of performing the rousing finale, "March of the League of David against the Philistines."

In a flash, I phoned Shura Cherkassky at the Pierre Hotel, where he was still half asleep. "Shura, Feltsman is sick. Do you have the *Carnaval* in your fingers?"

"But how wonderful, David," he said. "I get to play the Chopin section *and* the March. I'd love to. I'm playing *Carnaval* in Paris on Monday."

The logistics of the concert, along with its filming, were complicated. That afternoon, we all gathered for a rehearsal.

At eight sharp, the gala began. It took a full four hours. It was a piano lover's paradise. Nobody left. The unpredictable Cliburn, who had been detained in Atlanta, suddenly appeared backstage at eleven-fifteen. He made his speech, and his mother duly received her award.

I now introduced the 500,000th Piano's designer, Wendell Castle. The piano was unveiled, and the audience heartily cheered its outlandish design.

Finally, at nearly midnight, the wide-awake Albert Kim proceeded to play his selections note-perfectly. He loved every minute on stage, taking the lowest bows I've ever seen.

After the concert, hundreds of specially invited guests were treated to a party at Steinway Hall which lasted until three a.m.

At the reception, little Albert was exhilarated with his new celebrity. Richard nudged me. "Just think. This kid has started his career by replacing Horowitz. Not bad. A Carnegie Hall debut at nine. He better practice hard."

During the concert, the unhappy Mrs. Horowitz sat in a box with John Steinway. At the first intermission, John came backstage and whispered in my ear, "Wanda is a bitch tonight." But I thought, Why shouldn't she be? She didn't receive an award and her husband is sitting stubbornly at home. However, he sent a telegram of congratulations to Steinway which was read on stage.

The concert was now history. For me, it was a personal triumph, but nonetheless I was disappointed that this dazzling occasion was not capped off by Horowitz. It would have been the perfect "programming."

Just as he had not done the Juilliard program with me, I knew deep down that he wouldn't participate in the Steinway gala.

43

AFTER THE GALA

It was June 18, more than two weeks since the gala.

When I entered the drawing room, Wanda was watching "Wheel of Fortune," which she frequently had on just before the Maestro came down; the program bored me, but I enjoyed Wanda's attempts to get the right answers. She said nothing about the Steinway event.

When Horowitz appeared, the television was shut off. I wondered if he would mention the Steinway concert and hoped he wouldn't.

He greeted me with gusto. His first words were "Mr. Dubal, my father had a saying he used often. Nobody ever got hurt with what you didn't say."

"Your father, Maestro, was a wise man." I took this to mean, "Let's not discuss the Steinway gala."

Soon we went downstairs for dinner. Horowitz exclaimed, "I'm for Dukakis, of course, but I'm afraid he is too dull to win. Reagan's man will win. Did you know I was playing a concert in Boston after Martin Luther King was murdered? I played Funeral March from the Chopin sonata. I thought I should do it, and I did."

"Actually, Mr. Horowitz, I didn't know you did that. That was a superb gesture."

"Yes, I think so, too." Horowitz continued, "Do you think that my living in America for more than half-century improved the country?"

I said, "Naturally, it has improved the country. A country is only

243

as good as the quality of its people. The government should pay important people to live in it."

"I tell you, you are right. Maybe Dukakis will pay me. I pay a lot of money to the U.S. I believe in democracy. It's the best way."

Mrs. Horowitz nodded, "It's not so good, but the rest is worse."

We had finished our soup. I found it amusing the way Mrs. Horowitz used her silver dinner bell after each course. Although she tinkled the bell daintily, it seemed like a defiant gesture; strange, in egalitarian America, to call the servant with a bell. This tiny detail was one more way that the Horowitzes observed class distinctions as well as a vanished amenity of life.

I told them that I was enjoying reading Thomas Mann's diaries. "It seems both of you met him on November 25 and 27, 1937, when he was living in Switzerland. Do you remember?"

"Oh, yes," Wanda said. "He invited us for lunch. He was curious about what we thought about America and the events in Germany. He was in exile. He talked about Wagner and loved his music very much. He knew many conductors such as Bruno Walter, and was very interested that I was Toscanini's daughter."

"In the diary, he says he talked to Mr. Horowitz after a champagne supper. Do you remember what he said?"

"No," Horowitz said. "He was one of the big writers of the world. Everyone paid him respect."

Wanda said, "He was a typical German of the upper class. His manners were perfect."

"He was a passionate spokesman against the Nazis," I said, "and in the diary entry where you are mentioned, he was preparing a speech for America. He wrote, 'Democratic idealism. Do I believe in it? Am I only adopting it as an intellectual role?' He was skeptical about democracy and the artist's place in it."

"Yes," Horowitz responded. "There was once respect for the artist, and there was an elite who were really cultured. That is gone now."

"Absolutely gone," I said. "The artist now lives in isolation. Most people think that the artist, if he is not dangerous, is at the least a loafer, a drunk, a good-for-nothing, and a sinner. I love the story of the two ladies taking a walk in Oxford, Mississippi, pointing to a man on a rocking chair on his front porch. 'That man sitting there is Mr. Faulkner. He doesn't work.'"

After dinner, we retired to the living room. I asked, "Have you seen an improvement in the appreciation of music in the U.S.?"

"I don't know," Horowitz replied. "There are fewer people who play music. They play records, which gives people the chance to know more music. I think they used to complain more about difficult music. But once you go out of the big music cities, you never know what they will like. I've never played down to an audience, but I'm careful, too. They are paying their good money to hear you. I would never give them all Beethoven or Schubert, like Schnabel did. The public needs contrast. That is snob programming."

I said, "Schnabel once wrote to his wife from Seville, telling her that, while he was playing the hour-long *Diabelli Variations* of Beethoven, he felt this was really unfair: 'I am the only person here who is enjoying this, and I get the money. They pay and have to suffer.'"

Horowitz laughed. "Schnabel at least was honest. But I can't make people suffer."

"Yes, I agree. Well-planned programming is essential. Schnabel was a missionary. He thought of himself as an educator, but one must be careful not to drive people away."

Horowitz continued, "I remember a long time ago, my manager says to me that some people are complaining that my recitals are too difficult. 'They don't understand some of the music you are playing.' I was indignant. 'What are you talking about?!' I screamed. I was so angry. 'My recitals are easy to understand. After all, I am playing all season the Chopin G minor Ballade.' This man looks at me. 'Yes, Volodya, that's the very piece they don't understand.' So what can you do? If they don't understand the G minor Ballade, it's hopeless.

"But I tell you a wonderful story. I think in '42 or '43, I am going to play a recital in Gainesville, Florida. I had on the program the Prokofiev Eighth Sonata. It had never been heard down there. I wanted to try it out because I was to play the Sixth, Seventh, and Eighth Sonatas of Prokofiev at the Russian embassy in New York. So I look at the audience filling up, and I start to feel sorry for them. After all, the Eighth Sonata is very introspective and lyrical, and is nearly half hour long. Imagine this little town in Florida having to live through this. Today, the Eighth Sonata is hard to hear. Then, my God, what would they think? They never come to hear any pianist

again. I call the stage manager. I tell him, please go out on stage and
tell the people that Mr. Horowitz is not going to play the Prokofiev.
Instead, I will play Beethoven's *Waldstein* Sonata. He goes out and I'm
right at the curtain, listening. 'Ladies and gentlemen, tonight Mr.
Horowitz will not be playing the Prokofiev Eighth Sonata. Instead,
he will be playing the Beethoven 'Sonata in Waltz Time.'"

I laughed. "Maestro, it's a great story of musical ignorance."

Horowitz continued, "Maybe musical taste is on a higher level
today. I think my playing is more simple today. In the past, perhaps I
make more exaggeration because people did not know the music so
much. But today, they hear it on records, on radio, God knows
where. And so, since they know it better, you don't have to
exaggerate so much. You can be more direct."

Mrs. Horowitz said, "I must tell you, Mr. Dubal, I like your hair
cut shorter like this. It was too long."

"Thanks. But I'm always terrified when I get a haircut. I absolutely don't want to get my money's worth."

Horowitz said, "Did I ever tell you, when I play in Budapest, an
old lady came to me and wanted to give me some strands of Liszt's
hair? I'm sorry, but I tell her, 'No thanks.' She was very hurt. She
said, 'You play Liszt's music as it should be played, and I wanted to
thank you through this gift.' But I just couldn't accept. I found this
creepy."

"I understand, Maestro. But what is creepy to one age is not so for
another. Once, it was the fashion to give strands of hair. Some people
would have killed to have the hair of Byron, Chopin, or Liszt."

"As you know, I love Liszt. I travel everywhere with two photos of
Liszt. I showed you them in my room. But I don't want his hair."

"Maestro, you have his music. That's better."

Horowitz continued. "Do you know who I hear on the radio? He
played Chopin E minor Concerto very good. Maybe I should meet
him."

"Who was it?" I asked.

"Zimerman. But I see picture of him and he has beard. That I can't
stand."

Krystian Zimerman, Polish pianist and winner of the 1975 Chopin
Competition, never met Horowitz.

"Maestro, I think you just don't like too much hair. Perhaps

Zimerman would shave his beard for the chance of meeting you. But you are right, he is a fine Chopin player."

Horowitz continued, "Today, I practice a Chopin etude. But I must tell you, Chopin's etudes are impossible on the modern piano. Chopin would have changed lots of things if he have the Steinway. Of that I'm sure, oh yes! You can't play the etudes well if you follow Chopin's metronome markings. They are too fast."

"Mr. Horowitz, which are the most difficult of the Chopin etudes?"

"Ah, all are terrible. The double-note etudes are very difficult, especially Op. 25, No. 6. Everyone tries to show off the speed of their thirds, but the beauty of the piece is in the left hand. Of course, the thirds have to be played very nice, very evenly. For me, the most difficult of all is the C Major, the first one, Op. 10, No. 1. I cannot do that, and I can't do the other C Major, Op. 10, No. 7. Also, I can't do the A minor, Op. 10, No. 2. Richter told me he could never do it, either. But I hear Richter do the Scriabin Etude in ninths, Op. 65, No. 1. It's fantastic! He has a very large hand. I've always very much wanted to play that work. But I cannot do it."

"Maestro, your hand is big enough."

"No," Horowitz said, "My hand is good for chords, good for octaves, of course, but not the Scriabin Etude in ninths. My hand falls off, believe me. Each hand is totally different, and you must learn about your own hands. You know, composers are often cruel. What they ask us to do should be forbidden. The public, who knows nothing of what is required, knows nothing of the hell of the work required. The tears. I've torn out many pieces of hair when I was young. The most important thing is to work hard. Anton Rubinstein said, 'Don't tell me how talented you are. Tell me how hard you work.'"

"Maestro, you worked hard."

"You're damn right, I did. You must tell your students to work hard."

I continued, "I was reading a marvelous little book by Marguerite Long called *At the Piano With Fauré*. In it she says she received a postcard from the renowned pianist Francis Planté. Throughout his life, he was a fierce worker. The card read, 'The schoolboy still plodding away in his ninety-seventh year.'"

"I think I knew Long," Horowitz said. "She played lots of French music."

"Yes, she mentions in the same book that she met you around the summer of 1928. You had rented a house just to work on the B minor Chopin Sonata for three months."

"I remember," Horowitz said. "Pianists, you know, must not be bothered when they work."

"But tell me, Mr. Horowitz, did you ever feel like a prisoner of the piano, a slave to it?"

"Oh, sure, many times. These are the times of despair. But the piano always brings me back. It calls to me."

I said, "Vladimir Ashkenazy, an endless worker, calls it 'sweet slavery.' The most interesting way of putting it was Busoni's; he wrote to his wife, 'It is an effort for me to practice the piano. Yet one cannot leave it! It is like an animal whose head always grows again, no matter how many times one cuts it off.'"

Horowitz drew a deep breath. "Ah, Busoni was brilliant."

"By the way, Maestro, I've always wanted to know why you didn't play the Chopin B minor Sonata in public?"

"Oh, I played it one or two seasons, and I know it well. It's very difficult, very uncomfortable. The first movement is a miracle, but the other movements have problems. I have some trouble liking the finale. Chopin would have changed some things if he had our piano. No, the *Funeral March* Sonata is more for me."

Horowitz said, "It's eleven o'clock. Let's put the news on and see what's happening in the presidential race. The weather has been good. I will take a long walk tomorrow."

"Maestro, I'm going home now. Talking with you has made me want to practice. But unfortunately, living in a New York apartment makes it impossible this late."

Our evening was pleasant. The Steinway gala was over, and I would never again see Horowitz display anger.

44

HOROWITZ TEACHES

During May 1988, I began bringing students from my Juilliard classes to Horowitz, who no longer resisted. He was ready to teach again, and this activity was soon to become a major addition to his life.

The first student I brought was a young American who had ingratiated himself with me. At the time, he was my favorite student, and I chose him because I thought he was the pupil who would prove cleverest in talking to Horowitz. Unfortunately, he was not the most talented pianist in class. He tried hard to win Horowitz over, and it worked. Horowitz was charmed. But Wanda, for whom he had brought flowers, was skeptical of his cloying manner. For a while, he was convincing. But after a few visits, I became repulsed by his forwardness and realized that Horowitz would soon tire of him because he was just not good enough.

Other pupils followed. One of them, Keith Albright, a tall, light-haired Texan, was in awe of the Maestro. He was terribly nervous while playing the first movement of Chopin's *Funeral March* Sonata. Several serious mishaps occurred during the work's perilous path, but Keith forged on and Horowitz never twitched. Horowitz whispered to me, "He looks like Cliburn a little."

Afterword I told Horowitz that Keith had learned his *Stars and Stripes Forever* off the recording.

Horowitz's ears perked up. "Let me hear it!" he cried.

Keith played it through, mustering up considerable bravura. As he played, Horowitz grinned widely at me.

Keith did not realize that this transcription was Horowitz's nemesis. In the 1940s, people tore the roof down if Horowitz didn't play it. Indeed, after 1953, he never played it again in public.

When Keith finished, beads of sweat glistened over his face. He was now pleased, as he had vindicated his poor Chopin performance. The Maestro, whose uncanny ears detected several miscalculations in Keith's arrangement, left the couch and showed Keith where he was wrong. Keith's face beamed as Horowitz complimented him on his ear, skill, and playing.

What Keith actually did physically, in his pianistic layout, was more difficult than what Horowitz did. I looked and listened with delight. It was an illuminating lesson, showing how magnificently Horowitz understood pianistic effect.

In his transcriptions, Horowitz strove for maximum effect with the least amount of effort. It was a pity that no one—including me—could persuade him to write them down for publication. Studying them would be a revelation in pianistic know-how.

Horowitz had a little protocol he followed after I introduced the students. He already knew something about them through the photo and curriculum vitae they were required to send before coming to see him.

After the formalities, he would say, "Now I will show you that I can be an interviewer like Mr. Dubal," and the Maestro would question them on various topics: Are you interested in art and literature? Are your parents musical? Do you want to have a big career? What has been your experience so far? Do you have any siblings? What are your hobbies? Horowitz was a good interviewer and enjoyed asking these questions. It also made the pupils less nervous.

The evenings quickly slipped by and always went smoothly. If he wanted to see someone again, he would call him himself. Before bringing a student to him, I tutored the pupil on what to wear, how to speak, and what to play. Soon, I found myself looking at a student through Horowitz's eyes. In class, I wondered how Horowitz would like him. Did he look "normal"? Would he understand Horowitz? Was his technique good enough? I started rejecting worthy ones because they were physically uninteresting or because they would bore Horowitz.

Unfortunately, he was only interested in the boys. My many female students were off-limits. He said to me, "I am not homosexual, you know. But I have too many women around me every day. I need male company."

"I understand, Maestro. But," I protested, "some of the best pianists at Juilliard are young women."

"Ah! You know, they will all give up music for the babies," he snorted.

"Perhaps so." I added, "But you should hear a few of them."

Horowitz said, "Maybe later." He never did.

Most of the students visited only once. He could tell quickly if they had that extra spark which made them different.

"Bring me more," he would say. "Now, for me, only the young count."

By September, Horowitz had dispensed with seeing the student résumé. During that month, I brought over a young pianist whom I knew he would find exceptional. Eduardus Halim was then around twenty-seven years old. He had been in my classes for several years, and was a student of the Czech pianist Rudolf Firkušný. Earlier, he had studied with the late Sascha Gorodnitzki, a teacher who gave students excellent technical grounding. In class, Halim listened avidly to every word I uttered. He was an ideal student who saturated himself in the piano.

Because of the intense competition at Juilliard, students often balked at performing in my piano literature classes. Every performance in Room 549 would immediately be reported, bad or good, to fellow students. Eduardus had no such inhibition. He performed constantly, large and small works. His Schumann *Humoreske* was filled with ardor, and his Brahms *Paganini* Variations revealed a blistering technical mechanism.

In class, I sometimes played records of great pianists of the past, and Eduardus was hypnotized by Barère, Friedman, and Hofmann. He was at that stage where coming under the influence of Horowitz could prove not only electrifying, but quite dangerous artistically. It was Horowitz whom he idolized most. However, there was no doubt that Halim should have this chance.

I had shied away from bringing Eduardus because he was Asian. Horowitz, a man filled with nonsensical prejudices, had often said that Asians could only imitate like monkeys, that they could never really play creatively.

Although Horowitz had seen Halim's photo, he said, "Bring him. Let's hear what he can do." Perhaps he didn't think he looked Asian.

Halim was terribly anxious and excited on the evening he was to meet Horowitz. When I met him on the corner of Ninety-fourth and Madison, I found him wearing a bow tie. Horowitz was in a good mood and began interviewing the young pianist. I could see that Halim was at ease and I felt that Horowitz liked him. In his little interview, Horowitz had neglected to ask Eduardus where he was born.

"What did you bring to play?" Horowitz asked. Eduardus was prepared to play one of Horowitz's specialities, the Bach-Busoni Toccata, Adagio, and Fugue. As Halim played, Horowitz kept looking at me, making pleased facial gestures. Afterward Horowitz made some suggestions as to the pacing of the long work and gave him advice about differing levels of sound. Horowitz could hear that Halim was already too influenced by his own recording of the work and encouraged him to have confidence in his own conception. But Horowitz was deeply impressed with him.

Just as Eduardus sat down, Horowitz said, "Do you mind if I ask you a question?"

Eduardus replied, "Of course not, Maestro."

Horowitz, with the most exquisite naïveté imaginable, leaned over and asked, "By the way, Mr. Halim, are you a member of the yellow race?"

Eduardus simply smiled, saying, "Yes I am, Mr. Horowitz. I was born in Indonesia. My parents are Chinese." Eduardus looked at me and smiled.

I wanted to burst out laughing. Naturally, I had prepared Eduardus for this question. Horowitz went no further. But I think he was incredulous that Halim was Asian. I also believe that his prejudice was broken. Never again did I hear him make any remark about Asians being unable to play Western music.

In Eduardus Halim, Horowitz found a talent whose elongated, tentacle-like fingers he could not resist molding. The great pianist became fond of Halim, even allowing him to use his own piano at his New York debut at the Kaufman Auditorium. During the last year of Horowitz's life, he coached Eduardus some twenty times.

After the Asian barrier was broken, I brought to East Ninety-fourth another Chinese pianist in my class, Dan-wen Wei, a student of Martin Canin. At the time, he was twenty-two and, like

Eduardus, possessed a virtuoso technique. He could whiz through Chopin's Etude in thirds like a breeze. Dan also lived and breathed the piano. At about six feet, weighing around a hundred thirty pounds, Dan's long straight hair falls over his forehead nearly into his eyes. When he plays, he looks like he is in the throes of either panic or ecstasy. His mouth is never in repose, and often a gurgling kind of singing emanates from his gut. With Dan's attitude of casual confidence, I was certain that Horowitz would like him.

The Maestro received Dan cordially and began his questioning. Dan told him he was born in China and had only come to the United States in the last five years. Horowitz commented on his excellent English. I had suggested to Dan that he play a great deal for Horowitz that evening, and Dan was prepared to offer Bach's *Italian* Concerto, the Scriabin Fifth Sonata, and Chopin's Fourth Scherzo. Dan began with the *Italian* Concerto. During the slow movement, Horowitz looked at me and imitated Dan's extreme facial contortions. If Dan had seen this, I'm sure he would have lost all confidence and probably would have collapsed.

However, when Dan played the Scriabin, Horowitz's interest was aroused. He looked at me frequently, with approval written on his face. "Not bad!" Horowitz shouted from the couch. "Let's now hear the scherzo." Horowitz afterward made several pertinent remarks, which were always remarkable for their succinctness and absolute pianistic truth. Dan felt wonderful as we left that night.

Early in 1991 I asked Wei about his visits with Horowitz. Here is the interview:

DUBAL: What did playing for Horowitz mean to you? You knew him the very last year of his life.

WEI: It was the greatest experience of my life.

DUBAL: Tell me about your period of study with him.

WEI: The first time I went there, you were already there. You had dinner with him that evening. I was nervous as hell because I didn't know what to expect. I immediately felt I was in the presence of some greatness. There was no doubt that he was different. He made me feel at ease immediately. That was true throughout the year. I was always nervous before I went, but I felt comfortable the minute I saw him. I also felt that to play for him was one of the easiest things in the world. I don't know why. I can't explain it. You got the feeling that whatever you did at the piano, he would understand. He'll know what's good, what's bad, where you are. I felt this even before he said a word.

After the first evening, he called me. I was not home. My roommate, who was a great music lover, answered the phone. When the voice said, "This is Vladimir Horowitz," his legs started trembling. Horowitz said, "Just tell him his teacher called." When I called him, he said, "Why don't you come back and play for me again." Altogether, I had around fifteen lessons in the next eleven months. The lessons were two hours long, sometimes more.

DUBAL: One of the reasons he was easy to play for was he seemed amazed that anyone else could play the piano.

WEI: Yes, that's it. I felt if I can play this through, he will be impressed. I once said, "Maestro, this is a very difficult piece." He said, "What are you talking about. *Every* piece is difficult. The more you know, the more difficult it gets, so every piece is difficult."

DUBAL: What did he mean to you growing up in China?

WEI: His records had even reached China. He was the ultimate pianist, the great Romantic pianist. I always admired how he combined a Romantic way of interpreting music with individuality and style. So many people play the same way no matter what the piece. Not Horowitz. Everything sounded individual, each composer was different, and he also created such a sense of sonority. I felt this even growing up.

With him, I lived the real atmosphere. With Horowitz, you were in the middle of the whole Romantic tradition. He was a source of inspiration and encouragement which for me had no limit. I always felt hampered by conventional playing, but being with Horowitz, I no longer felt in the minority in wanting to project my individuality. He made me less afraid in trying out various ways, going in different directions.

DUBAL: Fifteen lessons of two hours each is a significant amount. Were you always prepared?

WEI: You don't go and play for Horowitz without preparation. I wanted to learn and play as many works as possible for him. Naturally, every piece is not really ready to play and he would know.

DUBAL: Horowitz had great musical wisdom.

WEI: Yes, it was beyond belief. He could remember everything. After playing a piece, he would go to the piano, open the music and say, here you did this, that's good. But he never said "don't do this" or "this is bad." He always said, "Maybe you try it this way," or, "Maybe you do this."

DUBAL: Because he was himself "maybe"—always in flux, always experimenting.

WEI: That's right. But his "maybe" was an amazing thing. Throughout the year, I was trying to learn the principles of his way of playing, his way of communication.

DUBAL: What would you say those principles are?

WEI: I'm still trying to learn the way he could create a lot of tension, which has a great deal to do with phrasing and touch. I feel Horowitz was the pianist who played with the most direct touch. Much of the time, I do a lot of unnecessary things before I play the note. With Horowitz, I always felt that when he *hit the note*, he knew what it would sound like. He didn't worry about it.

DUBAL: Yes, because he already had an exact sonorous image in his mind of what that sound would be.

WEI: Exactly. He knew what was going to come out. This takes great confidence.

DUBAL: You must have seen during your sessions the immense pianistic experience he had, almost as if the entire history of how to play the piano was within him.

WEI: Absolutely. If he played for you, you knew this. His mind worked at a tremendous speed, at a pace that you wouldn't believe, that you cannot even follow. He was a genius, a genius!

DUBAL: Horowitz went way beyond a musician who had great instincts and didn't think much.

WEI: Oh, yes. He knew exactly what to do. I remember once I tried to do a lot of things in the opening theme of Chopin's E Major Scherzo. He said, "This theme comes back many times. Here, the first time, you must be simple. Now, when it comes again, then you really start making something." That is what I mean about his principles.

DUBAL: He would say, "No, don't use rubato in the opening measures of a piece."

WEI: Yes, I once played the Liszt Second Rhapsody for him. I was trying to be fancy in the opening statement after the introduction. He said play it straight. A lot of people can count and play straight, but it's boring. But Horowitz figured out every possible way to put together a lot of surface color and a lot of different concepts of pedaling.

DUBAL: How did you perceive his personality?

WEI: Very simple and very complicated, too. I never knew what he would say. Once I was shocked when I said I wanted to play the Prokofiev Seventh Sonata. "I don't know it," he said. "What's that, how does it go? I sang the theme but he still said, "No, I never heard that."

DUBAL: He played many games. Of course he knew the piece. He played the American premiere.

Did you ever play the Liszt *Benediction to God in the Solitude* for him?

WEI: I did. He liked my playing of it. But he would never say you're fantastic or anything like that. If he said, "Not so bad," that was a high compliment. I was sure happy with "Not bad."

He had a great sense of humor. He thought I'd like to look at the curious Siloti edition of the *Benediction*, so he loaned it to me. But I would always forget to bring it back. He would say, "You forget to bring it back because you want to come back next time. You always want to see me, so you don't want to return the music."

He truly loved the *Benediction*. He had not played it himself. He wanted to show me something about it, so he sat down and tried to play it. The melody is in the left hand. But as you know, the right hand is so awkward and tricky, you can't really sight-read it and make a lot of sense. So he said, "I don't know the right hand. It's not important. I tell you what, you play the right hand, I play the left hand and I'll pedal it for you." It was an unbelievable experience. The second time around, he screamed, "That was good! That was good! Let's do it again." This time, I was trying to follow him, to try to feel how he created his amazing phrasing with his magical pedaling. The way he pedaled, you heard different sounds, a different way of creating on the piano. All of a sudden, I heard the *Benediction* with me being a part of it.

DUBAL: Somehow, he could mold a phrase in such a way as to make it sound new and original.

WEI: Yes, yes, and also every time it would be somewhat different. He was totally creative, always working at the music. Once he said, "I think I like the Chinese." You brought him Eduardus and me, and he liked us. He was being funny. He said, "I think I should only teach Chinese. Do you know why?" I said, "Why, Maestro?" "Because they are very talented and they work very hard, which is important. You have to work hard."

DUBAL: How did you react to his personality?

WEI: It was very easy to be drowned by him. He was such an influential character. In a way, it's dangerous. His way becomes part of you. And before you know it, you are doing everything he was doing.

The last time I played for him, he was about to make the last recording and he was very nervous. He became a fellow pianist. He had to get in shape and learn all those pieces. I sensed that he was nervous. I played to him the Schumann *Fantasiestücke*, and there was one part where he said, "How did you do that? It sounds so difficult. Is it really difficult?" I said yes, and he said, "But do you think if I practice, I can do it? Can I do it?" This was because he was about to record.

DUBAL: Yes, he knew he was Horowitz, and he always had to come up to that standard. How do you feel now after the experience of his teaching?

WEI: If you imitate him, you are in trouble. But by being with him, I achieved a certain kind of confidence. I am not as frightened to be a little freer and a little unconventional. But without his presence, I have to be careful because, on my own, I can distort the style. But with him there, I felt I could try things because he gave me guidance. What he gave me has to be digested. To understand his simple words will take a long time.

DUBAL: Did you notice that he had real psychological insight as to what to say to you about a piece?

WEI: Yes, he knew when to say what. He knew if he said too much right after you learned a piece, you would be confused and you would try to do everything without letting it digest. He knew that it took time to arrive at an understanding of the piece. But he always emphasized the fact that you had to work hard and that you need to play in public.

He worked extensively with me on the Chopin F minor Concerto. He knew the work very well. In one part in the last movement, he said he could not play where the left hand goes over the right. He said, "I can play the whole thing but not that little place. So I don't play it." Of course I didn't believe that he couldn't play it. I used to be sloppy in the concerto, and without him saying, "Don't miss all those notes," he made it clear he was not pleased. It's not true that he didn't care about wrong notes, absolutely not. When I played for him, the style was important, the phrasing was important, the sound was important, but the right notes also. Horowitz was always the craftsman first.

DUBAL: Did Mrs. Horowitz ever attend the lessons?

WEI: Only twice. Once he asked me to play the *Benediction* for her and she liked it. One time, he came down and said, "I have good news for you. I heard the *Benediction* on the radio by a famous pianist. It was slow and dry and I said to myself, I have a Chinese pupil who plays it much better."

DUBAL: Did you ever get any feeling of a big ego? Did you think he thought of himself as the ultimate manifestation of a pianist?

WEI: No, never. He knew, of course, he was different, but he never said anything like he was the greatest. He just wanted the best from himself.

DUBAL: I remember a story Mrs. Horowitz told me. "Mr. Dubal," she said, "this is a good story that represents the quality of the public. We walked into the restaurant, and the maître d' says, 'Mr. Horowitz, how does it feel now to be numero uno?' We looked at him. Mr. Horowitz asked, 'What are you talking about? What do you mean, Number One?' He said, 'Now that Liberace is dead, *you* are Number One!' Can you imagine? That is today's audience."

WEI: Mrs. Horowitz once came to my rescue. I wanted desperately to play the *Second Hungarian Rhapsody* for him, but he didn't want to hear it. Mrs. Horowitz said, "You play it. Why can't he?" And so I did. I miss him now as you must, too. I want to repeat, going to play for him was the greatest experience of my life.

Another tremendously gifted young pianist that I brought to play for the Maestro was Mark Salman. Mark had graduated from Juilliard a few years before, but seldom missed visiting my masters seminar on Wednesdays. Mark is a six-foot-three, strapping young man who was then twenty-six. He has an insatiable curiosity about music and enormous respect for Liszt's music. One day in class, I challenged him to learn Liszt's *Twelve Transcendental Etudes*, one of the cornerstones of Romantic piano music. Lina Ramann called them "an unparalleled, gigantic work of spiritual technique." Mark had them prepared for class soon afterward. Seeing that he liked challenges, I said, "Now bring in Book I of the Debussy Preludes." After he accomplished that, I said, "Isn't it time you learned Beethoven's *Hammerklavier* Sonata?"

Mark has a formidable technique, although not as flashy as Eduardus's and Dan's. He is quiet and deeply serious. I think he lacked that certain flair needed to arouse Horowitz and win him over. I was disappointed that Horowitz did not take more of an interest in him, and it was a pity he only saw him twice, as Mark was the finest musician that I brought to play for Horowitz. Here is Mark Salman's account of his first visit with Horowitz.

On July 18, 1988, David Dubal asked if I would like to meet and play for Vladimir Horowitz. I was excited but also intimidated. Horowitz had always been one of my major idols, and I have turned to him more often than any other pianist for ideas and inspiration.

Dubal gave me his address, told me to wear a jacket and tie, and when to arrive. As I rang the buzzer, my heart sounded like a bass drum. I had never before been so nervous, not even for my New York debut. A maid directed me up a narrow staircase, where I paused and breathed deeply. I thought many a pianist would kill to be in the presence of Horowitz. I only hoped I would be able to talk, let alone play for him.

Through the double doors, which were half opened, I glimpsed the Maestro sitting on the couch, avidly talking to his wife and Dubal. As I entered, Dubal jumped up to introduce me. Mr. and Mrs. Horowitz greeted me warmly. Horowitz's smile radiated, while I was instantly aware of Mrs. Horowitz's resemblance to her father.

I was seated opposite the Maestro on a sort of ottoman with a coffee table between us, which had various books on it. Dubal eased my way into the conversation, and although I felt my upper lip tremble, I was a little more relaxed.

Horowitz questioned me about my studies, my favorite composers, what repertoire I was most interested in, and whether I got nervous before playing. When I said, "Yes, I get very nervous," he replied with a real feeling of comradeship, "Oh, I do, too." Mrs. Horowitz added with a twinkle in her eye, "I get more nervous just listening."

Horowitz's voice was a rather hoarse, low, guttural growl, and I strained with all my might to understand him over the air-conditioning on this extremely hot evening. I felt intensely uncomfortable having to ask him to repeat himself.

To my utter dread, he asked me if I would like to try the piano. I was secretly hoping somehow to avoid playing for him. My fingers felt like spaghetti, and I had had almost no chance to touch a piano since I heard I was to visit the Maestro. Naturally, I had no choice but to comply, and I went to the instrument as a man condemned to hang.

I had told him I was interested in unusual and neglected Liszt pieces, and to get a feel of the piano I tried out one of Liszt's short slow pieces, *La Lugubre Gondola No. 1.* I had always heard that the action of his piano was so fast that one could blow on the keys and it would play. But to my dismay, the piano, a new Steinway, Horowitz told me, had one of the heaviest actions imaginable. I thought, How can an old man even budge such a piano?

I was more or less ready to play any of the *Twelve Transcendental Etudes.* Of course, Horowitz chose No. 10 in F minor, the one I felt most insecure about that day. Soon after I began, I realized that his bench, which was nonadjustable, was lower than any bench I had encountered. The new piano, the bench, and my nervousness caused me to play quite poorly.

Afterward, Horowitz was very kind. I apologized for the performance, but he dismissed my comment and said that he could tell that I could play the piece with technical ease. I felt encouraged, and asked him if I could use some music to sit on. I took several scores from the piano, which was covered with piles of music.

I now plunged into the first two etudes and followed those with the fiendish *Feux follets* and the exhausting *Wilde Jagd.* On completion, Horowitz said, "Very good. You can play piano."

Mrs. Horowitz sat quietly throughout and added her compliments. My nerves now vanished, and I realized that Horowitz was actually easy to play for. He seemed to care little about wrong notes and was totally concerned with musical ideas.

He then asked me to play something lyrical, suggesting Liszt's *Petrarch Sonnet No. 104*, a piece that Horowitz owned. I knew the composition, but I was far from being prepared to play it. He said, "Use the music. It's somewhere in that pile." I found it, and played it through, faking some of the runs.

He now told me to play *Jadis*, a late Liszt piece which is a nostalgic waltz. As pianists today neglect the color potential of the left pedal, or una corda, afterward he told me to use more soft pedal.

To my delight, he came to the piano and played *Jadis* for me, but in his own version. He told me he was thinking of recording it. Horowitz then pointed out to us that he felt Liszt only sketched some of his later works, and he couldn't resist filling out or adding certain colors and effects. He showed me some of his alterations of left-hand figurations and subtle harmonic changes. He had also added short cadenza-like passages in some of Liszt's pauses, which were very much in keeping with the composer's late style, and which added to the work's effectiveness. Unfortunately, the Maestro never recorded it.

I now turned pages for him as he played the Liszt Prelude based on Bach's cantata Weinen, Klagen, Sorgen, Zagen. Dubal came over to watch the score, and Mrs. Horowitz left her seat for the couch. This piece he recorded on his last record.

From this position, I was able to observe his hands. His flat fingers allowed him to contact the keys with the bottom of his fingers, and he seemed to stroke the keys rather than press them. His hands appeared to me to have broad palms, and each finger was long, thick, and strong at the base, tapering to the tip. This seemed to account for the great strength of his hands and his amazing ability to bring out individual notes within a chord. He demonstrated several technical things to me about tone production.

As the evening progressed, I saw that Horowitz's knowledge of the piano literature was considerable, and he seemed to know almost all the lesser-known works of Liszt. It was obvious that a large part of the public saw him only as the great virtuoso and gave him little credit for his knowledge or how thoughtful an artist he was.

Later, he improvised a bit, somewhat in Rachmaninoff's

style. Then he played some of Liszt's *Feux follets* and showed me a few facilitations which would ease its difficulties.

Coffee and cookies were served, and we settled down to conversation about the Golden Age pianists, such as Rachmaninoff, whom he admired without reservation. He said Rachmaninoff was the biggest pianist, the most emotional. His records, great as they are, still give little indication of the immensity of his conception and sound. He said that he liked Lhévinne and nobody could play some of the Chopin etudes better. Friedman, too, got high marks from Horowitz, but he said he never cared much for Godowsky. He was too detached and cool, but he played wonderfully for friends in a room. In a big hall, however, his playing lost its effect and flopped.

Dubal asked Horowitz what he thought of the celebrated pianist and Liszt pupil, Emil von Sauer. Horowitz thought his playing very elegant and told us that Sauer liked to look at the audience while playing. And if he struck a wrong note, he looked very surprised.

The talk turned to politics. I was surprised how much he knew about the race for President. He said, "I no longer play the piano. Now I am only interested in politics."

Mr. and Mrs. Horowitz seemed to get along marvelously. They often teased each other. Horowitz would comment favorably about Ronald Reagan, whereupon Mrs. Horowitz would say, "You only like him because you played for him at the White House. He is a second-rate actor and a second-rate President."

Mr. Dubal said that it was now past midnight, and we stood up to leave. The Horowitzes graciously expressed concern about my having to travel so late at night to Connecticut, where I live, but I told them I would stay in Manhattan, at a friend's. They told me that I was welcome to come again. Unfortunately, I only had one more visit with Maestro Horowitz, and I will never forget the privilege of being with him.

45

THE BIRTHDAY PARTY:
HOROWITZ AT EIGHTY-
FIVE

In mid–September 1988, I received an invitation from Mr. and Mrs. Peter Gelb for a birthday party at their apartment celebrating Horowitz's eighty-fifth birthday.

There were very few acknowledgments for this occasion because of the confusion over Horowitz's year of birth. Most sources read 1904, but Horowitz was actually born in 1903; he said he had falsified the date to avoid conscription into the czar's army.

Although this was a major anniversary, Horowitz didn't seem perturbed at its lack of observance.

He laughed. "I don't give a damn for attention on just one day of the year. I like attention every day of the year. When I am a hundred, I will make sure everyone knows. If I can still move."

I had just published an excerpt in *Keynote* magazine on Horowitz from my forthcoming book, *The Art of the Piano*. The article, scheduled to coincide with his birthday, was an overview of his recordings and the repertoire he performed. I was pleased with the piece, and I had read it to him just after it appeared. I didn't want any surprises in case he didn't like it. The article was a tribute to his art, although I made minor criticisms of several records I didn't especially care for. He listened avidly and often nodded his head in approval.

When I finished, he said, "I think you like my records more than I do."

I was glad Mrs. Horowitz was out when I read him my article. She might have liked it less. At eleven o'clock, she came home.

Horowitz said, "Mr. Dubal just read his article on me."

Mrs. Horowitz haughtily announced, "I've seen it. Somebody has already sent it to me." Wanda assaulted me with a litany of criticisms of the article. She protected her husband like a lioness her cub. Nor could she tolerate any criticism of his playing unless, of course, it came from her.

"But Mrs. Horowitz," I gently protested, "this article is laudatory in the best sense." However, I felt terrible that she was upset by it.

Mrs. Horowitz continued, "I didn't want Volodya to see it."

"Do you think I would have read it to him if I was not proud of it?" Horowitz slouched in his seat and said nothing.

Earlier in the summer, I had read him several other sections from my book, which he complimented me on. My editor hoped I could get a blurb from Horowitz. I wasn't happy about asking, but I did.

"No, I can't do it," he exclaimed, irritated. "Then others ask me."

"All right, Mr. Horowitz, I won't ask again." But he knew by the tone of my voice that I was hurt, and I sounded perturbed.

Next week, much to my surprise, Horowitz had prepared a statement for the book.

★   ★   ★

I had been a faithful guest at his home now for three years. My visits were often inconvenient for me.

The woman I was seeing at the time was upset because she was invited only once, as a courtesy. There was no doubt Mr. and Mrs. Horowitz preferred our threesome and were possessive of me.

Over the past years, the Horowitzes had asked me to attend certain formal occasions and parties; however, it was taken for granted that I would come alone. At this juncture in our relationship, I felt I should have the right to bring a guest to these events as others did.

After receiving the birthday invitation, I decided to ask Mrs. Horowitz if I could bring my friend. I was nervous making this request, just as I had been when I sought the book blurb.

I have always had trouble asking for even a trivial favor. For me, to refuse a favor is difficult unless I feel clearly exploited.

Mrs. Horowitz, however, had no such problem. When we were alone, I asked whether I could bring a friend to the Maestro's birthday party.

She looked at me furiously and said, "This party is only for Mr. Horowitz's closest friends and business associates."

Her refusal was an edict. "All right, Mrs. Horowitz, I understand."

"But you *must* come. That is important."

"I won't disappoint Mr. Horowitz on his birthday. Of course I'll be there."

I felt like a child who had been put in his place. I had experienced the same feeling that winter. The three of us had dined out. It had snowed earlier that day but grew much worse during supper. Usually, when it was late, Mr. and Mrs. Horowitz drove me home first. If the weather was bad, they went home, and then they had me driven home. At other times, I left them and took a taxi.

This time, Wanda, for some perverse reason, wouldn't allow the driver to take me home. "You will find your way. There must be cabs."

Mr. Horowitz was nervous about her decision. "Wanda, why the driver not take Mr. Dubal home after he takes us? It's terrible out. Maybe Mr. Dubal will not come back to see me," he said as he gave me a helpless grimace.

"No, Maestro. If that's what Mrs. Horowitz wants, that's what she gets."

It was late and there was no cabs nor buses in sight. Trudging home from the East Side to the West Side took me forty minutes. I was sopping wet and felt peculiarly empty.

The next morning, I received a call. "David, this is Wanda Horowitz. Did you get home all right?"

I told her I walked home and would probably get sick since my feet were totally wet and frozen.

On Horowitz's birthday, a black-tie affair, I arrived with my gift, a score of the Mozart Requiem and the complete recorded piano works of Busoni. I found Gelb's apartment crowded.

Everyone else there was with a guest or spouse. I was the only one alone, except for the conductor James Levine, who dropped in later. Giuliana and her husband, Tom and Lynne, Mr. and Mrs. Isaac Stern the Perahias, Mia Farrow and Woody Allen, and many others. Even Richard Probst, who, like me, was in the habit of being with the Horowitzes alone, brought his friend Codie.

The party was predictable. Horowitz and Wanda sat on the sofa with gifts and congratulations pouring in. Isaac Stern gave a fine impromptu birthday speech. Mrs. Perahia and Wanda talked intimately. Perahia told me Horowitz was always speaking to him about me, and I told Murray what a blessing it was for Horowitz to have him in his life and playing for him.

Perahia said, "I can't tell you what he has done for my playing."

During the party, Horowitz frequently beckoned me over to sit between him and Wanda. I felt more like a son than a guest.

Lynne Frost said, "You are the apple of Horowitz's eye."

"Yes, perhaps so. But I'm a second-class citizen here."

Richard Probst came over to me and said, "I wish somebody would introduce me to Woody Allen."

"I'll introduce you."

"Do you know him?"

"No, Richard, but nevertheless, I'll introduce you."

Both Mia Farrow and Woody Allen were timidly standing alone, looking desolate. The couple occasionally had dinner with the Horowitzes, and Wanda was fond of Mia.

During the time Allen was filming *Crimes and Misdemeanors*, Wanda asked Woody why he didn't use her in one of his films. The very next day, she was called and asked if she wanted to be a walk-on. She arrived on the set, and indeed, there is a very good shot of her in the film.

"Woody," I casually said, "this is Richard Probst, director of Concerts and Artists at Steinway & Sons."

It was a brief conversation. Knowing Allen loved to play clarinet, Richard told him that before Steinway, he had worked in Paris for Buffet Crampon, the famous clarinet makers.

Woody appeared interested. "Why did you leave the clarinet for the piano?" he asked.

"Because he wanted to move up to a greater literature," I blurted out.

Allen merely nodded. Probably everyone wanted to be witty for him.

He looked brighter when I told him I enjoyed his recent review in the *New York Times Book Review* of the autobiography of Ingmar

Bergman. Both Mia and Woody appeared to be loners and intensely private. They soon left.

I ended the evening talking to Giuliana, a woman I had grown fond of over the years.

Giuliana Lopes, middle-aged, Italian-born, with marvelous high cheekbones and a beguiling accent, possessed exquisite tact. She is a natural helper and had been in the Horowitz service for years. Daily, she took the subway from Queens to the Horowitz residence, where she functioned on so many levels that no title could adequately describe her various duties.

Always sensitive and caring, her devotion to the Horowitzes was invincible. Indeed, she was even more indispensable to Horowitz than to Wanda. She bathed him, pampered him, and brought the daylight of reality to many of his thoughts. However, she was always at the mercy of two high-strung, demanding people, and at times a suppressed anger surfaced.

I once remarked, "You know, Giuliana, Horowitz loves you."

"Mr. Dubal," she said sharply, "may I tell you that Mr. Horowitz is incapable of love. Make no mistake about that. And I don't understand. He is like two people, one is the man and the other is the great genius that he is." Nevertheless, Giuliana was always discreet in her occasional complaints.

"Why do you stay with him?" I asked her.

"I believe I stay because of the music. Because through his music, he gives to the world. And it is through his music that he gives love."

"I understand, Giuliana."

"By helping him and encouraging him, I feel valuable," she said thoughtfully.

Giuliana displayed her usual tact. As I left the party, she said, "Mr. Dubal, may I congratulate you on your article on Mr. Horowitz. Forget about what anyone else says. It's a wonderful piece, and very intelligent."

"Thank you, Giuliana. I appreciate your comment."

"I know you are upset tonight. Lynne told me why, and you have every reason to be. Of course, you should be able to bring to a party anyone you want."

I hugged Giuliana and went home.

46

THE END OF A
FRIENDSHIP

During October 1988, I frequently visited the Horowitzes. The
Maestro was becoming more and more involved with the students I
brought from Juilliard as well as with Perahia. Although Horowitz
was not playing concerts, he was stimulated to practice and he was
busy hearing the young pianists. He was forced to verbalize his ideas
to them and he was excited by his renewed interest in teaching.

Horowitz, it seemed, now wanted to hear new pianists all the
time, and I soon found myself wondering whom I should bring next.
I thought, What have I gotten myself into?

Aside from this, nobody was to know Horowitz was listening to
students. We both insisted on secrecy. The students were made to
promise not to breathe a word about playing for Horowitz, not even
to their own piano teachers at Juilliard. I felt that the opportunity of
visiting Horowitz was more important than petty school politics.

Soon, however, it became messy. Horowitz would forget his vow
of secrecy by telling other students that so-and-so had just played for
him. Of course, the students all knew each other, so the halls of
Juilliard were filled with Horowitz gossip, and naturally, these
students were dying to tell others that they were playing for him.

At that point, I decided to tell Joe Polisi, Juilliard's president, that I was taking some students to visit the Maestro. Joe was delighted and couldn't imagine how any of their teachers could object.

On November 3, I was afflicted with some allergic reaction from my contact lens or the solution. It spread to both eyes, and for ten days, I suffered excruciating pain. Both eyes were bandaged and I was in terror of going blind.

Naturally I couldn't visit the Horowitzes. Mrs. Horowitz called to see how I was progressing. Although it was not yet mid-November, she mentioned that I was to be invited to a grand wedding anniversary party on the twenty-first of December. I would be getting a formal invitation. Afterward, I wished she hadn't told me, as I knew already that I would have to confront them about my bringing a guest.

In early December, I received the engraved invitation.

On December 6, I went to dine alone with Horowitz. Mrs. Horowitz was in Milan. The time had come and I was going to take up the issue with Horowitz himself. I was quite nervous.

He greeted me with even more warmth than usual. "You look very good tonight," he said buoyantly. He proceeded to tell me that Perahia called him on Sunday from London, as he did every week. He had suggested that Perahia work on Beethoven's Thirty-two Variations.

He then reported to me Halim's progress. At that point, Horowitz thought his playing too skittish, fidgety, and nervous. "But," he said, "Halim will have a career. Oh, yes!"

I was trying to find the right moment to broach the subject of the anniversary party before the maid called us to dinner. After I told him about the next student I was bringing him, I managed to pull the invitation from my jacket.

"Do you know what this is, Mr. Horowitz?"

"No," he replied. "What is it?"

"It's the invitation to your and Mrs. Horowitz's anniversary party."

"Oh, yeah, Madame says this will be a big party. You come, of course."

"Mr. Horowitz," I said, "believe me, I am honored to be invited to your anniversary party. But I must tell you, I shall not come alone."

Horowitz sat there dumbfounded. He hemmed and hawed. "I will talk to Wanda. She'll be back from Italy on the weekend."

"Maestro, you can talk to Mrs. Horowitz all you want, but I shall not come to the party alone. I think you should decide this yourself and let me know."

His eyes flashed: How dare I put him in this stupid position? "You know Wanda is in charge of these things. She likes only married people. She's Catholic."

I said, "Come now, Maestro. Are Woody Allen and Mia Farrow married? And I can name other exceptions who are allowed to your parties. You know very well that you have no bourgeois morality. You have no rules at all. What is this nonsense about marriage? Maestro, what I'm saying to you is that I am not a second-class citizen in the Horowitz entourage."

There was no doubt Horowitz was rather upset at this confrontation. Just then, we were called to dinner.

"We go down now. I go peepee first. After a good dinner, you will feel better."

When he returned, he sat, as always, at the head of the table, with me at his left side. During his absence, he had regained his composure and started talking about the people who had been ostracized from his life.

I wasn't interested in his message, and I took him by the arm and looked straight into his eyes. "Maestro," I said slowly, "are you telling me that I can be ostracized, too?"

"Oh, no," he said cautiously, "not you."

We continued our meal in the most amiable manner. Horowitz was eating boiled chicken and potatoes cooked according to a Polish recipe. We both loved potatoes, and as he saw me gobble mine, he took some from his plate to give to me.

"Eat," he said.

Afterward we went upstairs and talked until it was time for the news. "Stay a while and listen to the news."

"No, Mr. Horowitz, I'm so tired I can't keep my eyes open."

"Well then, if no news, I'll play for you."

"Maestro, tonight, even such a gift as that holds no enticement." I couldn't believe I had said it. For three straight years, that had been the glory of my visits. Tonight I was refusing to hear the great Horowitz play.

"Then go home to sleep. I see you soon."

"Don't forget to talk to Mrs. Horowitz about what we discussed."

"I will," he answered glumly.

I hugged Horowitz and left. I never saw him again.

47

THE PASSING OF THE
MAESTRO

Monday came and Giuliana didn't call. Well, I thought, Mrs. Horowitz is back and is either angry at my attempt at rebellion or else they don't know what to do. However, it looked like I was not to be invited over that week.

As the anniversary approached, there was no word from the Horowitzes.

Tom Frost called, deeply concerned. "Why is this stupidity happening? This is awful. David, he needs you. Why are they so unreasonable? Will they cut off their noses to spite their faces?"

"Tom, what are they thinking?" I asked.

"I think they are banking on your coming. That you will change your mind, but they're afraid to call you."

"This is so silly," I complained, "because there can't be the excuse that this is an intimate party. They've invited everybody from socialites to ambassadors. Tom, I won't go," I said firmly. "I'm not their possession. I requested a reasonable and simple thing, to have the right to bring a guest. I deserve this much. If they simply must have their way, I am not going to give in to them."

I asked, "What else has Horowitz said?"

"He is worried now that, without you, he won't get to see any more students."

273

"How typical, thinking only of himself. What am I, a pimp to bring him students? I've brought him enough. Do you know how time-consuming this has been?"

"Believe me, I understand," Tom said. "We know how good you have been to him."

"I'm sorry, too, but I won't be there unless I get the call telling me that I can bring whomever I want."

"You know they won't do that. They can't put themselves in any position of wrong."

"Well, my friend, you carry on, then. Because nothing but that simple call will change my mind."

The call did not come.

The very afternoon after the party, I met Murray Perahia by chance in a drugstore. He had flown in for the celebration.

"David," he sighed. "Your absence last night was conspicuous. I heard about what happened. This is terrible. He'll die without you."

"Murray, that is extravagant, to say the least. I'm sure he will miss me a little, as I will miss him, but I cannot go there after being slighted."

Murray continued, "There is not a Sunday that I call him that he doesn't talk to me about you or who you have brought to play for him."

I said, "No, it's a matter of principle. I will not see him again."

As we said good-bye, I felt confused. I am basically not a stubborn person. I dislike men of principle. I would rather be judged by men of heart. But in this case, I was adamant.

★ ★ ★

The new year began and I was busier than ever, occupied with many projects and considerable travel. In no way did I regret my decision. In fact, I felt relieved and free. I badly needed the extra time for myself.

Many people envied such a friendship. I frequently heard the comment, "How lucky you are. If only I could be a fly on the wall. Imagine hearing the greatest pianist of all time play for you at his home."

It's hard to give up what others would love to have, what had also been exhilarating for me. However, I have come to realize that my defection from our friendship was deeper than my conscious reason of being slighted socially. I felt I was giving far more to the relationship than I was getting, and the excuse that I was being insulted was my way out.

As a child, I had to inspire myself. There were no important gurus, nobody to feed off, no real mentors, and I had developed a powerful need for a father in art, and that was Horowitz.

The more I thought about it, however, the more I realized that in many ways, both Mr. and Mrs. Horowitz had much in common emotionally with my own parents. As a boy, I had given endlessly to my father. Now, after three years with Horowitz, I felt that I was in the same position. My conscious excuse for leaving Horowitz seemed to me perfect. The break was clean. I had no guilt, remorse, or any anger.

When my book *The Art of the Piano* was published in the fall of 1989, I felt a lump in my throat as I saw the back of the jacket, with Horowitz's words in a box boldly proclaiming "For all those interested in the piano and pianists, this book will provide great insight and knowledge. It must be read by everyone who loves the instrument."

I swelled with pride and sent him a copy "hot off the press," with a letter thanking him and sending my love to both of them. I received no reply.

I didn't send a birthday card on October 1 for his eighty-sixth birthday, but I thought of him that day as I practiced. It had been ten months since our separation.

On Sunday, November 5, I was in Phoenix, Arizona, where I was to give the first piano concert in the new Herberger Theatre. As I shaved in preparation for the lecture-recital, the television news seeped in. The voice said, "Vladimir Horowitz, the great pianist, died earlier today." My face froze, my hands shook, and my heart pounded. I was dazed. My spiritual father was dead. The pianist of the century was no longer.

I felt hollow as I made the short walk to the hall. The concert began at seven-thirty p.m. I appeared in the already darkened backstage only two minutes before. I took a deep breath, walked to the piano, and played Schubert's *Mourning* Waltz and Chopin's *Farewell* Waltz. I went to the lectern and told the audience that Vladimir Horowitz had passed away that afternoon. I spoke of his great contribution to the history of the piano. I saw wet eyes in the audience.

On returning home the next day, I found many phone messages

from friends who had heard the news. I called Frost to find out about the funeral arrangements. He said Horowitz would be buried in Milan, but the body would be on view at the Frank Campbell Funeral Chapel on Madison Avenue.

"Should I call Mrs. Horowitz?" I asked.

"I don't know," he said. "Just the other day, she was talking disparagingly of your book and threatened to send it back to you."

With that, Lynne took the phone, saying, "David, it's not about your book. They were still hurt that you left them."

The next day, I went to the funeral home with Eri Ikezi, a young pianist and the woman in my life. There had been long lines all day. Eri was upset at his passing; he was, for her, as for so many other pianists, the major symbol of the pianistic art.

We walked up to the casket. He looked like wax. I thought, Dear Maestro, your turbulent life is over. May you rest in peace.

The poignancy of the moment was enhanced by a tape Tom had made of Horowitz playing. I spotted Lynne sitting alone. She hugged me and wept bitterly.

"Please take me to see him," she asked. "I haven't been able to go up yet. Mrs. Horowitz is here in the side room of the chapel. When she comes out, go to her."

In a moment, Wanda appeared with Giuliana, and I went over to her, kissed her, and said, "Our hero is dead." I told her that I had paid tribute to him in Arizona on Sunday night.

She held my hands and, looking at me sadly, said, "You missed a lot this year."

"I know I did," I said. "Can you forgive me?"

"There is nothing to forgive. You missed a lot," she repeated.

"Mrs. Horowitz, do you want to see me in the near future?" She replied yes. I kissed Giuliana, who looked like the bereaved widow as well.

On November 10, I received a copy of an obituary by Byron Belt, which appeared in two hundred cities. I was gratified that Mr. Belt wrote at the end:

> Pianist and author David Dubal became very close to the very private Horowitz while preparing a magnificent series of radio interviews some years back.
>
> Some of that insight is reflected in Dubal's latest book, *The Art of The Piano: Its Performers, Literature, and Recordings*.

Not surprisingly, the Horowitz entry is the longest and most detailed in analyzing the man and his music.

Dubal concludes his study by commenting, "Throughout his career, Horowitz gave us indelible performances of many works in the repertoire, always revealing new avenues of color and detail. His recordings are precious documents of the art of piano playing. Horowitz has shown us more completely than anyone else the glory of this instrument in all its range and sonority."

★ ★ ★

As 1990 began, my long career at WNCN ended. The radio station I dearly loved had been inching its way downhill. WNCN no longer pursued a sophisticated, civilized format. There was cynical contempt for art and the public. It had become a crass, vulgar business machine with a nonstop action sound for an idealized yuppie.

Horowitz had once said to me, "If you play one more piece of Telemann on your station, I'll die."

I started to believe what Baudelaire had written: "The spirit of every businessman is completely depraved."

Slowly, over the years, my position was eroded until I became merely a figurehead. On January 20, I resigned.

Immediately after my break with WNCN, I plunged into my book *Conversations With Menuhin*, which had to be sent to the publisher, Heinemann, in London, by May 1. Throughout this time, Mrs. Horowitz was on my mind, and I called several times, but somehow we both put off seeing each other.

In May, Eri and I were in Italy. In Milan, we went to pay respects at the famous Cimitero Monumentale, where Horowitz was buried in the Toscanini tomb. At that time, there was still no indication he had been buried there.

I laughed when Lynne Frost told me that, because Horowitz was Jewish, the powers at the cemetery didn't want him. However, Mrs. Horowitz called the Vatican, saying, "Horowitz, toward the end of his life, was leaning toward Catholicism." This did the trick.

Around that time, I received a call from Peter Goodrich, the new director of Concerts and Artists at Steinway, asking me to lunch. He told me of Steinway's plan to send Horowitz's famous piano to many cities and asked if I would like to do a program to complement the tour. I would play on his piano, talk about him, and create an audiovisual program with segments of the master's playing. I thought it a marvelous idea. Horowitz, it seemed, was back in my life.

My program was successfully launched at Steinway Hall on January 17, 1991, to an overflow house. The very next day, the piano began its nationwide journey.

The Maestro had taught technicians exactly what he wanted from his piano, and he had jealously guarded it since 1943. Steinway sent on tour only one other pianist's instrument: Paderewski's.

Modestly named CD 503, Horowitz's is the 314,503rd piano made by Steinway (CD stands for Concert Department). It is a gorgeous instrument, with the largest tonal range imaginable, and because it was Horowitz's, the instrument's mystique seems for many to be almost supernatural. CD 503 is by no means an orphan; it is loved everywhere. People want to touch it, kiss it, play on it, and be photographed with it.

Mrs. Horowitz was unhappy about commercializing her husband's piano. She said, "I don't care now if the piano is in a bordello. But at least *you* are doing the program. You understood him and loved him."

I hope Horowitz doesn't mind that I play his piano. At times, I feel touching it is sacrilegious. But his spirit is most definitely with me. I have found myself saying, before performing, "Maestro, I hope I play *your* Scriabin etude well. Don't be angry with me if it's not worthy of you."

For me, there is no escaping him, nor do I want to.

AFTERWORD

AN APPRECIATION

To the world, Vladimir Horowitz was the virtuoso pianist par excellence, as Heifetz was for the violin. As with his nineteenth-century forebears, Paganini and Liszt, Horowitz's playing was often described as diabolical. No doubt if he had lived in Paganini's time, the superstitious would have crossed themselves as he passed by. Once, when I was talking to the violinist Wanda Wilkomirska, she said, "Horowitz is the best. He is better than anyone, any violinist, any singer, any pianist. Oh, but he is also not human!"

Horowitz did things at the piano which just did not seem possible to other pianists. One of his interpretive achievements was the very rare ability to capture in piano playing the eerie, the sardonic, the frightening, and the perfidious. He was a man who daily fought his demons. The dark side of his temperament was channeled into his art. His "souped-up" arrangement of Mussorgsky's *Pictures at an Exhibition* at moments sounds ghoulish. Don't listen at midnight with the lights off. Or in his amplification of Liszt's transcription of Saint-Saëns' *Danse Macabre*, one "sees" the rattling of skeletons in the graveyard. Horowitz portrayed the sound of bells with a moonlit spectral radiance in an evocation at once metallic and seductive.

I shiver when he puts his hand to Scriabin's vertiginous scores. His playing of *Vers la flamme* is a conflagration. The tension is maddening, choking. For four minutes, Horowitz has his listener in his deadly grip. Or listen to the Horowitz recording of Scriabin's Tenth Sonata: The sun relentlessly beats upon the flesh, the gigantic trills burn the eyelids. ("Look into the eye of the sun when you listen to my *Poem of Ecstasy*," Scriabin once shouted to a listener.) Such extravagant music demands the untrammeled temperament of a Horowitz.

For a journey to perfidy, listen to his performance of Scriabin's Ninth Sonata, known as *The Black Mass* and composed in a fit of sinister inspiration. The composer found it a "falling from grace." The nearly insane Scriabin feared his creation and would not touch it. Horowitz, however, touches it, and the sulfurous smell of evil seems to reek in every measure. Horowitz is a necromancer, his smile sickening, slime on his fingers. Sir Sacheverell Sitwell once said, "Liszt had the glamorous eye," but surely Horowitz had "the evil eye" as well. He plays *The Black Mass* in a shroud.

Another Horowitz feat of black magic is the Scriabin Fifth Sonata. Here, F-sharp Major and B Major blend into a hypnotic and smoldering perfume. Horowitz virtually explodes in pent-up erotic passion. Its languid sultriness is almost lewd. For comparison, listen to the same sonata in Richter's marvelous, finely chiseled reading. It is mother's milk to the Dionysian orgy in which Horowitz engulfs us.

The psychic energy Horowitz poured into such scores was only equaled in very different idioms by Schnabel in some slow movements of Beethoven and Schubert, and by Toscanini in Beethoven's Seventh Symphony and Verdi's Requiem. Horowitz played Scriabin with a nervous exaltation, and he saw a frightening vision. And it must be noted that Horowitz was a superb architect. His ability to cover up flaws in a musical structure was admirable indeed.

But Horowitz is a poison mushroom, a musical addiction. Too much of him is bad for the purely musical instinct. He seduces one from the simple and beautiful, from a sense of normalcy. Horowitz worship is a cult, a contagion, and he has been a dangerous force for many a pianist who has tried to be a "little" version of his idol.

Horowitz was a law unto himself. Technically, he was supra-normal. His mechanism was so vast, and yet so pinpointed, that he must have felt his nervous system to be on fire. He was in a state, so to speak, of constant articulation. Horowitz, however, like all true virtuosi, was obsessed by the conquest of his instrument. He liked telling me that Busoni said, "To be more than a virtuoso, one must first be a virtuoso," and Horowitz would add, "There are few enough real virtuosos."

Although the Romantic composers were his lifeblood, Horowitz was attracted to many styles. At home, he went through various composer moods, in which Fauré, Clementi, Haydn, or Scarlatti would be his daily bread, as Mozart was in his last years. He was concerned with correctness of idiom. For Scarlatti, he would call in the harpsichordist Ralph Kirkpatrick for consultation. When Debussy occupied him, George Copeland, a Debussy specialist, would discuss the French master with him.

In his own way, Horowitz was a humble interpreter, always searching for the musical style. He never consciously violated a score, but like all truly original artists, he had his iconoclastic side. This originality bothered many conservative critics. Horowitz, they explained, is not a musician. He can't really interpret the great Classical masters. Yes, it was conceded with condescension, he could play Liszt well. For them, he remained the man with the fastest, loudest octaves, an image he could never quite dispel.

Yet Horowitz's recordings of many Classical works hold up brilliantly. Some of his Beethoven playing is riveting, especially the Sonata, Op. 10, No. 3 and the *Pathétique* Sonata. Horowitz's Haydn is quirky and characteristic, his Clementi sonatas noble, while his Scarlatti sonatas are unequaled in their rhythmic tensions.

Horowitz's Schubert was never congenial to me. A 1953 disc of the great B-flat Sonata is strange, although fascinating. It is not the lovable, tragic Schubert felt by Schnabel, Kempff, Haskil, Hess, or Curzon.

Nor is his Mozart the kind that passes for the usual. It has been condemned for being too flexible; he paints with almost an impressionist's palette, and the strokes of magical color he lavished on Mozart may eventually change the "straighter way" we have been accustomed to while listening to the Salzburg master. Certainly, the Horowitz Mozart is as colorful as Glenn Gould's is dry and ironic. Hearing them both, Mozart would have been fascinated by the flexibility of his idiom.

Horowitz was not merely a musician, but an artist who used the piano as his medium, his subjects being the composers he loved. Basically, his was not a re-creative mind, but a creative one. His playing was highly subjective, and I'm sure that we would be shocked by Mozart's playing, or by Beethoven's, Paganini's, Chopin's, or Liszt's. These were not just great musicians; they were each massive geniuses who played with unimagined creative force.

Horowitz understood above all else that music had to be "projected"; it had to be implanted into the listener's very being. He could make his audience hushed, listening spellbound to every note. The pianist Arthur Loesser must have had the Russian in mind when he begged students "to put some makeup on the music. You've got to get it across the footlights to the audience, or you'll lose them." Horowitz felt that the musical purists are a little clan of pedants, who had no understanding of the reality of public music making. They should stay home and read the score silently.

Horowitz was a master of playing in large halls. He had a wonderful acoustical sense and understood how sound fills space. He studied the properties of each hall before a concert; he knew every crack in the wall. If his piano were moved a few inches, his acoustical equilibrium could be fatally disturbed. He needed a rich-sounding hall and was sadly serious when he said to me, "I have my integrity, you know; I won't play in bad hall for a million dollars."

Of course, his quest for excellent acoustics was a luxury only he could afford. When the refurbished Carnegie Hall opened, he played one piece at the gala opening. He shouted to me, "I will never play there again!" To him, it spelled one more forum for his art that was now closed to him. The Horowitz arena was small, and he told me, "Someday I'll only be able to play at the Amsterdam Concertgebouw," a hall he felt was ideal: not too bright or dry, but mellow-sounding throughout.

The piano is officially labeled a percussive instrument, but its nature and its raison d'être is as an instrument of "inflection" that can achieve shadings through a variety of touch and dynamics. It is for this reason that the piano was the chief confidant of the Romantic composers. (Just think of a Chopin nocturne on the harpsichord.) Horowitz was unrivaled in producing a wide range of tone colors, which he accomplished through a perfect judgment of finger pressure and an uncanny use of the pedals.

Horowitz never used the pedal without thinking, never instinctively as do so many pianists. It was always part and process of his overall conception of a score. Nor was it used as merely an amplifying or blending apparatus. Pianists often try to disguise defects or improper technique by overpedaling. Horowitz hated this, calling it dishonest playing. He never used the pedal where the fingers alone should be doing the work. He played for me pedal-less, demonstrating that the piano need not be impersonal or "soulless" without pedaling. He condemned the avoidance of the una corda (the left pedal), of which, like Cortot, he was a great exponent.

Horowitz's hands were long and lean. But they were by no means gigantic, as were the hands of Arthur Rubinstein, Josef Lhévinne, or Rachmaninoff. They were muscular, yet softly supple and quite young-looking, even at age eighty-five. His basic hand position—with fingers outstretched, or literally straight out—looked, and was, unorthodox to those taught to curve their fingers. However, genius never does as others do, and very early, he found the best use of his hands. Somehow, he was able to achieve a fantastic clarity and evenness in passagework. (His *"jeu perlé,"* he told me, was the envy of Rachmaninoff.) It seemed that with his fingers straight forward, he could caress and knead the keys with more pressure. He often played with slightly curved fingers as well. He had a tremendously long and powerful fifth finger. Once he exclaimed, "One needs a strong 'pinky' for the Rachmaninoff Third Concerto."

Obviously, a great deal of his technique came from a fabulous inborn and unique motor system, bound to a rhythm of elemental steadiness. His sonority could pierce the eardrum, and his softest sigh could reach the farthest corner of the hall. When listening to him, I was often reminded of the phrase "A nightingale cooing in a thunderstorm,' uttered by Rossini when he first heard a Steinway piano. It has surely been through the art of Horowitz that we have best understood the coloristic potential of the modern piano.

Although Vladimir Horowitz lived to see his eighty-sixth birthday, his death on November 5, 1989, spread like a shock wave through the world of music. He had become the most beloved pianist in the world.

When Horowitz was born, there were fewer than one billion people in the world, but scattered among them were dozens of great virtuoso pianists. Today, with an exploding population nearly eight times that of 1900, we can claim very few pianists capable of moving an audience on the deep levels of a Horowitz.

After the birth of Ferruccio Busoni in 1866, only thirty-seven years elapsed until Horowitz, Rudolf Serkin, and Claudio Arrau, all born in 1903. Those few preceding decades saw an astonishing outburst of pianistic talent which produced what has been called the Golden Age of piano playing. (These were Golden Ages in violin playing and the art of singing as well.)

To understand properly this sadly disintegrating tradition, it is necessary to name only the more important of the pianists born in this period. They include Ignacy Jan Paderewski, Emil von Sauer,

Moritz Rosenthal, Harold Bauer, Leopold Godowsky, Frederic La-
mond, José Vianna da Motta, Eugene d'Albert, Alexander Siloti,
Alexander Scriabin, Edouard Risler, Sergei Rachmaninoff, Josef
Lhévinne, Marguerite Long, Ricardo Viñes, Josef Hoffman, Ernö
von Dohnányi, Alfred Cortot, Ossip Gabrilowitsch, Mark Ham-
bourg, Harold Samuel, Egon Petri, Artur Schnabel, Percy Grainger,
Ignaz Friedman, Wilhelm Backhaus, Arthur Rubinstein, Myra Hess,
Benno Moiseiwitsch, Clara Haskil, José Iturbi, Walter Gieseking,
Alexander Brailowsky, Guiomar Novaes, Simon Barère, Robert
Casadesus, Solomon, Maria Yudina, Mischa Levitzki, Vladimir
Sofrontisky.

These and many more were Horowitz's immediate predecessors.
They were all renowned, had thriving, influential careers, and
played to sold-out halls. These artists were comfortable as part of an
honored tradition and a branch of high culture. Most important,
these pianists possessed an indescribable individuality. Not one
resembled any other.

In 1991, Horowitz's great contemporaries, Serkin, Arrau, and
Wilhelm Kempff, died. For many, this was the end of a vanishing
race of giants. The last vestige of a great tradition passed on. Was it
any wonder that the Horowitz I knew felt isolated? Nor is it
surprising that the many young pianists whom I teach today feel
alienated from society and the richness of their tradition. Many of
these young musicians do not even know the names of the pre-
Horowitz pianists that I have listed.

The French philosopher Roland Barthes writes, "The human
subject has changed: intimacy and solitude have lost their value, the
individual has become increasingly gregarious, he wants collective,
massive, often paroxysmal music, the expression of *us* rather than of
me."

The solo piano recital has fallen victim to this attitude and shows
signs of eventual extinction.

The necessary intimacy between the individual and his or her
instrument and the endless hours of quiet needed to develop are no
longer available in our hectic, noisy world. The romance of the single
individual on stage communing with a piano has been replaced by the
amplification and mass hysterics of pop music, promoted endlessly.
This amplified musical fascism produces an environment that gives
little scope to study the inward serenity of Bach, the romantic
solitude of Schumann, or the ethereal ecstasy of Debussy.

Only when a society values, respects, and protects the individual's worth and his privacy can there be the possibility of major talents blossoming. It cannot happen in isolation or the poor artist will be considered a "freak," and will indeed feel like one. At best, he will be called an eccentric, a word which was so often applied to the older Horowitz, both as a man and musician.

The word *eccentric* has become a polite euphemism for "crazy." Nobody called Paderewski, Busoni, Schnabel, Rachmaninoff, or Godowsky eccentric. For another Golden Age to be nurtured, there must be a sophisticated, open-hearted, and open-minded audience to sustain and maintain a large group of instrumentalists of high artistic caliber.

During Horowitz's last thirty-five years, he took a major stand against the hysteria that his own concerts produced through his own often unchecked virtuosity. He was a born showstopper, and part of the success of his programs and his immense public acclaim were due solely to the fact that he could use his unique powers to seduce the lower musical impulses of his primarily superficial audiences.

Musical excitement is a heady brew, and Horowitz, an addictive personality, was almost swallowed up by his own potion. Virgil Thomson was probably correct in his estimation when he wrote in 1950, "One sees fewer and fewer known musicians at his recitals, more and more a public clearly not familiar with standard piano repertory."

Aesthetic awareness was generally not a priority at a Horowitz concert. His quest for glory nearly eclipsed him as an artist. A lesser person would have been content to use such ability to astonish, make money, and be famous. Horowitz, however, knew the meaning of André Gide's statement, "The pianist is well aware that the less I understand, the more I shall be impressed."

To his credit, he spent much time after his retirement in recovering, defining, and promoting neglected masters such as Scarlatti, Clementi, and Scriabin. He had already taught us how magnificent such usually poorly played composers such as Liszt and Rachmaninoff can sound. In his last years, he discovered new pianistic colors which he applied to his every-growing admiration of Mozart.

His last venture in recording still reveals Horowitz's deft finger nimbleness in the Chopin *Fantaisie-Impromptu*, a spry and humorously fetching Haydn sonata, and an otherworldly lyricism in two late Chopin nocturnes.

On this last recording, he plays the almost desolate prelude by Liszt based on a theme from Bach's Cantata No. 12, *Weinen, Klagen, Sorgen, Zagen*. In this work, the pianist weeps and laments. This was the last music he recorded, only two days before his death. He was working at his beloved instrument until his final breath. It was this Liszt-Bach prelude which he once again played only hours before passing away. At eighty-six, Horowitz died too young.

The pianist Richard Goode said, "When you think of Horowitz, you can never lose sight of his personality, his own inner law. He was a phenomenon. What happened was something between him and the instrument. It was that magical act between him and his fingers and the keyboard, his imagination, and that weird sound world that only he knew how to unlock."

The finest homage to his memory will be to listen often to his interpretive genius through his large recorded legacy. This will forcefully remind us of a musician who followed his own path. Through labor and love, he forged a body of recording that has the power to stir the human heart. For future generations, pianists will be gloriously reminded of what a piano is capable of producing technically, as well as its possibility of poetry and dynamic range.

Yehudi Menuhin, the great violinist, said this to me about Horowitz: "He was a man who was as concentrated on his keyboard as any human being had ever been. Horowitz had a genius of his own, in the mastery, in the touch, in the expression. He was a man driven by this instrument. He was possessed by it. This kind of possession is something we need in the world. We need people like that because there are certain things that happen in art only when you can give all and everything you have, including your life. Horowitz had this."

HOROWITZ ON
COMPACT DISC
A DISCOGRAPHY

BACH–BUSONI

Toccata, Adagio, and Fugue, BWV 564
  CBS M3K 44681

Horowitz felt Bach was not suited to large halls. But I suspect that since he grew up in the decline of Russian Romanticism, "pure" Bach was not much to his taste. The ripe arrangements of Bach–Busoni were in fashion during his youth, and he gravitated to Busoni's wonderful transcription of the great *Organ Toccata*. It was in his repertoire by age seventeen, and he used it in 1965 for his Carnegie Hall "comeback" recital. The performance is in the grand manner.

BARBER, Samuel

Sonata
  RCA 60377-2-RG

Horowitz recorded Barber's only piano sonata in 1950. From the moment of its release, the recording has inspired countless pianists to attempt its many difficulties.

The Barber Sonata is the most performed of any American piano sonata. In it, Horowitz is dashing, playful, and dramatic. In the fourth movement, a fugue, there is a joyous overflow of energy and zest.

In 1977, when I was preparing broadcasts of Barber's music, the composer, who was especially conscious of "performance," called me to make certain I would use the Horowitz recording of the sonata. Barber said, "To this day, I can't get over it."

BEETHOVEN, Ludwig van
    Thirty-two Variations in C minor
        EMI USA CDHC 63538

    Sonata No. 7 in D Major, Op. 10, No. 3
        (LP) RCA LM-2366
        LSC-2366

    Sonata No. 8 in C minor, Op. 13 ("Pathétique")
        CBS-MK 34509

    Sonata No. 14 in C-sharp minor, Op. 27, No. 2 ("Moonlight")
        RCA 60461-2-RG
        RCA 60375-2-RG
        (LP) CBS-MK 44797

    Sonata No. 21 in C Major, Op. 53 ("Waldstein")
        RCA 60375-2-RG
        CBS Cassette MT 31371

    Sonata No. 23 in F minor, Op. 57 ("Appassionata")
        RCA 60375-2-RG
        CBS MK 34509

    Sonata No. 28 in A Major, Op. 101
        CBS-MK 45572

    Piano Concerto No. 5 in E-flat Major, Op. 73 ("Emperor")
        RCA Victor Symphony
        Fritz Reiner, conductor
        RCA 7992-2-RG

Although Horowitz was ambivalent about Beethoven, he nevertheless made a significant contribution to Beethoven recording. Horowitz generally preferred the early and middle periods to the late style. He told me he had carefully studied Liszt's arrangements of the Beethoven symphonies and found in them the ideal transference of Beethoven's orchestra to the piano.

When I told him I admired his performance of the *Emperor* Concerto, he said, "That record is not bad."

It is tight, lean, and heroically cast.

His 1932 venture into Beethoven's Thirty-two Variations is tightly packed with tension and drama.

His *Waldstein* and *Appassionata* Sonatas are glittering and high-powered, though somewhat self-conscious. The later CBS releases are less projected.

The three recordings of the *Moonlight* are interesting to compare. Horowitz is generally not comfortable in the first two movements, but the finale is immense in its surging restlessness. The 1972 CBS version is not only explosive, but also defines the work's structure with a newfound spaciousness.

The early (1796) Sonata in D Major, Op. 10, No. 3, finds Horowitz inspired in the great slow movement in D minor. The pianist presents the pathos of a Greek tragedy with a sound only he could achieve. His recording of the *Pathétique* Sonata is a magnificent and large conception.

Horowitz's lone recording from Beethoven's third period is an expressive interpretation of the sonata, Op. 101, one of the most technically difficult of the entire cycle. The performance of the first movement is from a Queens College recital in 1967; the rest is taken from a Carnegie Hall concert days later. The result is one of the finest recordings of this enigmatic work. The first movement is stated with a disarming simplicity. The march movement brings to the surface the weirdness inherent in the score, while the fugal playing is exultant.

BIZET–HOROWITZ

Variations on a Theme From "Carmen"
  RCA 7755-2-RG
  CBS MK 44797

The *Variations on a Theme From Bizet's "Carmen"* takes the Gypsy Song from Act II for its theme. Horowitz made slight changes in his CBS version of 1968. I prefer the earlier 1947 performance on RCA. The *Variations* are clever and the playing unique.

BRAHMS, Johannes

Piano concerto No. 2 in B-flat Major, Op. 83
  NBC Symphony Orchestra
  Arturo Toscanini, conductor
  RCA 60523-2-RG

Horowitz recorded little Brahms. He can be heard on CD in a virile presentation with Nathan Milstein of the Brahms Violin Sonata, Op. 108 (RCA 60461-2-RG). The tiny A-flat Waltz, Op. 39, No. 15 is available on LP.

The lovely B-flat minor Intermezzo, Op. 117, No. 2, can be heard on the CD containing the Brahms Second Concerto. The inter-mezzo, recorded in a live performance in 1951, is played without the tenderly passionate Brahmsian musings and questionings. It is, however, well balanced and convincing.

The Brahms Second Piano Concerto is the only four-movement concerto in the active repertoire. The 1940 Horowitz–Toscanini collaboration is now more than half a century old. It is a stern reading, lean and muscular, at times almost strident and percussive, but fresh and bracing. One hears Toscanini's no-nonsense, unsenti-mental approach. Horowitz said it was more Toscanini's conception than his own.

The conductor, known for his quick tempi, dispatches the con-certo in 44:00, four to six minutes longer than the average. There is not a shred of weltschmerz. We hear a more remote Brahms, but one that glitters with detached intensity performed with raw passion.

Because of Horowitz's sparse use of pedal, the reading, especially in the first two movements, exudes a feeling of bitterness. It is a performance that many find unidiomatic—one either loves it or hates it—but it is an important view of a sublime masterpiece.

CHOPIN, Frédéric

Andante Spianato and Grande Polonaise in E-flat Major, Op. 22
    RCA 7752-2-RG

Ballades:

No. 1 in G minor, Op. 23
    RCA RCD1-4572
    RCA 60376-2-RG
    CBS MK 42306
    CBS M3K 44681

No. 4 in F minor, Op. 52
    RCA RCD 14585

Barcarolle in F-sharp Major, Op. 60
    RCA 7752-2-RG

Etudes:

E Major, Op. 10, No. 3
  RCA 60376-2-RG
  CBS MK 42306
C-sharp minor, Op. 10, No. 4
  RCA 60376-2-RG
  CBS MK 42306
G-flat Major, Op. 10, No. 5
  RCA 60376-2-R6
  CBS MK 42306
F Major, Op. 10, No. 8
  CBS M3K 44681
C minor, Op. 10, No. 12
  CBS MK 42306
A-flat Major, Op. 25, No. 1
  Sony Classical SK 45818
E minor, Op. 25, No. 5
  Sony Classical SK 45818
C-sharp minor, Op. 25, No. 7
  RCA 7752-2-RG
  CBS MK 42412

Impromptu No. 1 in A-flat Major, Op. 29
  RCA 60376-2-RG

Introduction and Rondo in E-flat Major, Op. 16
  CBS Cassette MT 30643

Fantaisie-Impromptu No. 4 in C-sharp minor, Op. 66
  Sony Classical SK 45818

Mazurkas:
F minor, Op. 7, No. 3
  CBS MK 42306
A minor, Op. 17, No. 4
  CBS MK 42306
C-sharp minor, Op. 30, No. 4
  M3K 446181
  RCA 60376-2-RG
D Major, Op. 33, No. 2
  CBS MK 42306

D-flat Major, Op. 30, No. 3
  CBS MK 42306
B minor, Op. 33, No. 4
  CBS MK 42412
E minor, Op. 41, No. 2
  CBS MK 42306
C-sharp minor, Op. 50, No. 3
  CBS MK 42412
C minor, Op. 56, No. 3
  Sony Classical SK 45818
F-sharp minor, Op. 59, No. 3
  CBS MK 42306

Nocturnes:
E-flat Major, Op. 9, No. 2
  RCA 60376-2-RG
F minor, Op. 55, No. 1
  CBS MK 42306
  RCA 60376-2-RG
E-flat Major, Op. 55, No. 2
  Sony Classical SK 45818
B Major, Op. 62, No. 1
  Sony Classical SK 45818
E minor, Op. 72, No. 1
  CBS MK 42412

Scherzo No. 1 in B minor
  RCA 60376-2-RG
  CBS MK 42306

Sonata No. 2 in B-flat minor, Op. 35
  CBS MK 42412
  RCA 60376-2-RG

Polonaises:
A Major, Op. 40, No. 1
  CBS MK 42306
  CBS MK42412
F-sharp minor, Op. 44
  CBS M3K 44681
A-flat Major, Op. 53
  CBS MK 42306
  RCA 7755-2-RG

Polonaise-Fantaisie in A-flat Major, Op. 61
   CBS MK 42412
   RCA 7752-2-RG

Prelude in B minor, Op. 28, No. 6
   CBS MK 42306

In the genres of the polonaise and mazurka, Horowitz is at his finest as a Chopin interpreter. He has a real flair for the pomp of the polonaise, and his readings of the A Major ("Military"), the A-flat, Op. 53 ("Heroic"), and the Polonaise-Fantaisie are enthralling. His greatest achievement in the polonaise form is a nerve-racking performance of the Polonaise in F-sharp minor, Op. 44. His 1945 recording of the *Andante Spianato and Grande Polonaise* has become a classic.

Horowitz is surely one of the greatest of mazurka players: impish, painfully nostalgic, employing a wide variety of touch and an exotic rubato.

In the nocturnes, Horowitz is sultry and voluptuous. His nocturnes are never innocent, but dense with a musky atmosphere and a passionate eroticism.

In both of his recordings of the *Funeral March* Sonata, the pianist reveals a Byronic Chopin burning with frustration and blood-curdling rhetoric.

Horowitz recorded the G minor Ballade four times. Each one is different; all are vivid. His recording of the Fourth Ballade is convincing, with many original moments.

His interpretation of the Barcarolle is uncomfortable; the waters are troubled, the crooning and warblings sound artificial.

Although he recorded all four scherzi, only No. 1 has been transferred to CD. Horowitz hurls himself into the mighty coda.

Horowitz was highly successful with the Chopin etudes that he recorded. His final disc presents a highly original view of the E minor Etude, Op. 25, No. 5. His *Revolutionary* Etude shows a swirling, propulsive left hand, all of the notes perfectly welded together with an extra drive and cutting edge.

In the Rondo, Op. 16, the pianist is most infectious and elegantly sparkling in this uncharacteristic and happy composition.

At times, there is a clash of personalities between Chopin and Horowitz. The great virtuoso could overwhelm the delicate Pole. His phrasing can sound unnatural, even hysterical, yet every performance compels my attention. He presents a deeply emotional, highly charged, virile portrait of Chopin.

Horowitz was deeply attuned to the Polish master's despairing rage. In every piece, there is the hand of a creative musician passionately basking in the poetry of this incomparable literature.

CLEMENTI, Muzio

Sonata quasi Concerto in C Major,Op. 33, No. 3
Sonata in G minor, Op. 34, No. 2
Sonata in F minor, Op. 14, No. 3
Sonata in F-sharp minor, Op. 26, No. 2
Rondo from Sonata Op. 47, No. 2
    RCA 7753-2-RG

All that Horowitz recorded of Clementi is here on one compact disc. Horowitz had great faith in this music and never tired of perusing the nearly sixty sonatas. His recorded choices offer a fine view of Clementi's style. One quickly realizes why Beethoven admired the Italian.

Clementi adapted the C Major Sonata from one of his piano concertos. The sonata is a major work of twenty minutes, full of muscular virtuosity. Horowitz is most happy with the score and performs it with tremendous brio.

The large-scale G minor Sonata is a remarkable work of storm and stress. Beethoven must have studied its structure carefully when it appeared in 1788.

The Sonata in F minor is smaller in length, about fourteen minutes, as is the Sonata in F-sharp minor, which is the most romantic of the sonatas. Here, we have vintage Horowitz. How well the pianist brings to the surface the passion lurking in these scores. Especially fine is the finale of the F minor sonata, played with Horowitz's uncanny rhythmic tension.

CZERNY, Carl

Variations on an Aria by Rode, "La Ricordanza," Op. 33
    RCA 60451-2RG

Czerny left over three hundred sets of variations and potpourris on eighty-seven operas of the time. The disc was recorded in 1944. In this piece, Horowitz finds a delightful vehicle for his inborn sense of style in this type of early Romantic pianistic figuration. *La Ricordanza* is nine minutes of suave piano playing.

Once, while listening with Horowitz to this recording in the last variation, he nodded almost in surprise, saying, "Good fingers there."

DEBUSSY, Claude

Etude No. 11, Pour les arpèges composés
EMI-USA-CDHC 63538

L'Isle joyeuse
CBS-MK 42305
M3K 44681

Serenade for the Doll
CBS-MK 42305
M3K 44681
RCA 7755-2RG

From 1928 to 1976, Horowitz recorded around half an hour of the French piano literature. Wonderful readings of Poulenc's Toccata and Pastourelle, recorded in 1932, are available on the EMI CD with the Debussy etude.

In 1947, he added to his tiny Poulenc repertoire the delightful Presto in B-flat, which can be heard on CD RCA 60377-2-RG. On the same disc is the 1976 recording of Fauré's great Nocturne in B minor, Op. 119, played with depth. Unfortunately, RCA did not release on the CD Fauré's Impromptu No. 5, Op. 102, which was the nocturne's companion piece for the original LP, RCA ARL1-2548.

Horowitz was interested in Debussy's etudes and knew six of the twelve. Earlier in his career, he often programmed four of them in recital. His recording made in 1932 of *Pour les arpèges composés* is a marvel of execution.

The 1966 live performance of *L'Isle joyeuse* is positively orgiastic.

"Serenade for the Doll" from the *Children's Corner Suite* was one of his favorite encores. He made four recordings of it, each lighthearted and gracious.

In 1963, he recorded for CBS three Debussy preludes from Book II: *General Lavine—Eccentric, Bruyères*, and *Les Fées sont d'exquises danseuses*, which is the highlight of the three. They have not been transferred to CD. They first appeared on CBS MS 6541.

HAYDN, Joseph

Sonata in E-flat Major, Hob. XVI/52
  EMI-USA CDHC 63538
  RCA 60461-2RG

Sonata in F Major, Hob. XVI/23
  CBS M3K 44681

Sonata in C Major, Hob. XVI/48
  CBS MK 45572

Sonata in E-flat Major, Hob. XVI/49
  Sony Classical SK 45818

These four sonatas by Haydn form an important segment of Horowitz's Classical discography. The pianist immensely enjoyed the Austrian's quirkiness, which appealed to the capriciousness of Horowitz's temperament.

His early 1932 recording of the great E-flat Sonata, No. 52, has been a model for its warmth and the plasticity of the pianism. He recorded it again in 1951 for RCA, in a slightly more orchestral style.

The Sonata in F Major is a fine work with one of Haydn's most lyrically engaging slow movements. The pianist told me he had received many letters regarding the slow movement, which he plays with lavish expressiveness. It was recorded at a live recital in 1966.

The C Major Sonata is a strangely fascinating two-movement composition. The first movement, Andante con espressione, is eight minutes and based on variation technique. The three-and-a-half-minute Rondo gallops from Horowitz's fingers. This splendid reading took place at the Philadelphia Academy of Music in 1968.

The ample eighteen-minute, three-movement E-flat Sonata, No. 49, is contained in Horowitz's last recording. It is Haydn-playing which bubbles with a playful jauntiness and is flush with life. The long Adagio e cantabile movement is blessed with Horowitz at his most songful.

KABALEVSKY, Dmitri

Piano Sonata No. 3, Op. 46
  RCA 60377-2RG

The Third Sonata in three movements is a remarkable synthesis of Kabalevsky's balanced art within the guidelines of the Prokofiev mold. The sonata is charged with Russian feeling. Horowitz plays it to the hilt, examining each dynamic marking with exactitude and building to shattering climaxes. The finale is especially effective, and is reminiscent of the composer's ballet, *The Comedians*.

LISZT, Franz

Au Bord d'une Source
  RCA 60523-2-RG

Vallée d'Obermann
  CBS M3K 44681

Sonetto 104 del Petrarca
  RCA 60523-2-RG

Ballade No. 2 in B minor
  RCA 5935-2-RC

Consolation No. 3 in D-flat
  RCA 5935-2-RC

Funérailles
  RCA 5935-2-RC

Valse Oubliée No. 1
  Deutsche Grammophon 419217-2-GH
  RCA 7755-2-RG

Prelude on "Weinen, Klagen, Sorgen, Zagen"
  Sony Classical SK 45818

Mephisto Waltz No. 1
  RCA 5939-2-RC

Scherzo and March
  CBS MK 45572

Impromptu
  Deutsche Grammophon 419-217-2-GH

Sonata in B minor
  RCA 5935-2-RC
  EMI USA-CD-HC 63538

LISZT–HOROWITZ

Hungarian Rhapsody No. 2
   RCA 60523-2-RG

Hungarian Rhapsody No. 15
   RCA 7755-2-RG

LISZT–SAINT-SAËNS–HOROWITZ

Danse Macabre
   RCA 7755-2-RG

It is in Liszt that the sonorous imagery of Horowitz's art finds all of its variegated splendor. The Horowitz comprehension of the grief-stricken *Funérailles* has never been equaled. The range of nuance, the subtlety of his timing, the massiveness of his left-hand octaves make his performance the finest ever recorded. My heart quakes when I listen to it.

Horowitz's 1932 recording of the Sonata in B minor retains its importance. Although the Liszt Sonata was prized by Busoni, d'Albert, Friedheim, and others, it did not enter the world repertoire until Horowitz's recording. In 1977, he recorded it again, but without the lithe, pantherlike spring; instead, the score sounds exaggerated and grandiloquent.

Other valuable Liszt performances are the *Vallée d'Obermann*, with his own discreet changes and touching up of the text. It is a ripe expression of Horowitz's Byronic Romanticism.

The neglected and fearsomely muscular Scherzo and March is unique among Liszt's compositions. It is humorously diabolical and akin to Alkan's extraordinary and bizarre piano music. In 1967, Horowitz recorded it, throwing all caution to the wind. There is a mocking spirit and the daredevil virtuosity which is so essential to bring this music to life. Horowitz renders the *Mephisto Waltz* with some Busoni additions as well as his own; it is a Liszt with sarcasm and humor.

He is in top form in a monumental reading of the B minor Ballade.

There are also Horowitz's versions of four of the *Hungarian Rhapsodies*. Each is a reworking of the original, although No. 6 contains only a bit of touching up for added effectiveness. In this, the Horowitz octaves are unbelievable. It seems that RCA has not yet transferred to CD the Sixth Rhapsody, which was recorded in 1947 on 78s and transferred to LP RCA LM 2584.

His amazingly clever reworking of the celebrated Second Rhapsody near the end utilizes three themes at once. It is a wondrous transcription which would have delighted Liszt.

In No. 15, the *Rakóczy March*, Horowitz much improves Liszt's original. His sober arrangement of No. 19 remains on LP CBS M35118.

Horowitz also made a few definite improvements in Liszt's transcription of the Saint-Saëns *Danse Macabre,* recorded in 1942. It is a must in any collection. In these performances, Horowitz displays perhaps the most astounding sonority in history. No matter the extent of the "virtuosity," however, it is his control, his very coolness, that is so exciting. One hears everything clearly. His rhythmic sense seems so right, and his reflexes are peerless. Horowitz's use of the pedal is ingeniously calculated and often quite sparse, with all sorts of finesses wrought with the una corda pedal. The virtuoso's touch defies description. It is a sound that only a piano can make, and that only Horowitz can summon out of it.

MENDELSSOHN, Felix

Etude Op. 104, No. 3 in A minor
    CBS-MK45572

Variations sérieuses, Op. 54
    RCA 60451-2-RG

Scherzo a Capriccio
    RCA 7755-2-RG

Three Songs Without Words:
    Elegie, Op. 85, No. 4
    Spring Song, Op. 62, No. 6
    The Shepherd's Complaint, Op. 67, No. 5
    RCA 7755-2-RG

MENDELSSOHN–LISZT–HOROWITZ

Wedding March
    RCA 7755-2-RG

I once asked Horowitz, "Mendelssohn is a composer you like?"
He abruptly answered, "No!"
I continued, "But you have recorded several works."

"Yes, some pieces work. Mendelssohn is neat."

Notwithstanding his comment, Horowitz's small Mendelssohn discography is enchanting. He plays the *Scherzo a Capriccio* with elf-like spirit.

The Mendelssohn etude possesses pristine evenness in left-hand passagework.

The three *Songs Without Words* have the fragrance of early German Romanticism.

His own reworking of Liszt's paraphrase of the celebrated *Wedding March and Variations* has that beguiling rhythmic control which is one of the hallmarks of Horowitz's art.

The treasure among his Mendelssohn discs is a high-voltage, seething, and technically impregnable 1946 performance of Mendelssohn's greatest piano work, the *Variations sérieuses*, Op. 54.

MOSZKOWSKI, Moritz

Etude in F Major, Op. 72, No. 6
   RCA 7755-2-RG

Etude in A-flat Major, Op. 72, No. 11
   RCA 7755-2-RG
   CBS MK 44797

Etincelles, Op. 36, No. 6
   RCA 7755-2-RG
   Deutsche Grammophon 419499-2GH

Horowitz's performances of two Moszkowski etudes and *Etincelles* are lighthearted fluff tossed off with nonchalant ease.

MOZART, Wolfgang Amadeus

Adagio in B minor, K. 540
Rondo in D Major, K. 485
Sonata No. 3 in B-flat Major, K. 281
   Deutsche Grammophon 427772-2

Sonata No. 10 in C Major, K. 330
   Deutsche Grammophon 423287-2

Sonata No. 11 in A Major K. 331
   CBS-M3K 44681

Sonata No. 12 in F Major, K. 332
  RCA 60451-2-RG

Sonata No. 13 in B-flat Major, K. 333
  Deutsche Grammophon 423287-2

Piano Concerto No. 23 in A Major, K. 488
  La Scala Orchestra
  Carlo Maria Giulini, conductor
  Deutsche Grammophon 423287-2

The Adagio in B minor is one of Mozart's most profound utterances. Horowitz thought about it for years; his recording of the adagio is more dramatic than the usual reading.

The same disc presents sparkling playing of the D Major Rondo, actually a sonata movement with one subject.

The Sonata in B-flat, K. 281, is played with a fetching lilt; it was recorded at his home early in 1989.

The Sonata in C Major, K. 330, forms part of the disc *Horowitz in Moscow.* He played it in public often and captures its radiant charm with a confident ease.

The Sonata in A Major, K. 331, was recorded live in 1966. It is a rather heavy interpretation; even the celebrated *Rondo alla Turca* lacks the right kind of clangor. Horowitz's earlier rendition from 1946, on RCA 7755-2-RG, is more suitable to the rondo's spirit.

The Sonata in F Major, K. 332, is a 1947 recording played in a highly inflected and Romanticized style. His rendering of the graceful andante is especially Italianate and operatic. The finale, an unbuttoned rondo, shows off Horowitz's incomparable finger control.

The Sonata in B-flat, K. 333, was recorded in Milan with the Twenty-third Piano Concerto. Horowitz plays with formal unity and high seriousness.

The piano concerto performance possesses a youthful verve. Horowitz's tone in the slow movement is gorgeous. The finale is taken at a spirited tempo and is played with a technique of extraordinary suppleness.

MUSSORGSKY, Modest

Pictures at an Exhibition
  RCA 60449-2-RG

Horowitz enlarged Mussorgsky's sound and texture in the *Pictures*. Purists persist in hating it, but the impact is awesome and is so perfectly Horowitzian in manner that it must be judged on his terms.

He recorded it twice: in 1947 in the studio, and in 1951 at a concert at Carnegie Hall. Fortunately, RCA's compact disc reissue uses the live performance, which is most thrilling.

The disc also contains Horowitz's beautifully stated transcription of Mussorgsky's song "By the Water."

PROKOFIEV, Sergei

 Toccata, Op. 11
  RCA 60377-2RG

 Sonata No. 7, Op. 83
  RCA 60377-2RG

The recording of the motoric toccata, made in 1947, is clangorous and justly famous.

The 1945 disc of the Seventh Sonata has brought many pianists to this score, making it the most often performed of the composer's nine piano sonatas. Horowitz has shaped each phrase to his critical requirements. The first movement shows the pianist's acute structural sense, and in the exciting third movement finale, marked precipitato, he is not intent on speed but on a cumulative display of infinite rhythmic movement. He literally implants in the listener his beat, which remains in the auditory organ long after hearing the recording.

RACHMANINOFF, Sergei

 Sonata No. 2 in B-flat minor, Op. 36
 Moment Musical in E-flat minor, Op. 16, No. 2
 Prelude in G Major, Op. 32, No. 5
 Polka V.R.
 Piano Concerto No. 3 in D minor, Op. 30
  RCA Victor Symphony Orchestra
  Fritz Reiner, conductor
  RCA 7754-2-RG

 Piano Concerto No. 3 in D minor, Op. 30
  London Symphony Orchestra
  Albert Coates, conductor
  EMI USA CDHC 63538

Piano Concerto No. 3 in D minor, Op. 30
New York Philharmonic
Eugene Ormandy, conductor
RCA RCD 12633

Prelude in G-sharp minor, Op. 32, No. 12
Moment Musical in B minor, Op. 16, No. 3
Etude Tableau in E-flat minor, Op. 33, No. 5
Etude Tableau in C Major, Op. 33, No. 2
Etude Tableau in D Major, Op. 39, No. 9
Sonata No. 2 in B-flat minor, Op. 36, No. 1
CBS Cassette MPT 39757

Horowitz recorded the Third Concerto three times. The 1930 version with Coates was severely truncated to fit onto nine 78 sides. Horowitz himself discounted the performance, saying he had only an hour to record it. Nonetheless, the performance has had many admirers and is unaffected playing, less turbulent than the other two recordings.

The 1951 disc with Reiner is the pianist's most characteristic reading: demonic, searing, technically daring. The 1978 live performance is marked by excessive and self-absorbed melancholy.

In Horowitz's recording of various solo pieces by Rachmaninoff, he concentrates on the epic side of the music far more than the composer's recordings reveal. In the climax of the *Etude Tableau* in E-flat minor, for instance, Horowitz, lifts one from one's seat. In the Etude in C Major, his freedom of phrasing is exquisite, as is the shimmering light in the G-sharp minor Prelude. The E-flat minor *Moment Musical* is boiling in its agitation.

Horowitz's playing always evokes an orchestral instrumentation. But unlike many pianists who play orchestrally, he never leaves his listener longing for the actual orchestra, so completely does he understand the piano and its plangent sonority.

Both versions of the B-flat minor Sonata present the work in monumental fashion.

SCARLATTI, Domenico

Six Sonatas
From the Metropolitan Opera House
RCA RCD 14585
Seventeen Sonatas
CBS MK 42410

Horowitz adored Scarlatti unconditionally. Once, when we were speaking of him, he went to find Scarlatti's own preface to the thirty-three sonatas published during his lifetime of the six hundred he composed. Horowitz gleefully read:

Dear Reader,
Whether you be dilettante or professor, do not expect any profound learning, but rather, an ingenious jesting with art to accommodate you to the mastery of the harpsichord. Neither consideration of interest nor of ambition, but obedience alone spurred me on to publish these pieces. If they prove agreeable to you, then only more gladly will I obey other commands to favor you with more simple and various styles. Therefore, show yourself more human than critical, and thus you will increase your own pleasure."

Horowitz looked at me and said, "That means if you don't criticize the music, you will feel better. I love that!"

On playing Scarlatti on the modern piano instead of the harpsichord, Horowitz said, "The harpsichord cannot achieve the continuity of tone that the piano can. On the piano, I still try to play the music in the framework of Scarlatti's period, yet I never want to imitate the harpsichord; I only want to show the public how the music sounds on the piano."

Indeed, Horowitz's interpretations are a lesson in the transference of harpsichord music to the modern piano. He employs a large set of dynamics, and the pedal is used ingeniously, in washes and dots and dashes.

Horowitz packs these priceless, four-minute binary gems with drama. One hears intrigue, gossip, the clatter of Madrid cobblestone, the pomp of court, castanets, Spanish dance forms, all etched with a breathtaking finger control and spacing of notes. It is a living, breathing Scarlatti which, once heard, can never be forgotten.

SCHUBERT, Franz

Sonata in B-flat Major
    Deutsche Grammophon 435025-2GH

Impromptu in G-flat Major, D. 899, No. 3
    CBS MK 42305

Impromptu in B-flat Major, D. 935, No. 3
  Deutsche Grammophon 419217-2GH

SCHUBERT–TAUSIG

Marche Militaire
  Deutsche Grammophon 419217-2GH

SCHUBERT–LISZT

Soirées de Vienne Nos. 6 & 7
Serenade
  Deutsche Grammophon 427772-2

Horowitz's largest Schubert undertaking is the live performance of the B-flat Sonata from February 25, 1953, just before his retirement. His performance lacks the heartbreaking lyricism of Schubert's last sonata. It is on compact disc RCA 60451-2-RG. His second version, released in 1991, differs in details and is more expansive.

In 1973, he recorded four impromptus for CBS, available on LP M 32432, the best being the Impromptu in F minor, D. 935, No. 1.

Listed above is the beautiful G-flat Impromptu, played with a large, singing tone. The 1985 performance of the B-flat Impromptu, a golden set of variations, is played with beautiful limpidity.

The two *Soirées de Vienne* are Liszt paraphrases on Schubert waltzes; they are relaxed and nostalgic. The Schubert *Marche Militaire*, arranged by the formidable Liszt disciple Carl Tausig, displays Horowitz's penchant for marches. There is biting humor within the pianist's characteristic sonority.

The Schubert–Liszt *Serenade* is played with much rubato and lushness, so different from the refined performance by Rachmaninoff. His performance of the famous *Moment Musical* in F minor is fatuous.

SCHUMANN, Robert

Arabeske, Op. 18
  CBS M3K 44681
  CBS M3K 42409

Blumenstück, Op. 19
  M3K 44681

Fantasy in C Major, Op. 17
CBS M3K 44681

Fantasiestücke, Op. 111
RCA 6680-2-RG

Humoreske, Op. 20
RCA 6680-2-RG

Nachtstücke, Op. 23, Nos. 3 & 4
RCA 6680-2-RG

Kinderscenen, Op. 15
CBS MK 42409
RCA RCD1-4572
Deutsche Grammophon 435025-2GH

Kreisleriana, Op. 16
Deutsche Grammophon 419217-2GH
CBS MK 42409

Sonata No. 3 in F minor, Op. 14
RCA 6680-2-RG

Toccata in C Major, Op. 7
CBS MK 42409

In Schumann, Horowitz's creative imagination is fired. Here he finds a kindred spirit, childlike but complex, thorny, caressing, fragmented, and full of trickery and whimsy. In no other composer has Horowitz so laid bare his heart.

There are splendid performances from the early 1930s of the Arabeske, *Traumeswirren*, Toccata, and the *Presto Passionato* to be heard on EMI USA CDHC 63538. The later recording of the Toccata is fuller with more musical meaning.

The great C Major Fantasy is tonally glorious; the first recording of *Kreisleriana* from 1969 is unforgettable in its intensity. The 1986 recording is more flexible and mellow.

Horowitz's *Humoreske* fully realizes the rare potential of this vernal masterpiece.

The Sonata No. 3, subtitled "Concerto Without Orchestra," is neglected and important Schumann. The performance is throbbing, fiery, and tender.

The *Kinderscenen* were never far from his fingers, and he performed the cycle throughout his life with telling effect.

SCRIABIN, Alexander

Sonata No. 5, Op. 53
Preludes, Op. 11, Nos. 1, 10, 9, 3, 16 13, 14
Prelude Op. 15, No. 2
Prelude Op. 16, No. 1
Prelude Op. 13, No. 6
Prelude Op. 16, No. 4
Prelude Op. 27, No. 1
Prelude Op. 51, No. 2
Prelude Op. 48, No. 3
Prelude Op. 67, No. 1
Prelude Op. 59, No. 2
Sonata No. 3 in F-sharp minor, Op. 23
Etude in B-flat minor, Op. 9, No. 7
Etude in C-sharp minor, Op. 42, No. 5
Etude in D-sharp minor, Op. 8, No. 12
   RCA 6215-2-RG

Etude in C-sharp minor, Op. 2, No. 1
Etude in F-sharp minor, Op. 8, No. 2
Etude in A-flat Major, Op. 8, No. 8
Etude in D-flat Major, Op. 8, No. 10
Etude in B-flat minor, Op. 8, No. 11
Etude in D-sharp minor, Op. 8, No. 11
Poem in F-sharp Major, Op. 32, No. 1
Etude in F-sharp Major, Op. 42, No. 3
Etude in F-sharp Major, Op. 42, No. 4
Etude in C-sharp minor, Op. 42, No. 5
Feuillet d'Album in E-flat Major, Op. 45, No. 1
Sonata No. 9, Op. 68 (The Black Mass)
Two Poems, Op. 69
Sonata No. 10, Op. 70
Vers la flamme, Op. 72
   CBS MK 42411

Horowitz is spiritually linked to the mercurial and mystic impressionism of Scriabin. The pianist knew exactly how to bring to life that master's flickering, flamelike spirit, its vertiginous, supercharged nervosity and quivering eroticism.

The early etudes—Op. 2, No. 1 and Op. 8—portray yearning, while later ones from Op. 42, especially No. 5, capture Scriabin's quest for breathlessness. No. 5 is marked affannato. The preludes are epigrams of the most varied and fleeting moods.

Horowitz's recordings of the Sonatas Nos. 3, 5, 9, and 10 are the zenith of all Scriabin playing. These performances possess a devastating verisimilitude.

The Sonata No. 3 is declamatory and spasmodic.

One can see a blinding light in the trills of the Tenth Sonata. The composer said the work was "born from the sun." Wild, orgiastic rhythms combined with caressing languor spark a diabolical sensuality in the Fifth Sonata.

Horowitz made two recordings of the Ninth Sonata, *The Black Mass*. Alfred Swann calls the work—couched in the most hideous, grimacing harmonies—"a veritable picture of Dorian Gray!" The 1953 disc is actually three minutes faster and more satanic than the 1965 performance with its milder colors. Horowitz draws from these scores every molecule of their meaning, and his passion exhausts the listener.

Other great Scriabin performances are the Two Poems, Op. 69, played with incisive capriciousness, and the extraordinary *Vers la flamme*, which he plays with pent-up fury: a purification by fire.

SOUSA–HOROWITZ

　Stars and Stripes Forever
　　RCA 7755-2-RG

Horowitz told me that, invariably, bands play military marches too fast. Horowitz's adaptation of Sousa's march is electrifying. He manages to make the piccolo smile, and what rhythmic sweep his playing has.

TCHAIKOVSKY, Peter Ilyich

　Piano Concerto No. 1 in B-flat minor, Op. 23
　　NBC Symphony Orchestra
　　Arturo Toscanini, conductor
　　　(1941 studio recording) RCA 60449-2-RG
　　　(1943 live performance) RCA 7992-2-RG

From opera to symphony, Horowitz dearly loved Tchaikovsky. The two recordings of the Piano Concerto are immortal: steely, disciplined, and burning with a volcanic passion. The studio recording from 1941 was recorded in Carnegie Hall. The 1943 performance was live from Carnegie, during the celebrated Tchaikovsky War Bond Concert. RCA released it only in 1959.

Horowitz's only excursion into Tchaikovsky's solo piano music is the eight-minute Dumka, Op. 59, recorded in 1942. It is a pungent reading and should not be missed. RCA reissued it in 1968 on an LP called *The Young Horowitz* (LM 2993), which contains his dazzling 1928 recording of Dohnányi's Capriccio in F minor, Op. 23, No. 6 and a remarkable Paganini–Liszt Etude in E-flat from 1930.

The album also includes Horowitz's own *Danse Excentrique*, composed in 1921, a light piece with a dash of pepper and a dance hall flavor.

INDEX